FIGHTING BACK

D0885648

BY THE SAME AUTHOR

THE REGENERATION OF BRITAIN
SPEECHES
ARGUMENTS FOR SOCIALISM
ARGUMENTS FOR DEMOCRACY
PARLIAMENT, PEOPLE AND POWER
THE SIZEWELL SYNDROME
OUT OF THE WILDERNESS: DIARIES 1963–67

FIGHTING BACK

Speaking Out for Socialism in the Eighties

TONY BENN

HUTCHINSON
LONDON MELBOURNE AUCKLAND JOHANNESBURG

© Tony Benn 1988

All rights reserved

This edition first published in 1988 by
Hutchinson, an imprint of
Century Hutchinson Ltd, Brookmount House,
62–65 Chandos Place,
London WC2N 4NW

Century Hutchinson Australia Pty Ltd
PO Box 496, 16–22 Church Street, Hawthorn,
Victoria 3122, Australia

Century Hutchinson New Zealand Limited
PO Box 40–086, Glenfield,
Auckland 10, New Zealand

Century Hutchinson South Africa (Pty) Ltd
PO Box 337, Berglvei,
2012 South Africa

British Library Cataloguing in Publication Data

Benn, Tony, *1925–*
  Fighting back: speaking out for socialism
  in the Eighties.
  1. Great Britain. Political events,
  1979–1987
  I. Title
  941.085'8

ISBN 0–09–173792–3

Phototypeset by Input Typesetting Ltd, London
Printed and bound in Great Britain by
Mackays of Chatham Ltd

Contents

This book is lovingly dedicated to my life-long friend and partner in socialism, Caroline; to all our family; and to those around the world, known and unknown, whose lives have been devoted to the improvement of society and the unending struggle for peace.

Introduction

The years since 1979 have been characterised by a major attack on ideas which for over a generation had been generally accepted as part of a national consensus: the idea that any Government would seek to maintain full employment; the idea that the welfare state would exist to help all those in need; the idea that those in government work for detente.

But in the eighties new and much harsher attitudes have taken root in the British Establishment, and the policies that have flowed from them have carried the day in three consecutive general elections.

With Labour in Opposition and socialists on the defensive, millions of people in Britain have suffered severe hardship and humiliation. Many battles have been fought to defend jobs, living conditions, essential public services and industries, and people have had to struggle to protect their democratic rights and civil liberties, at both local and national level.

In this decade too, the Labour Party began a long process of re-examination of its own philosophy and organisation, under three different leaders. Each of these leaders, in their own way, attempted to move the Party closer to the new Centre-Right of British politics, and to isolate and neutralise those socialists who would not follow their lead.

This is the background against which the speeches, articles and transcripts contained in this book have to be read, for they were all part of a fight back against the onslaught of the new Right. I hope that in their different ways they will each help to give an insight into what really was at stake during the great struggles of the Eighties. I hope, too, that they will identify the outline of a new, and very different, politics that may emerge in the 1990s and beyond.

Setting these years of struggle against my own experience over a much longer period, it seems that several factors have surfaced which have great implications for the future.

The first is the rediscovery that moral values must be addressed and considered and discussed if we are ever to change the policies which now prevail. Without some conscious sense of community and internationalism, we will never be able to develop the collective strength to change our prospects in the years to come.

The fact that a moral approach has been so neglected in electoral politics, particularly by the Labour movement, for so long, and that the choices offered between the parties have been so managerial in character may, in part, explain why we are facing our present difficulties.

A second neglected factor has been our failure to study and understand the nature of the institutions under which we are governed. Most of these were developed for quite different purposes in very different periods of history, and with a view to advancing the interests of wholly different groups to those whom Labour represents.

Most of these institutions are centralised and secretive in their nature. Their power has been enormously increased by the growth of technology, which has armed them with weapons, information systems, and other implements of social control which they use quite ruthlessly to protect their privileges and their interests. Perhaps the strongest force at work in British politics today is deliberately stimulated fear – of breakdown of law and order, of riots, of dole queues, of foreign invasion – which freezes people into accepting a situation which they should not for one moment tolerate.

When our children and grandchildren look back on the 1980s, they are bound to ask themselves how it was that so many people in this generation were apparently content to live in a society that was so authoritarian, and acquiesce in policies that were so damaging. They will blame us for our craven subservience to those who imposed it all.

But the undermining of democracy and civil liberties in Government, finance, industry, the trade unions and the Labour Party itself is now being questioned. The democratic challenge to those power structures has led to many increasingly fierce debates in which the Establishment has needed all its new-found powers to defend itself.

The rediscovery of social morality and the renewal of democratic protest, expressed in part in the bitter strikes and campaigns of the eighties, will have to become central themes in the future if we are not all to be driven back to the wilderness, policed by new technocratic authorities. And there are signs of hope emerging if we look for them: changes in the socialist countries, the strong liberation movements in South Africa and elsewhere which are committed to free speech and development.

The eighties will be remembered for the courage of those who stood up for themselves and their principles: the women at Greenham Common, the printers, the miners, the teachers, the nurses, the leaders of the black communities.

Readers of this book should be encouraged by the example of those who have fought back heroically, and who will continue to fight in the years ahead to repair the damage done. We must all strive to reconstruct our society in a way that offers each and every one a better life in a more peaceful world.

Tony Benn
Chesterfield
May Day, 1988

Editor's Note

The 1980s have witnessed deep divisions in British society. The Labour Party and socialists generally have been on the defensive, while the Labour movement has been undergoing a painful reassessment.

The choice of extracts in *Fighting Back* reflects Tony Benn's personal advocacy of a broad and radical socialist response to all the crises which have preoccupied the decade: the Falklands War, during which he was a leading voice against both Conservative and official Labour Party policies; the Miners' and Wapping disputes; the Conservatives' renewed commitment to the special relationship with the USA, and all that this implies in international relations and nuclear policy; and the growing obsession with 'state security'.

Within the House of Commons Tony Benn has made influential, sometimes decisive, contributions during the 1980s, most notably in the Zircon Debate of January 1987. Few people will have heard or read more than the brief snippets of Parliamentary proceedings given by television, radio and the press, so Parliamentary speeches form a significant proportion of the book. Their inclusion will, in effect, provide the opportunity to follow in full the arguments pursued over particular issues.

In this connection I would like to acknowledge the Editor of *Hansard*, for kindly allowing us to reproduce proceedings so extensively.

I would also like to thank Kate Mosse, Editor at Century Hutchinson, without whose considerable ability, advice and hard work this book would not have been possible.

Ruth Winstone
March 1988

1
THE STALEMATE IN
BRITISH POLITICS

Fifty Years of Consensus Rule

The administrations which have governed Britain in modern times may perhaps best be classified not by reference to the traditional electoral cycle, but by identifying four different periods of consensus, which have followed one after another. The first, the pre-war consensus, underpinned the National government and lasted from 1931 to 1940; the second, the wartime consensus, ran from 1940 to 1945 when the coalition was in power; the third, the welfare capitalist consensus, lasted from 1945 until 1976; and the fourth, the monetarist consensus, which began when the Labour Cabinet accepted the IMF terms, has lasted from then until the present day. To lump governments from different parties into the same categories may seem strange, but, looking back on all the various policies that have been followed by successive administrations, it is the similarity between them, quite as much as the differences, which now seem to be so strikingly obvious.

The pre-war consensus, marked by unemployment and appeasement, ended with the formation of the coalition in May 1940, and brought both Churchill and Attlee together, each of whom had been in direct opposition to the National government throughout the thirties, and the mix of ideas that resulted was a most interesting one. Churchill had been a radical minister in the great reforming 1906 Liberal Government and he called back his old colleague Sir William Beveridge, who had worked with him then at the Board of Trade: they found it relatively easy to operate the wartime consensus, designed to plan the economy for victory and provide for the basic needs of the people. All of this fitted in with the moderate Fabian ideas which were brought into government by Attlee, Dalton and Morrison, and the few Liberal ministers.

Thus, while the Labour landslide of 1945 marked a turning point in British politics, in the sense that it was the first occasion when Labour won an overall majority, it is also true that a great number of the policies it followed had already been agreed in outline during the war years, and this 'welfare capitalist consensus', built around a mild Keynesianism, bore more resemblance to Roosevelt's New Deal than to socialism. The boom which followed the war was strong enough to put industry on its feet again, to end unemployment, to pay for the welfare state, and, above all, to strengthen the trade union movement, which could use the bargaining power that full employment confers on labour to wrest concessions from capital. Labour's New Deal found wide support amongst the politicians and the electorate in the years that followed, although the breadth of that support was often concealed beneath the sharp personal exchanges between the parties, especially at election times.

But the Civil Service mandarins, brought up in the same wartime tradition, together with the Establishment generally, knew and accepted what was going on: the business community felt reasonably safe so long as there was a broad continuity of policy on which they could rely; and the Labour voters recognised the improvements which they enjoyed, as compared to the prewar years.

Labour policy could then, in one sense, be interpreted as a plan to save capitalism, by incorporating the trade union leadership within the governing group, in return for measures that were important to their union members. The experience and mechanisms of wartime planning made this task a relatively easy one, but it all rested upon the continuation of the postwar boom itself, which provided a market for goods for reconstruction, here and worldwide, at a time when our major industrial competitors – Germany, Japan and Italy – had been virtually destroyed. Thus the huge task of conversion from military to civil production was made possible, and unemployment virtually disappeared, although physical shortages were still experienced.

In the field of foreign and defence policy most of the concessions were made by Labour to the Conservative view of the world. Ernest Bevin, as Foreign Secretary, whose suspicion and dislike of the USSR matched that of Churchill himself, offered one example. Attlee offered another, since he decided, around the time of the Berlin airlift, to build a British atom bomb, and invite the United States to establish bases here, in both cases without telling the full story to his Cabinet, Parliament or the people, thus laying the foundations for a policy that Churchill accepted, welcomed and extended when he returned to power in 1951. Indeed, after 1951, when Labour was defeated, neither Winston Churchill nor Anthony Eden made any serious attempt to return to prewar Tory economic policies, and Harold Macmillan, the veritable 'wet' grandfather of welfare capitalism, lived to become the beneficiary of the very ideas he had advocated as a Tory rebel twenty years earlier in his book *The Middle Way*. Britain, he told us, had never had it so good.

With this slogan Macmillan won a landslide victory against Hugh Gaitskell in 1959 and the Labour leadership then began a long, and highly publicised, revisionist retreat from socialism, in which Harold Wilson, James Callaghan and Michael Foot all played their parts. But under these shifts at the top of politics other factors were at work in industry and the economy, which were actually undermining the foundations of our postwar prosperity, and were destined to change British politics more fundamentally. British capitalism, denied its traditional imperial markets, and reluctant to invest in the necessary re-equipment, began to fall behind in the race for markets, and became victim of a series of balance-of-payments crises, which were dealt with, by parties of both colours, by means of 'stop and go', a form of macro-economic masochism that undermined both business confidence and the power of labour. Both Wilson, after ditching the National Plan in 1966, and Heath, after his U-turn in 1972, tried to counter this decline by policies designed to tempt, or bribe, industrialists to invest, coupled with solemn warnings to the trade unions not to use their bargaining strength to raise wages, backed by anti-union legislation.

British membership of the Common Market was then presented as the route to recovery and growth within a wider European framework in which, we were all assured, capitalism could be revived; but when the OPEC oil crisis occurred in 1973, all the underlying weaknesses of our economic system were exposed.

It became clear that the economic base on which the 'welfare consensus' depended had finally collapsed, actually ending half-way through Labour's term of office, when the IMF demanded, and received, assurances that public expenditure would be cut, supposedly to restore business confidence. At the end of its twenty-one-year life span, it was clear that the welfare consensus had neither revitalised British industry nor retained public support with the electorate, which successively defeated Wilson, Heath and Callaghan, who had all tried to make it work, thus paving the way for the election of a very different kind of Conservative Government.

Though its seeds had been planted earlier, the monetarist consensus was born three years before Mrs Thatcher came to power, since the Tories, nursing their defeats in 1974, had resolved to elect a leader who would return to the old orthodoxy and settle their own score with the unions. Meanwhile the Labour Party at the grass roots, after its defeat in 1979, resolved to fight more vigorously for its own people, and insist upon more socialist policies and a more accountable leadership. The years from 1979 to 1983 saw the full flowering of these movements back to class politics, and then, in each party, countervailing forces began to emerge. The wets in the Tory Party, who did not question the basic tenets of monetarism, but feared for the electoral consequences if it was applied too harshly, came together slowly and hesitantly, partly because of the power of the Prime Minister, and partly because the Falklands War gave a huge boost to the flagging popularity of the government in 1982. For Labour the counter-revolution of the Right was more traumatic when 10 per cent of the Parliamentary Labour Party actually resigned in 1981 and formed a new party, the SDP, which, along with the Tory wets and the Labour Right, seemed to be agreed that politics should be steered back towards safer arguments about who was best able to administer the economic system that monetarist policies had created.

In the light of this it can be argued that the history of the last forty years has been the story of one long attempt, by all parties, to save British capitalism, by the use of different policies each of which carried at the time a wide measure of public support. Of course the monetarist consensus has been much the harshest, but when it emerged the crisis of British capitalism had become much more serious, and, if it was to survive, such measures were necessary – though it should be noted in passing that at no stage did the Parliamentary Labour Party ever seek to blame the crisis upon the nature of the system, always preferring to focus its attacks upon the record of ministers.

The unions had already been weakened by rising unemployment, by incomes policies, and more recently by crippling legislation, and the Labour leadership itself had long since abandoned any serious socialist critique of the economic system as such, and had fallen back on its claim to be able to run it better. Capital, by contrast, had by 1976 recovered its self-confidence, had developed much stronger international links, and now had a government ready to use the full apparatus of the state to enforce its interests against any group, whether in the unions or Labour local authorities, which tried to resist the policies that were being applied. Though it would be wrong to describe these policies as ever having won a positive and enthusiastic consensus of support, there was, in the absence of any clear socialist alternative, a broad spectrum of opinion that the surgery being applied was inescapable. In that sense the acceptance that for capital to survive it had to recover the ground it had lost to Labour in the post-war years became widespread, and an antisocialist, anti-union and anti-democratic alliance was created, in the formation of which many Labour leaders, some of whom joined the SDP, played a key role, especially in their denunciation of those who engaged in extra-parliamentary struggles or advocated radical policies.

The polarisation and confrontations that these class policies produced were certainly reflected in the thinking of the wider Labour movement, but they were not articulated in the presentation of the case in the House of Commons, where an informed consensus began to develop in which the Tory wets, the SDP–Liberal Alliance and the Labour right were content to limit the argument to the question of which of them was best qualified to administer an unchanged economic system. It is certainly true that many people in the Conservative Party and the Alliance, and some inside the Labour Party, backed by the majority of the Establishment and political commentators, now believe that it may be possible to reconstruct our political system on the old Victorian, or modern American, principle that Whigs and Tories, Democrats and Republicans will for ever play the game of ins-and-outs, within the broad framework of the policies and institutions evolved during the monetarist consensus which any successor will inherit from the Thatcher administration. In that sense, despite all that has been said about the destruction of the consensus by Mrs Thatcher, there still is a wide measure of agreement among parliamentarians as to how the political future might be shaped.

But, despite the renewed evidence of the traditional huddling together at the top, the economic prospects as oil revenues and the privatisation windfall profits run down are poor, and the price that has been paid by millions of people in unemployment has created a much stronger resistance to the government of the day than we have seen since the 1930s.

So far the strength of this feeling has been mainly articulated outside Parliament, and if it forces its way upwards then we are heading for a very different sort of politics. Politicians of all parties, who are now seeking to retain or gain office in a basically unchanged system, may find that the next real radical challenge comes from outside the formal system: there are forces which will seek to be heard and will make demands and back them up with organisational strength. That should neither surprise nor alarm socialists, for looking back over the years since the war it is arguable that our problems today really derive from the failure of consensus and the failure to give the country the chance to face up to the basic reforms that are necessary in its industrial, economic and political structures if social justice is ever to be achieved. Indeed our whole history shows that every period of change has been heralded by some pressure from underneath or outside the House of Commons, Whitehall or the City of London.

Those who believe that the power of labour has been finally eroded by changes in the make-up of the working class may be ignoring the emergence of new and significant social forces, each experiencing oppression of some kind and all with strong demands to make; and the residual feudalism which still hangs like a cloud over British society, together with its modern technocratic counterpart, virtually guarantees that class will remain on the agenda, even though it may take many forms. Those who want Britain to be governed by a consensus, and believe it can be, might also reflect upon the massive apparatus of state repression which has had to be assembled and used to protect the monetarist consensus from the many challenges to it which have emerged.

Any political leader, or group, on the Left who has the effrontery to argue – and mean it – that an election might actually be used to advance socialism or democracy is immediately put beyond the pale, and an Establishment veto is placed upon that person or that group. Those who act as guardians of the outer limits of so-called legitimate debate include the City, the Whitehall mandarins, the Chiefs of Staff, the security agencies and, above all, the mass media, whose co-operation, however limited, is necessary for traditional electioneering. These domestic centres of Establishment power have strong allies in the IMF, the EEC, NATO and the multinationals, all of whom have enormous influence in shaping British policy through direct and indirect means. No Conservative Government need ever fear falling foul of these external forces, since it would be unlikely to want to do anything that would anger them. But that is not true of the Labour Party and the Labour movement which have consistently demanded policies which would bring them right up against both the national and international establishments. Successive parliamentary Labour leaders and Labour ministers have understood precisely how far they would be allowed to go in radical talk without incurring the wrath of those who wield real power.

Of course, some Labour leaders have in the past actually shared the views of the Establishment, and they have justified their policies to the Labour Party by using the all-too-familiar language of 'facing the harsh realities of office', and being ready to 'take responsibility'. So far, every Labour Prime Minister has had to reach an unwritten and unspoken understanding with certain key people in order to have had any prospect of becoming acceptable and being treated as legitimate.

These understandings cover a wide range of subjects, on each of which there have been bipartisan arrangements of one kind or another for many years, and at least since the war. For example, to have any chance of even the minimum of fair media coverage every Labour Prime Minister has had to assure, or reassure, the proprietors that no Labour government would ever touch their personal power over the newspapers that they own and control, and in return they are guaranteed support against the rank and file of their party. Similar assurances have been sought, and from time to time given, to permanent secretaries, military and security chiefs, to the City, and to Brussels and Washington that Labour would confine itself to the administration of the status quo in return for counter-assurances that there would be no serious attempt at destabilisation.

This is the real political consensus that underpins what we call parliamentary democracy in Britain: absolute freedom to put up alternative candidates to run the system, if, but only if, accompanied by secret assurances that the essential nature of that system will not be challenged or altered. This is how the British constitution really works, and understanding the way it works, to maintain a continuing consensus for the status quo, may help to explain why democracy and socialism have been successfully kept off the political agenda, under governments of all persuasions, since 1945. Yet, despite all that, the pressure for more democracy and for the ideas of socialism are strongly felt, and widely shared. But, like early trade unionists, the Chartists and the suffragettes, they will only secure their objectives by organised strength and by pressing them onto reluctant parliamentarians and a frightened Establishment, who will only concede when they realise that they can no longer hold the line. It has often happened before.

The Party and the Government

Many of the gains won by working people over a hundred years or more of struggle are now being reversed. The welfare state is being steadily dismantled; full employment policies have been abandoned and replaced by policies of mass unemployment to frighten workers into subservience; trade union rights and the rights of women are being taken away.

Fundamental civil liberties are going, one by one, and it is clear that the police and the army are being prepared for a repressive role.

Even the ballot box through which we should control our policies in Parliament has been by-passed by Common Market membership, the presence of American missiles, the power of the IMF and the multinationals.

One of the most powerful forces in bringing all this about has been the mass media with its hostile propaganda against the Labour movement.

We have to make the recognition of what has happened the starting point for our strategy to recover lost ground and prepare our next advance towards peace, jobs and socialism.

In analysing these events socialists have to strike a balance between the need to describe the sources of Establishment strength, which makes our task look very difficult, and the need to build up the confidence of our people that radical change can actually be achieved if we organise effectively.

The Inherent Strength of Labour and the Weakness of the Establishment

There is always a danger that a socialist analysis may have the effect of discouraging effort, because it focuses on the apparent strength of those who now occupy positions of power, so that we may accidentally underestimate our strength and hence doubt our capacity to defeat those centres of power.

Nor must we allow other factors to deflect us, such as the betrayals by ex-Labour leaders; the failures of previous Labour governments; or hesitancy inside the PLP about conference policies. Similarly, our anxieties about the pressure that will be put upon future Labour governments must not lead us to suppose that socialist policies cannot be implemented.

The spread of pessimism would play into the hands of the Tories whose most powerful weapon against us is demoralisation, and if we over-emphasise the difficulties that lie ahead we could unintentionally reinforce that same message and undercut our own movement.

Ironically, members of the Establishment know that we are much stronger than we sometimes believe ourselves to be, which is why the huge and sustained campaign takes place against the Labour movement twenty-four hours a day, seven days a week, fifty-two weeks a year.

But they recognise that the swing of the political pendulum will bring an opposition into power from time to time, and they want to be sure that when that happens it is as harmless as possible and that it does not engage upon the radical reform which they fear.

The media, voicing this view, therefore differentiates very sharply in their coverage between the leaders of the parliamentary party and the trade unions whom they call 'moderate' and who get a good press, and the overwhelming majority of the Labour Party members and active trade unionists, whom they have decided to call 'extremists'.

This Establishment strategy should help us to understand the source of our real strength, which lies with those who are the recipients of this continuous barrage of abuse.

Far from being extremists, this majority is in fact making most moderate and modest demands – for good jobs and homes and schools, adequate health care, dignity in retirement and peace – none of which can be met within the framework of wealth and power as it exists today in Britain.

It is also necessary to understand the real weaknesses of the British Establishment when faced with a strong challenge. In March 1974, after the miners had defeated Ted Heath, Labour was elected as a minority government and the forces of the British Establishment really believed that they were witnessing the re-run of the General Strike which, this time, they had lost: and they were prepared to make enormous concessions.

Today the Tory Establishment must question why it seems to be getting away with so much, and meeting so little real resistance.

We might well be asking ourselves the same question, and if we do we shall quickly realise that, just as all our gains were made by struggle, so, when we stop struggling, those gains are all taken away again. If we ask ourselves where those early struggles began, we shall discover the obvious truth that all campaigns for social justice and social change begin at the bottom and only reach the floor of the House of Commons much later, when popular demands are translated into Acts of Parliament by a Labour majority.

To talk of extra-parliamentary activity today is to run the risk of being accused of being anti-parliamentary, whereas the truth is that Parliament itself was never democratic in its origins and it was only by popular struggle that Parliament was made democratic.

The power base of the Tory Party is, and always has been, extra-Parliamentary, since the landowners, big business, the bankers, the media and the military have no independent basis of democratic power and the power they exercise is all outside Parliament.

We should not therefore agonise over our commitment to popular campaigns to win public support for a House of Commons made up of a majority that will work for Labour as strongly as the forces of the Establishment work for the interests of capital.

It is for this reason too that we should be looking to the Labour Party and the trade union movement to provide the driving force for the next great advance in our society.

Though founded by trade unions and socialists to advance the interests of working people in Parliament, the Labour Party remained, for over half a century, very much the junior partner of its own parliamentary leadership.

Ramsay Macdonald saw it as little more than an electoral organisation, and even in the 1930s the Party never succeeded in establishing its own distinctive position on the future of socialism. The Left made most of the running but the constituency parties even had to fight for the right to elect their own representatives to the National Executive.

Then came the war and the coalition, in which Labour ministers had to be responsible for the decisions of a Cabinet headed by Mr Churchill, while the Party itself remained outside the corridors of power.

The post-war Labour Government, despite all its achievements, reached its decisions without much regard to Conference
or the NEC. Then, from 1951 to 1964, came a long period in
opposition during which the parliamentary leadership under
Hugh Gaitskell began a major campaign to rid the Labour Party
of its Clause Four commitment to socialism, and turn it into a
modern version of the Liberal Party.

The defeat of this right-wing strategy marked a turning point
in the party's fortunes, for had it succeeded Labour would now
be the SDP and the party would have split.

The election of Harold Wilson in 1963 was seen by the party
as a manifestation that this could never happen, and the confidence of the rank and file rose sharply, encouraged by the
election victory of 1964 on a good and radical manifesto.

But the hopes of the party were dashed by the policies
followed by the Wilson Government which soon dropped its
manifesto commitments and came into conflict not only with
the party and the Left, but also with the trade unions, which
had been radicalised by shop-floor activity and the election of
some new and tougher trade union leaders.

After Labour's defeat in 1970, both trade union and party
opposition to the consensus policies of the Wilson Government
came together to hammer out new policies between 1970 and
1974 – through the party itself rather than in the shadow cabinet
as traditionally happened.

Emerging from this process, 'Labour's Programme 1973' went
forward the following year, was formally endorsed and formed
the basis of the campaign document jointly published by the
NEC and the Shadow Cabinet early in 1974, before it was known
that a general election would take place.

When Heath dissolved Parliament in February as part of his
campaign against the miners, that campaign document became
in effect Labour's manifesto.

The commitments thus entered into by the new Labour
Government with the electorate were in a real sense a reflection
of the growing role of the party and the unions, as well as
the Shadow Cabinet, and the parliamentary leadership lost –
temporarily – the sole control of policy that it had exercised
almost unchallenged in earlier years.

However, as we now know, many of these policies were not
implemented in practice by the 1974–79 Labour Government.

In the summer of 1974, the Cabinet issued a number of White
Papers and when the October 1974 manifesto was published,
Wilson insisted that these White Papers, some of which had

watered down our policies, replace the commitments that had appeared in the earlier manifesto of March 1974. Then, in March 1975, the Cabinet decided to accept the terms of the re-nego-tiation of Britain's Common Market membership, without even waiting to consult Labour MPs or the specially convened confer-ence – both of which were opposed to the acceptance of those terms.

The significance of that particular decision was twofold: by recommending Britain's continuing membership of the EEC Wilson made it impossible, and also illegal, for the 1973 Programme to be put into effect, and the way it was taken was intended to re-assert the primacy of the parliamentary leader-ship over the party and the unions.

From then on the task of replacing party policy with the Cabinet policies which Wilson and Callaghan wanted was rela-tively easy.

A major Cabinet reshuffle was carried through as soon as the referendum was out of the way and, with new ministers in charge, opposition from within the Cabinet was largely neutral-ised. Critics within the party were sternly lectured on the need for loyalty, and this left the trade unions as the only possible source of influential support for the manifesto policies for which they had voted at successive party conferences.

But the unions were caught by other pressures which rend-ered them much weaker than might have been expected. An economic crisis of a very familiar kind – a carefully orchestrated run on the pound – occurred as soon as the referendum was over and was made the excuse for introducing wage restraint.

Some union leaders may have been influenced by the fear that if they were to resist, the government would fall and be replaced by a Tory Government. But for whatever reason, the TUC went along with the Cabinet's proposals, and they carried their members with them for a while.

After a whole succession of cuts in public expenditure had been made, the pressure on working-class living standards reached breaking point and the winter of 1978–79 marked the end of the alliance that had so proudly launched the victory of four years earlier.

But in re-telling this familiar story of those unhappy years, it is necessary to recall that the party and the unions were not inactive during that time. While they remained loyal to the Labour Government in terms of supporting it in the Commons and the country, and did nothing to imperil its continuation in office for fear of opening the way to Mrs Thatcher, the work of campaigning to bring about a change of policy continued.

It was indeed during those years that the so-called Alternative Economic Strategy was pushed, both inside and outside the Government.

The Renewal of the Party, 1979–82

After Labour was defeated in the election of 1979, the party and the unions knew exactly what they wanted, and they went about the business of securing a change of policy in three key areas. First, they insisted upon the adoption of the Alternative Economic Strategy as the official policy of the party. Second, they wanted the party to pledge itself to take Britain out of the Common Market in order to allow that alternative strategy to be carried into effect. Third, they secured the abandonment of the nuclear weapons programme and the acceptance of a non-nuclear defence strategy.

Within a year or two of Labour's 1979 defeat, all these – and many other – policy changes had been carried through Conference, all with the requisite two-thirds majority, but the painful lessons concerning the relationship between the PLP leadership and the movement outside were not forgotten.

Thus in parallel with the policy changes came a campaign for greater democracy within the party to bring the PLP closer to the membership at constituency level and to strengthen the role of Conference. The long drawn out battle over reselection and the successful attempt to create an electoral college for the leader and deputy leader drew its support from a clear majority in the party.

The party is now therefore in a position where it has re-established its right to make policy and to secure sufficient accountability to give it a reasonable prospect of getting that policy put into effect.

But a manifesto that meets our aspirations and a constitution that is more democratic is only the beginning of the battle for change. Indeed, there is a danger that in working so hard on these essential changes we have had to look inwards at the expense of a campaign to build public support and were vulnerable to the charge that we were divided at a time when the campaign against the Tories should have taken top priority.

Labour must now re-establish itself as the true leader of a

progressive alliance working alongside all those who are fighting for a just society.

It is obvious that the Labour Party, as a political party, has electoral objectives which are necessary to secure a government with a majority to carry through the changes in law, administration and policy that are needed. But the Labour movement must be more than an electoral organisation and must campaign on a broad front with other groups that retain their autonomous nature, just as the trade unions do, even though many of them are affiliated to us.

We also need to have respect for the various socialist groupings that exist and are proliferating, even though some of them are very critical of the Labour Party. The socialist newspapers and the activists who gather round them are schools of thought which may illuminate the many problems which we may have to face in the future, and some of the issues associated with socialism.

Unless we take this very broad view of our constituency we cannot hope to mobilise the majority necessary to do what has to be done, for when a Labour government is in office it will need to have an active and informed body of public support if it is to beat off the attacks which its opponents will mount against it: that support has to be won now, and held, and it can only be done by having a clear view of the alliance we need, and being candid and open about this opposition.

From Defeat to Victory

I believe that the main causes of our defeat in 1983 were that over the years the parliamentary leadership became separated from the party, and that we have conceded basic arguments which no socialist party can afford to concede and still expect to win.

If Labour is to rebuild its strength and its unity for the future, as it must, we owe it to each other to say what we believe has happened and why; and how we think the party should approach its tasks over the next few years. Nothing must be allowed to obscure the political issues and the choices we must make.

Our starting point must be the economic background against which the election was fought and the political situation it created. After years of relative decline Britain was especially vulnerable to the world recession. Welfare capitalism, which had been created after 1945, ceased to be a viable proposition. A severely weakened market economy could no longer 'afford' to sustain full employment, pay for the necessary public services or 'allow' free trade unionism to practise collective bargaining.

A choice had to be made between the maintenance of unrestricted, international capitalism and a shift towards a more rationally and, where possible, a more internationally responsible system for the greater development of world resources. Within the United Kingdom, the need was for greater equality and more democratic control over our economy.

This choice was not forced upon us by extremist pressure from an allegedly revolutionary Left, but by the bankers, and in particular by the IMF which virtually blackmailed the 1976 Labour Cabinet into making cuts in public expenditure and clamping down on the trade unions by imposing a rigid policy of wage restraint upon them. The decision to give way to that pressure was justified by Labour's Cabinet majority, on the grounds that the Alternative Economic Strategy would lead to a siege economy.

Two years later, that Government then actually found itself besieged by its own political allies during the so-called 'winter of discontent', which defeated Labour a few months later. The incoming Conservative Government, armed with an electoral mandate, then proceeded to implement the bankers' policy with a will.

Unemployment was deliberately stimulated because it achieved everything that the new Government wanted to do. The dole queues controlled wages, undermined trade union bargaining power, limited imports, made further cuts in the public services seem 'inevitable' and boosted profits.

It divided working people – men from women, black from white, the employed from the unemployed – and it created a climate of fear which became the most powerful Tory weapon in the 1983 election campaign. When challenged to justify what was happening, the Tories chose the same argument that Labour had chosen – namely that it was the 'unavoidable' result of the battle against inflation. They were able to point out that when Labour had been in power it had completely rejected the very same alternative strategy that it was now arguing should be implemented.

Fear is a potent political weapon and it certainly played a major part in our defeat; for when people get frightened they become suspicious, cautious and conservative, and vote accordingly. If hope is to replace fear, people have to be able to believe that there is an alternative. Unfortunately for us, the electorate did not believe in Labour's alternative – and wondered whether we all believed in it either.

That is where we have to start – with what we believe and how that belief differs from the analysis of the Tories and the SDP/Liberal Alliance.

From 1979 the Tories used fear of foreign enemies to win support for their defence polices. The unceasing cold war propaganda to which we have been subjected over the last four years, conducted with the willing co-operation of the BBC, the IBA and Fleet Street, paid rich dividends in terms of electoral gains to the Tories.

Without any hard evidence being produced in support of it, many people were persuaded that the Soviet Union was actively planning an attack upon Western Europe, including Britain, and was only held in check by the massive American military presence in this country, and by huge stocks of US and British nuclear weapons. By falsifying figures of the East–West arms balance, and by ignoring the crushing of human rights within the Western sphere of influence – including Turkey and Latin America – the complexities and dangers of the present international situation were over-simplified to the point of crude distortion. People were presented with a stark choice between 'Capitalism and Freedom' on the one hand and all forms of 'Socialism and Tyranny' on the other. Thus the public were led to believe that Britain was engaged in a holy war which required a permanent crusade and the maintenance of this country on a semi-war footing.

Unfortunately, Labour did not offer a serious alternative analysis of world politics. People remembered that the post-war Labour Government had originally invited America to establish its bases here without insisting upon a British veto over their use; had built the hydrogen bomb without telling Parliament; and that the Chevaline project had been similarly authorised without even the Labour Cabinet having been fully informed. This record made our manifesto commitments to a non-nuclear defence strategy seem unbelievable.

It must also be said plainly that the support given by the Shadow Cabinet and a majority of the NEC to the Government's decision to send the task force in the spring of 1982 fatally undermined Labour's claim to be the advocate of internationalism and peace, and also hindered Labour's capacity to combat jingoism.

We were thus unable to criticise the Government effectively for its failure to negotiate with Argentina before the invasion, for its handling of the military operations or for its conduct since. In this context, the attempt to make an election issue of the sinking of the *General Belgrano*, or to call for a new inquiry, lacked credibility. We have to learn these lessons now, in case the same choices have to be made in the future over, say, a crisis in Gibraltar or Hong Kong. Labour must have a socialist framework of analysis if it is to be able to respond correctly to the world situation and the pressure of events.

Another contributory factor to Labour's successive defeats derives from the still unresolved problem of the relationship between the party and its representatives in Parliament, which has given the impression of disunity. The conference was strongly behind the manifesto policies; the main centre of opposition to them was in the PLP. In particular, the Shadow Cabinet consistently declined to put forward Labour's conference policies by tabling explicit opposition motions in support of them.

Thus, in the years leading up to the election itself, there was no proper parliamentary advocacy of those policies. The case for a non-nuclear defence strategy; for the closure of US nuclear bases; for British withdrawal from the Common Market; for the full alternative economic strategy, was simply not put in the Commons.

Hence Parliament was never properly used to develop a public understanding of, or support for, these central manifesto items upon which the election was eventually fought. Until the relationship between the party and the PLP is resolved, the party as a whole will continue to be presented as forever divided between Labour at conference and Labour in the Commons. And the electors will not know which to believe.

These explanations for our defeat will not be accepted by everyone in the party. We shall be told that our policies were unacceptable because they were too 'extreme', and that the main reason for our defeat can be traced back to what has happened within the party since the Tories came to power. It will be implied that if only we had stuck to the policies of 1979 (pro-market, pro-nuclear, pro-wage restraint and so on), and had left the constitution alone, if only the 1981 deputy leadership election had not taken place, if only the expulsions of the Left had happened earlier and on a wider scale, the SDP defectors would still be in the party and Labour would have romped home to an electoral victory on a title of popular revulsion against Tory policies.

Such an argument has to be spelled out for its inherent absurdities to become apparent. It must also be evident that if any attempt were made to carry this strategy of reversal through, it would meet with the opposition of the majority of the party. To argue along these lines is to encourage a grand illusion – a new myth that does not stand up to a moment's serious examination.

First of all, we were beaten in 1979 with the very policies to which we are now invited to return, when the SDP were all still with us. Second, such an argument assumes that policy commitment must be subordinated to the polls or the election results, without regard to what we believe, or to our capacity to win support for it by sustained public campaigns. Third, the demand for a policy change now is, in the main, coming from those who never supported such policies in the first place.

It also overlooks the fact that over the next few years, as the economic, social and political crisis deepens, events will almost certainly confirm the relevance of, and necessity for, what we wrote in the manifesto. Furthermore, no one will ever believe the Labour Party again if we are now ready to drop the very policies which we put forward in the election campaign.

Finally, if the situation calls for the further development of our policies, or changes in them, the whole movement is entitled to play its proper part in the decisions through conference.

So this is no time for the British Labour Party, in the depth of a real crisis for British capitalism, to announce to the world that it has decided to abandon its socialism – perhaps in the vain hope that some of its leaders might secure ministerial office in a non-socialist coalition government.

There is overwhelming grief within the party at Labour's defeat, and a consciousness that millions of people who needed a Labour government in power will be suffering directly as a result of what has happened. We must do everything we possibly can to protect all our people, including the trade unions and Labour local authorities, by supporting them in their struggles for jobs and homes, for education and good health, dignity in retirement and for peace.

We cannot confine our work to the parliamentary arena, nor should we forget that campaigns for social justice have always begun outside Parliament. The present media campaigns against extra-parliamentary activities are devices intended to defuse the pressure for social change. We should set ourselves a clear target of achieving, within the next year, a million members drawn from amongst Labour voters identified through canvass returns. And we must start at once on a campaign to establish workplace branches all over the country. This will feed the experience of those in paid work more directly into the constituencies and encourage more individual trade unionists to affiliate to the party by paying the political levy. In such ways will the links between the unions and the party be strengthened at a time when new anti-union legislation threatens to weaken them.

We must also recognise that a mass party, if it is to win and hold the confidence of the public, has got to listen to and campaign actively on behalf of the people whom it seeks to represent.

We must be there when we are needed in the communities where people live and work, to help them in struggles for their rights. Our support must be equally available to assist women who work in the home and lack the protection of a trade union against domestic exploitation, and to support people under pressure because they are black, disabled, old, gay or hold unpopular views.

As socialists, we know that popular rights and social justice cannot be achieved without a major change in the power structure of society, and of its values. Indeed, it is the awareness of that fact that has brought many radical Liberals to see the relevance of socialism, and has brought some of the best of them into the Labour party.

With the growing complexity of an industrialised society, campaigning for social justice has, in recent years, also developed outside the political and trade union structures that Labour has built up. Many single-issue pressure groups have evolved non-party responses to some of the biggest problems in society. They are fighting for the rights of women, for ethnic communities, for justice for the old, for a decent environment, for peace, and represent important initiatives that the Labour Party should be encouraging. Most of these groups are critical of one aspect or another of the values of capitalism. Some have come into being out of frustration at the bureaucracies that have disfigured the welfare state, and because we have not been as active as we should have been.

As socialists, we should also take an interest in the many socialist groups that have appeared on the scene, often with their own newspapers and campaigns. These schools of thought – some using the language of revolution – are usually highly critical of the Labour Party, and the immediate reaction of some Labour members and party officials is to organise a witchhunt against them and then expel anyone associated with them. In fact, these sects are an indication of the growing interest in socialist ideas. They should be regarded as ideological pressure groups along with the explicitly non-party community action groups to which I have referred.

Though the direct affiliation to the Labour Party of such groups or sects would enlarge our own perception and contribute directly to our policy-making, we have to accept that even if they remain autonomous they may have many common interests with us. Joint campaigns with them would provide exactly the sort of progressive alliance that we shall need if our own aspirations to represent the majority of people in this country are to be realised. The evolution of such an alliance should be a high priority for Labour in the immediate future. Once established, it would be better able to identify a whole new range of social needs, evolve policies to meet them, win public support and raise legitimate expectations that are capable of being realised.

The Tories, the Liberals, the SDP and the mass media which, lumped together, are really the voice of the combined British, Atlantic and Common Market establishments, are united in their determination to eliminate socialism from the nation's political agenda. Our objective, by contrast, is to move socialism back into the centre of discussion about the future. The case for socialism must be firmly rooted in daily experience; when people are allowed to learn what socialists are saying, its relevance becomes apparent. Indeed it should be our long-term purpose to persuade all parties, and all groups, that any discussion that leaves the socialist analysis out of account is not likely to lead to a solution.

A few years ago, every major political party in Britain was, to a greater or lesser extent, monetarist and accepted the existing institutions of the state uncritically. Our aim should be that, in the future, socialist ideas have as wide a currency and become a normal part of our understanding of all political choices.

I believe that the most interesting and relevant arguments over the future will be the arguments that take place about the many different ways in which democracy and socialism can be applied. If the British Labour party keeps faith with its own long commitment to those ideas we can avoid the mistakes which led to our defeat in 1983. And we shall also stand the best chance of winning a majority Labour government at the next election, which must be an aim we all have in common.

Parliamentary Democracy and the Labour Movement

In stating its faith in the role of Parliament, the Labour movement has never forgotten that its main strength has always remained outside Parliament, and that, under capitalism, even when Labour has a parliamentary majority, the real levers of economic and financial power are also outside Parliament, and are not subject to the direct, or indirect, control of the electors or the MPs whom they have chosen.

This has always been the case and it is even truer today. While the power of the multinationals, the international bankers, the military, the civil service and the mass media have increased significantly they have correspondingly become more and more internationalised in the IMF, the EEC or NATO.

The Labour Party is absolutely committed to uphold the principle of government, and all social change, by the consent of the people, which forms the basis of our democratic faith. Further, we have never been afraid that the democratic process might prevent us from realising our objectives, but rather that the institutions which we have in Britain may not, in practice, be sufficiently democratic to allow the will of the people to be translated into action.

Although we are always told that Britain is a democracy and that we have the 'Mother of Parliaments' at Westminster, the form of government under which we live is a lot less democratic than we may realise.

Official government publications have described our system of government as being a 'Constitutional Monarchy' which is not at all the same as democracy, since it means that we are, in law, governed by the Crown, but that, by custom and practice, that Crown power, or most of it, is exercised by ministers in a majority in the House of Commons following every General Election, for so long as they can get its legislation through that House.

The reality is that the British constitution is composed of three elements: a hereditary monarch, a House of Lords which is in part hereditary and in part appointed by patronage, and only one House, the Commons, over which the electors have any control. In that sense the British people have only succeeded in winning the right to elect one-third of our system of government, while the other two-thirds are still feudal in character.

Against this it is argued that, in practice, the Crown will always accept the advice of any Prime Minister with a Commons majority elected by the whole nation, and that the powers of the House of Lords are now very limited.

This however is not the whole story as when the Prime Minister does use the powers of the Crown, this often can be done under our constitution without any reference to the House of Commons at all. For example, it is a royal prerogative to make war or sign treaties. Further, matters sent to the Privy Council for decision do not come to the House of Commons at all, therefore the reality is that MPs can do nothing whatever to stop them.

There have been two recent examples of this: in 1972, Ted Heath signed the Treaty of Accession, under which Britain was taken into the Common Market, and did so without the text of that Treaty even being published beforehand, and without any formal ratification of it later by the Commons. Similarly in 1982 Mrs Thatcher took Britain into armed conflict with the Argentine over the Falklands without having to seek the approval of the House of Commons.

The Crown – personally – retains an unfettered discretion in respect of three of the most powerful prerogatives of all: the power to dismiss any Prime Minister, at any time; the power to dissolve Parliament and call a General Election; and the power to invite any person to form a government.

These prerogative powers were actually used in November 1975 to dismiss Gough Whitlam, the then Labour Prime Minister of Australia, even though he had a clear majority in the House of Representatives, simply because the Senate would not enact legislation passed by the House of Representatives. What happened then was that the Governor-General used the Royal prerogative to effect a 'constitutional coup' against an elected Labour Prime Minister, and destroyed both him and his Government in the process.

There is therefore absolutely no legal, or constitutional, guarantee that such a coup would not be repeated in this country if the House of Lords were to create a constitutional crisis by refusing to pass Bills that had the support of a Labour majority in the House of Commons, towards the end of its term of office, when there was nothing that the Commons could do to override the Lords obstruction, or if the Crown were to dissolve Parliament.

Equally important is the absolute discretion of the monarch to decide whom to call to form a new government at the beginning of a Parliament where no political party has an absolute majority, or to dissolve, or refuse to dissolve, Parliament when asked to do so by a Prime Minister. The fact that the armed forces, judges, bishops and all ministers and Members of Parliament are required to take an oath of allegiance to the Crown, and that there is no parallel oath of allegiance to the decisions of the House of Commons or their constituents, could also be very significant in any circumstances in which the Crown decided to intervene. Moreover the powers of the electors and their MPs have been fundamentally weakened by British membership of the Common Market, since all Common Market laws take precedence over all laws passed by the British Parliament, if the two conflict. Further all British judges are obliged to uphold, and enforce, the EEC laws in British courts, even if it means ordering British ministers to stop obeying laws passed by our own, elected, British Parliament.

Britain's membership of NATO, and, in particular, the secret agreements under which American forces are based in Britain with their own nuclear weapons which they can use without explicit agreement of the British Government or Parliament, also constitute a grave limitation upon the rights of the British people to govern themselves, and hence undermine many of our claims to be a democratic country.

These are all very fundamental questions which throw an important beam of light on the weakness of our democracy, and will explain why some of the recommendations made have to be quite radical.

The whole of our system of government rests upon the power of the Prime Minister, who, on appointment, assumes complete control of the entire ministerial, Civil Service and military apparatus, and sustains that power by an almost unfettered right of patronage.

Prime Ministers enjoy the personal right to choose the Cabinet, and recommend it to the Crown, and when the list has been approved by Buckingham Palace those ministers take a personal oath of allegiance to the Crown, as Privy Councillors,

over and above the oath they have already been required to take
as Members of Parliament. They then become Her Majesty's
Government, and everything that they do, thereafter, is done
in the name of the Crown, from whom derives their sole authority to take charge of the Government departments to which
the Prime Minister has appointed them. All ministers are there
during the Prime Minister's pleasure, and can be promoted,
moved or sacked, at his or her discretion, without any reference
to the House of Commons or MPs who have no power at all to
approve, or disapprove, individual ministerial appointments.

The power of prime ministerial patronage is staggering, and
stretches throughout the whole of our system of government.
The Prime Minister acts in the name of the Crown, and exercises
almost all its powers, not only over ministers but also in the
appointment of all civil and military chiefs, ambassadors, archbishops and bishops, judges, the chairmen of all nationalised
industries, including the BBC and the IBA, but to top it all has
the personal power to put people into Parliament for life – as
members of the House of Lords – all without any need to refer
to the House of Commons, which in these matters is completely
impotent.

For any democrat, and for the Labour movement which bases
itself upon the principle of election and accountability, this
degree of personal power, even if exercised by a party leader,
ought to be absolutely unacceptable, and would be, if people
were allowed to know what really goes on. For it means that
when Labour wins an election, its leader is, in effect, taken
away, and given power over the party, as well as the state, in
a way that runs quite contrary to the democratic traditions of
the party itself, and its affiliated trade unions. Further the situation is more serious when one remembers that the proceedings
of the Cabinet are protected by the Official Secrets Act, which
effectively excludes the party, as well as Parliament and the
public, from knowing what is being discussed until after the
decision has been announced, by which time it may be too late
to have any influence. All Cabinet ministers are also tied by
the notion of collective Cabinet responsibility, which the Prime
Minister can impose or suspend at will, binding them to all
actions taken by the PM or any minister even if these are in
direct conflict with the policies of conference, or even of the
party manifesto upon which the Government was elected.

Next we come to the House of Commons itself into which a
new Labour MP will be catapulted as into some nineteenth-
century gentlemen's club with its own quaint practices and

funny rules and an atmosphere that is as cosy as it is unreal. New MPs soon realise that the Speaker gives priority, in calling members to speak, to those who are Privy Councillors – i.e. ministers who have been the recipients of earlier patronage. MPs will also learn that, though they have been elected, they are still firmly on the wrong side of the Official Secrets Act, and that even ministers from their own political party may appear to be working more closely with their own civil servants than with their parliamentary and political colleagues.

In every Parliament the overwhelming majority of Labour MPs work conscientously on behalf of their constituents and the party but the successes that they have are in spite of and not because of the traditions of the House. When Labour is in office, the Labour Party itself is in no sense in power and is kept outside the decision-making machinery of the State. And, since a great deal of decision-making is made in Cabinet committees, the composition of which is left entirely to the PM, and the existence of which is a closely guarded secret, sometimes even from other ministers, not even Cabinet ministers always know what is going on. For example, no matters which involved the exercise of the Crown's prerogative by the Prime Minister will ever come before the Cabinet, unless the PM wishes them to do so, and the Prime Minister has the right to control the Cabinet agenda.

The relationship between the Government and the Labour movement does however go far beyond these matters, in that, as the Prime Minister is the ultimate head of the security services, he or she has the ultimate responsibility for the supervision of all left-wing activity in the party and trade unions, as was quite clear during the 1966 seamen's strike when Harold Wilson was told of the existence of 'these politically motivated men' by the Special Branch and used the information to denounce the strikers. Further, trade union leaders certainly had their phones tapped when Labour was in power as did others whose names may never have been reported to ministers.

There is also the question of the very close links of the Treasury and the Foreign Office with the TUC, probably first established when Ernest Bevin was a minister, and the equally close links between the Foreign Office and the International Department of the Labour Party itself. The reason why it is important for all this to be known and understood by the party is that, unless it is, Labour MPs may not realise how the country is really governed and local parties may not understand how little influence a backbench MP may have when Labour is in office.

It is now provided that the first Cabinet formed after a Labour victory will be composed of those people who were elected to the previous Shadow Cabinet, but this avoids the real case for regular elections to the Cabinet itself; this is that, if such elections were to take place when Labour was in power, then all Labour Cabinet ministers would be a great deal more sensitive to the Party Conference, because they could be removed if they consistently ignored the policy of the party. Further, the absence of any proper standing orders means that there is no regular way in which Labour MPs can determine the policies followed by Labour governments.

It would not be possible to conclude this account of the workings of Parliament without some reference to the way in which the media handles British politics.

The lobby system, in Parliament, is devised, so it seems, to observe what is really happening and to present a picture of political debate that rotates around the personalities involved, and to pump out the briefings conveyed, on a confidential basis, by those who know how to play the system to their own advantage with a word – unattributable of course – in the right ears, knowing that the source will be protected.

Lobby journalists and MPs both benefit from this way of working, in that the politicians are protected and the journalists know that they can pick what they want without much effort, and get confidences in return for a few favourable mentions. Indeed one of the worst effects of the system is that information that ought to be made available from a named source to the public at large, and to Parliament in particular, is leaked on a back-door basis in the corridors and bars, so that only those who know the rules really understand what is being said, and who is saying it, while the pretence of Government secrecy can be maintained and the public can be kept in the dark.

It goes without saying that the normal media bias against the party in the country and the trade unions is also in evidence in all parliamentary reporting but the illusion of some balance is maintained by the support they give to those members of the PLP who attack the party and the unions themselves.

The proprietors who dictate the political line of their newspapers, and the broadcasting chiefs, are richly rewarded for all that they do, in this direction, by the lavish award of honours, including peerages, which encourages them to moderate their criticisms of the parliamentary leadership, in the hope of becoming 'Press Lords' themselves, as many do. This is one reason why the lobby system should end. Also, if the televising of the House of Commons is allowed it will permit people to hear and see major debates on TV in the same way as they now can hear and see the party conferences.

A Freedom of Information Act would also help by rendering much of the leaking and briefing unnecessary in that journalists acting in good faith would be able to convey to their readers or viewers what was really being discussed in the Whitehall machine and in the Cabinet.

Against this background the argument for parliamentary reform is a compelling one. The following recommendations are put before the Labour movement in the hope that they will be discussed in constituency parties, in trade union branches, in political education sessions and publicly so as to given an opportunity for the discussion to be broadened out to include those who do not serve as MPs but look to Labour MPs to advance the cause of socialism through Parliament.

1. All Crown prerogatives to be subject to the decision of the House of Commons, including powers of dissolution before the end of a Parliament, the power to invite a person to form a government, and the power to declare war or sign treaties, etc.

2. The abolition of the House of Lords and the transfer of its work to the House of Commons, whose procedures would need to be modified to allow that extra work to be undertaken.

3. The repeal of Section Two of the 1972 European Communities Act to restore control of all legislation to the House of Commons, and to safeguard against the risk that the British courts might interpret European law in a way that frustrated the will of the British electors.

4. Cancellation of the agreements under which the United States of America retains nuclear bases in the United Kingdom which, at present, permit the President of the USA to make war from British territory without the consent of the British Government or Parliament.

5. The passage of a Freedom of Information Act so that Members of Parliament, and the public, may have access to all but a very narrow range of genuinely sensitive or secret Government information.

6. The introduction of a system under which all major public appointments have to be submitted in advance to the House of Commons for approval, before those appointments can be confirmed.

7. The introduction of a ministerial committee system under

which all Labour ministers would take with them, into their departments, a number of Labour MPs chosen and elected by members of the PLP specialist backbench groups who would act as advisers to the minister and form, with him or her, a departmental Cabinet in order to be sure that each department responded to the wishes of the electorate as reflected in the manifesto set before the people in the previous General Election.

8. The election, on an annual basis, of all Labour Shadow Cabinet and Cabinet ministers by the electoral college that meet at annual conference.

9. The ending of the practice under which Privy Councillors enjoy priority in being called in Commons debates.

10. The granting of power to all MPs to table documents in the House of Commons Library – which is a form of publication covered by parliamentary privilege – a right which is now confined to ministers, but cannot be exercised by MPs.

11. The introduction of legislation that would reduce the life of a Parliament from five years to four.

This is an important amendment because the pressure for closer links between the electorate and the House of Commons is a real and legitimate one, and a shorter Parliament would represent a better way of strengthening the bonds than proportional representation which would have the effect of loosening those links through the establishment of coalition-type governments in a multi-party system in a succession of hung Parliaments. The Levellers and the Chartists called for annual Parliaments and this pressure for more regular elections has recurred from time to time, and it should now be put back upon the political agenda.

12. The Palace of Westminster to be brought under the House of Commons alone, to make it more accessible to the electors who come to visit MPs and to see that the necessary facilities, including creches, for all those who work in the building are provided.

13. The law to be changed so that any MPs that leave the political party on which they were elected must recontest their seats at the earliest possible date. In the interim all Labour candidates must be asked to sign a solemn pledge that they would resign their seats in these circumstances.

All these demands are for radical democratic reform and would be strongly resisted by those in the Establishment who, though protesting their commitment to parliamentary democracy, in reality are totally opposed to the granting of any more powers to the House of Commons or to the electorate for fear that this would threaten their privileges.

SOURCES

FIFTY YEARS OF CONSENSUS RULE
First published in *Ruling Performance: British Governments From Attlee to Thatcher*, ed Peter Hennessy and Anthony Seldon, Basil Blackwell, 1987
THE PARTY AND THE GOVERNMENT
Paper by Tony Benn, April 1983
FROM DEFEAT TO VICTORY
First published in *New Socialist*, September 1983
PARLIAMENTARY DEMOCRACY AND THE LABOUR MOVEMENT
Extracts taken from Campaign Group pamphlet, 1984

2
PROPHETIC
VOICES

Positive
Dissent

At present we are encouraged to believe that politics is all about personalities, or the managerial policies of those personalities, and it is in that way that they are regularly reported. You have only to look at the primaries in America to see where that leads you.

There can be no denying the importance of the character of those who exercise political power, nor the relevance of detailed policies that may be implemented by them. But nobody is indispensable and changed circumstances may force changes of policy. What matters much more is the mechanism by which decisions are made – whether by the imposition of decisions taken at the top, or by a democratic decision of those who are being governed. And the foundation upon which all societies must rest is necessarily a moral one deriving from the attitudes that people take about their duty to their fellow men and women. It is at that fundamental level that religion and politics come together and ethical considerations become all-important. And that must also be the starting point for any examination of the role of positive dissent in society. Many of our political rights were won as a result of earlier struggles to establish the parallel right of conscience in religious faith. Indeed it is no exaggeration to say that many of the battles which are now being fought out as political battles were, in earlier centuries, seen as religious battles between those of differing religious faiths.

In that context the role of non-conformity and the non-conformist conscience must be our starting point when we seek out the roots of radical dissent. It is an essential part of our tradition. It has enriched both our religious and our political life and is an essential ingredient in making us what we are; and in allowing us to be what we can be. And I would like therefore to excavate those foundations like a political archeologist.

It is not possible to speak of these matters without going straight back to the Old Testament, because the ideas from which dissent in both religion and politics in Britain have sprung come directly out of the Bible.

The history of the Jewish people before the birth of Christ provides endless examples of prophetic warnings against kingly power and the abuse of that power, and offer to us an external frame of reference to which we can relate our own experience and from which we can acquire some direct personal guidance about what is right and what is wrong.

For example, I quote from the prophet Amos:

> But let judgment run down as waters; and righteousness as a mighty stream.

Righteousness is seen as an independent force flowing through our lives and thoughts. The prophet Micah:

> He had shewed thee O man what is good: and what doth the Lord require of thee but to do justly and walk humbly with thy God.

And of course in the New Testament when Jesus was asked by one of the scribes 'what commandment is the first of all?' St Mark's Gospel records his answer:

> The first is Hear O Israel: The Lord our God, the Lord is One: and thou shalt love the Lord thy God with all thy heart, and with all thy soul, and with all thy strength. And the second is this. Thou shalt love thy neighbour as thyself. There is none other commandment greater than these.

It isn't good enough to say if only the rich are good and the poor are patient it will all be put right in the next world. It isn't an adequate answer in the world we live and it is not surprising that this social message has spread well beyond Christian denominations.

H. G. Wells, in his *History of the World* – and remember Wells was an atheist – described the revolutionary effect of Christ's teaching on him in a most remarkable passage in his book 'In what he plainly said,' this is Wells writing of Jesus:

> Is it any wonder that all who were rich and prosperous felt a horror of strange things, a swimming of their world at His teaching? He was dragging out all the little private reservations they had made from social service into the light of a universal religious life. He was like some terrible moral huntsman, digging mankind out of the snug burrows in which they had lived hitherto. In the white blaze of this kingdom of His there was to be no poverty, no privilege, no pride and precedence; no motive indeed and no reward but love. Is it any

wonder that men were dazzled and blinded and cried out against Him? Even His disciples cried out when he would not spare them the light. Is it any wonder that the priests realised that between this man and themselves there was no choice but that He, or priestcraft, should perish? Is it any wonder that the Roman soldiers, confronted and amazed by something soaring over their comprehension and threatening all their disciplines, should take refuge in wild laughter and crown Him with thorns and robe him in purple and make a mock Caesar out of Him? For to take Him seriously was to enter upon a strange and alarming life, to abandon habits, to control instincts and impulses, to essay an incredible happiness.

I consider this is one of the most remarkable passages in the English language and for Wells the message was clearly political.

Thus I come to the first characteristic of a dissenting conscience, the awareness of the difference between right and wrong and of a duty that is implanted directly and does not require the interposition of priest or prelate, to mystify the message, or to draw the faithful into a position of subservience to a clerk in holy orders before we can follow the teaching of the Almighty. The priesthood of all believers.

Not unnaturally such an idea was not welcome to those enjoying the positions of power in the Church or State when their authority and power rested upon just such a process. Martin Luther's challenge to the Church of Rome drew some of its force from just such a belief in the inner light of faith against authority imposed by the Bishops. But it would be wrong to equate such a challenge to the Papacy with the ideas of toleration. Because neither Luther nor John Knox, nor the Presbyterians, nor for that matter some of the Non-conformist denominations which grew out of the Reformation, were any more tolerant of dissent within their own ranks than were the Popes towards their own dissenters.

Dissent, independence and the whole idea of conscience as an inner light, and I might add as being above the law, must of necessity be seen as standing apart in all churches, all chapels, all denominations and indeed from all organised religion and political organisations too.

This is the second characteristic of a dissenting conscience. It stands apart from structures and feels free to challenge not only their doctrine and practice, but even their credentials and authority on the basis of tests applied from inside the heart and mind and soul.

I hope I have said enough to establish that dissenters are

likely to enrage both the priesthood and the political authorities in any society which establishes its religion and regards an attack upon the doctrine of the Church or upon the conventional political wisdom both as heretical and as subversive at one and the same time.

The history of the religious persecutions of the independent churches in the sixteenth and seventeenth centuries in Britain is full of examples of intolerance, and it still is, although the targets are new and the penalties are different.

Richard Fitz and his separatist congregation were arrested in 1567 for treasonable opposition to Elizabeth I's Act of Uniformity. Later the Brownists and the Congregationalists and the Baptists were persecuted. Barrow and Greenwood who carried on Browne's work were executed in 1593 for asserting that 'Christ is the only Head of His Church and His laws no man may alter'. But if the established Church was intolerant so too were the Puritans.

After the Restoration of Charles II sterner action still was taken against the Non-conformists. Presbyterians, Independents and Baptists who were ejected from their livings by the 'Great Ejectment' and in 1665 the 'Five Mile Act' effectively rusticated Non-conformist ministers.

Even in 1689 when the Toleration Act was passed it excluded the Unitarians from its provisions and civil disabilities were placed upon these denominations and upon the Catholics and continued for some time. At that time Papists were seen by many as Marxists are today – traitors by virtue of their faith.

To end the history at this point would be to give a very incomplete account of the subject of this lecture. For it might give the impression that dissent was the prerogative of Non-conformists and that the possession of a conscience and a stubborn adherence to its calling was a special feature of the free churches. Nothing could be further from the truth.

Catholics as well as Baptists and Congregationalists can lay equal claim to have thrown up their martyrs of conscience who should be recognised as such. And if the final proof of any person's faith must be sought in his readiness to die for it, then history will record the death of many of all denominations who cited as the reason why they were ready to die that they were asked to act against their consciences.

Sir Thomas More, sentenced to death in 1535, was asked if he had anything to say and when he began to defend himself the Earl of Norfolk said: 'Sir Thomas, you show your obstinate and malicious mind'. More replied:

Noble Sir, it is not malice or obstinacy that makes me say this: but the just necessity of the cause obliges me to do it, for the discharge of my conscience: and I call God to witness that nothing but this has excited me to it.

If you turn now from Catholic to Independent, Thomas Harrison, a Major-General in Cromwell's Army, the son of a butcher, executed on 13 October 1660 at Charing Cross, spoke from the scaffold before he was hanged, drawn and quartered:

I have again and again besought the Lord with tears, to make known His will and mind unto me concerning it, and to this day He hath rather confirmed me in the justice of it, and, therefore, I leave it to Him and to Him I commit my ways; but some that were eminent in the work did wickedly turn aside themselves, to set up their nests on high, which caused great dishonour to the name of God and the profession they had made.

The authentic voice of a political leveller.

Or to turn to another classic, this time David Lewis, Bishop of Llandaff, hanged, drawn and quartered on 27 August 1679, at Usk in Monmouthshire, said on the scaffold that he had been asked to admit to a plot. If he would admit to a plot then he would be excused.

Discover a plot I could not, for I knew of none; conform I would not, because it was against my conscience. Then by consequence I must die, and so now, dying, I die for conscience and religion.

Or if you want one last one, Richard Rumbold who was a Republican, executed in June 1685, at the Gallows in Market Cross in Edinburgh, hanged, drawn and quartered after the Monmouth Rebellion, said this on the scaffold; very memorable words they are if we are to build the bridge between religious and political dissent.

I am sure there was no man born marked of God above another; for none comes into the world with a saddle on his back, neither any booted and spurred to ride him.

The revolt against authority was not of course confined to matters of theology, but extended into politics from the earliest times.

Everyone remembers the words of John Ball, that turbulent priest – now they would call him a militant of course – who supported Wat Tyler at the time of the Peasants' Revolt in 1381: 'When Adam delved and Eve span who was then the gentleman?'

Where in the Old Testament do you find any authority for

the class system? John Ball was hanged, drawn and quartered. Now they do it in Fleet Street, but it has the same general effect.

In 1522, a Burford Lollard paid £1 for an English Bible (not many people realise it was illegal to read the Bible until the sixteenth century), so that he could read it with his friends, many of them weavers. One of them, John Edmunds, told a Witney man in Oxfordshire 'to go and offer his money to God's own image, which was the poor people, blind and lame'.

John Edmunds and his followers were forced to kneel on the altar steps at Burford Church, with faggots on their shoulders, and the faggots were no doubt burned to heat the branding irons with which this group of Bible readers – twelve men and nine women – were branded on the cheek at the end of prayers to teach the congregation *not* to read the Bible.

It is not only in the religious area, in the area of theology and faith, that dissent began to make itself felt.

I must ask you to follow me over the bridge that links Christianity to Humanism. And a very difficult but important bridge it is to understand, because it is the bridge that links and also divides those who believe that God created man and those who believe that man invented God. A very important, substantial, dominant theological distinction. But the ethical lessons drawn by people on either side of that bridge are very similar if they are both based upon the idea of brotherhood as a moral imperative.

The concept of brotherhood, however, on whatever theological superstructure it rests, forms part of the same external frame of reference to which conscience can refer. Take first the theological critique of injustice. This one is from the Christian side of the bridge. During the Civil War in 1649 a Royalist historian reported with horror what were the opinions of the people in revolt against King Charles I. In Chelmsford he discovered such a group of Levellers, and this is what he said they were saying. It's a quotation of their opinion:

> The relation of Master and Servant has no grounds in the New Testament; in Christ there is neither bond nor free. Ranks such as those of the peerage and gentry are ethical and heathenish distinctions [I agree with that]. There is no ground in nature or scripture why one man should have £1,000 per annum, another not £1. The common people have been kept under blindness and ignorance [and that still goes on] and have remained servants and slaves to the nobility and gentry. But God hath now opened their eyes and discovered unto them their Christian liberty.

Now that is the Christian view, but carry it to the Diggers or true Levellers and you come to the beginning of the crossing of the Humanistic end of the bridge to which I have referred. Here is not the New Testament that is the basis, at least not the Christian interpretation of creation, but the idea that man was created by Reason. So now take the same critique from the Humanist end. And this is what Gerrard Winstanley said on 26 April 1649, in his pamphlet 'The True Levellers' Standard Advanced':

> In the beginning of Time, the great Creator, Reason [not God but Reason] made the Earth to be a Common Treasury, to preserve Beasts, Birds, Fishes and Man, the Lord that was to govern this Creation: for Man had Domination given to him, over the Beasts, Birds and Fishes: but not one word was spoken in the beginning, that one branch of mankind should rule over another.

Now you compare the two critiques from either side of that divide and it doesn't take much analysis to realise that with the spirit of these ideas religion got drawn into the vortex of political controversy. Even the Methodists were denounced by the Authorities.

In 1792 the Mayor of Liverpool wrote to the Home Secretary in these words:

> In all these places are nothing but Methodist and other Meeting houses, and thus the Youth of the Country are training up under the instruction of a set of men not only ignorant, but whom I believe we have of late too much reason to imagine are inimical to our happy constitution.

I should think that sort of letter is on its way again! That is to say there were trouble-makers and militants and wreckers and all the things that the media now denounces in others.

I came across another passage. The Duchess of Buckingham wrote to the Countess of Huntingdon, whose connection was very much a part of this tradition:

> I thank Your Ladyship for the information concerning the Methodist preachers; their doctrines are most repulsive and strongly tinctured with impertinance and disrespect towards their superiors in perpetually endeavouring to level all ranks and to do away with all distinctions. It is monstrous to be told that you have a heart as sinful as the common wretches that crawl upon the earth.

Now we are beginning to get to the heart of political dissent. Let us remind ourselves that these ideas which had been fashioned in the Dissenting tradition in Britain were carried straight over in 1776 in the American Revolution.

We hold these Truths to be self-evident that all Men are created equal, that they are endowed by their Creator with certain inalienable Rights, and that among these are Life, Liberty and the Pursuit of Happiness. That to secure these rights Governments are instituted among men deriving their just powers from the consent of the Governed.

The inalienable right to equality in political power is where they all came from – traditions which I have tried to describe – but of course they went beyond the basic democratic argument. In the Chartists' Association of 1842 you find these ideas taking a directly political form, but still referring back to their Christian origins. And this is why this bridge is so important, but it is a bridge which can be crossed and re-crossed and regularly is.

This is what the Chartists said in 1842:

The great political truths which have been agitated during the last half-century, have at length aroused and degraded and insulted White Slaves of England to a sense of their duty to themselves, their children and their country. Tens of thousands have flung down their implements of labour.

Your taskmasters tremble at your energy and expecting masses eagerly watch this great crisis of our cause. Labour must no longer be the common prey of masters and rulers. Intelligence has beamed upon the mind of the bondsman, and he has been convinced that all wealth, comfort and produce, everything valuable, useful and elegant, have sprung from the palm of his hand; he feels that his cottage is empty, his back thinly clad, his children breadless, himself hopeless, his mind harassed and his body punished that undue riches, luxury and gorgeous plenty might be heaped in the palaces of the taskmasters, and flooded into the granaries of the oppressor. Nature, God and Reason have condemned this inequality, and in the thunder of a people's voice it must perish for ever.

If we are to go back to Victorian values we have some pretty good ones of our own. In 1897 Keir Hardie wrote a Christmas message in the *Labour Leader*, and he too drew heavily on the teachings of Jesus.

When I think of the thousands of white-livered poltroons who take the Christ's name in vain, and yet not see His image being crucified in every hungry child, I cannot think of peace. I have known, as a child, what hunger means, and the scars of those days are with me still and rankle in my heart, and unfit me in many ways for the work to be done. If the spiritually-proud and pride-blinded professors of Christianity could only be made to feel, and see, that the Christ is here present with us, and that they are laying on the stripes and binding the brow afresh with thorns, and making him shed tears of blood in a million homes, surely the world would be made more fit for His Kingdom.

Very powerful words they were and with them positive Christian dissent was restated with immense political strength.

But now I want to turn to dissent in that great part of the world which, as far as established religion is concerned, is formally atheistic in character. It would be wrong just to talk about the West. Let us look at dissent in the East.

Within the Communist world there are now many courageous dissenters (and this is what's interesting to me at any rate), who are citing Marx against Stalin in the way Christ was cited against Kings and Bishops by many of the Dissenters I have quoted.

I have chosen on extract from a speech made at Charles University in the Prague Spring of 2 May 1968 by Ivan Svitak, and this is what he said about Marx:

> Marx was not and is not and never will be the inventor and theoretician of totalitarian dictatorship that he appears today, when the original meaning of his work – true humanism – has been given a thoroughly Byzantine and Asian twist. Marx strove for a wider humanism than that of the bourgeois democracies that he knew and for wider civil rights, not for the setting-up of the dictatorship of one class and one political party. What is today thought to be the Marxist theory of the state and the Marxist social science imply an ideological forgery, a false contemporary conception, as wrong as the idea that the orbits of heavenly bodies are circular.

What I find interesting about that passage, and there are many others like it, is that in the humanistic or non-Christian tradition you see the founder of the faith cited against the practitioners of the faith.

Let me quote now from Milan Machovec who was a Marxist professor in Prague and organised many dialogues between Marxists and Christians. He wrote a book called *A Marxist Looks at Jesus*, and if you haven't read it I can most strongly recommend it. 'The attentive reader of this book', he says, 'will realise – perhaps to his surprise – that I am a self-confessed Marxist and yet I write about Jesus with enthusiasm and passion.' In it Machovec, who was a considerable theological scholar, wrote:

> Jesus' disciples understood him and believed in him, not because he had thought things out speculatively, or put great ideas before them, but because he embodied the lived future in His own being. Hence the emphasis on action ('Go and do likewise') rather than dogma.

Machovec believes that the central point in Jesus' teaching makes a binding claim on man in his present:

It is not remotely fantastic or mythological [that's how he's speaking of Jesus]. On the contrary it says that a man can become truly human, and can live to the fullest extent of his powers, on condition that the present is not viewed as an end in itself but is open to the positive and far reaching vision of the future.

Then he goes on to say something very political which directly challenges the Christian churches by referring them to the teachings of Jesus. This is where the complexity and interest of it becomes so riveting.

One may even wonder whether the disciples of Karl Marx who, 1800 years after Jesus, set in motion a similarly far reaching and complex process with as yet quite unforseeable consequences, but similar aspirations, to a radical transformation of social relationships, and a future conceived in a radically different way, may not in fact have the greatest right to regard themselves as the authentic perpetuators of Old Testament Messianism and early Christian desires for radical change. Many Marxists, but also many self-critical modern theologians, are aware of the fact that concern for the future – that longing for liberation and radical change once found in Christianity – has been taken over almost exclusively by Marxism.

Now I'm not asking anybody to accept the quotations. I've picked them to make the point, but you can see the strength of an argument that puts such a view forward. This is what he says about Christianity:

You can corrupt the heritage, overlay what is best in it, push it in the background, but those who seek it out tomorrow will find life and new hope beneath the layers of dirt and the petrified outlines – simply because they are attuned to it. Thus in Christianity the dogmatised image of Jesus Christ has never been able thoroughly to banish the image of the man, Jesus of Nazareth.

Machovec himself of course suffered for that view, because he was dismissed from his post after the Russian occupation of Czechoslovakia in 1968.

And it is within that same tradition we find others who move freely across the bridge from matters of Christian faith to matters of social action. I refer to the statement now made by the Latin American Bishops at their conference at Puebla in Mexico in 1979. They said life in the continent is 'a type of abomination'. They supported the workers and peasants in their rights to form trade unions. They denounced torture, exile and the kidnapping of dissidents and they said of the Church in politics that religious duty included a more just and free and a more peaceful society. And they also said, 'Now is the time for Latin America to warn developed countries that they should not immobilise us, hinder our progress, nor exploit us but help us.' Liberation Theology with priests armed with the Bible in one hand and *Das Kapital* in the other as preached by the 'Church of the Poor' against the hierarchical Church is even stronger in its impact. Here we can begin to see a confluence from East and West and North and South of ideas which have their roots in the Bible that we study and the New Testament from which we're taught. And with the World Council of Churches supporting liberation movements, we can begin to see the blend and mixture of what a political message of dissent in religious and political terms really means.

Look at today's dissenters to see what happens to them. We find in all religions dissent against doctrines and actions imposed by the authorities of the Church. We find in all states dissent against the doctrine and the actions of the State. In many faiths – Christian, non-Christian, humanist and socialist, we find people who are prepared to suffer the ultimate penalty for their beliefs. And I pick them out as a mark of my respect, the women at Greenham Common who are prepared to be mocked for their testimony for peace. In view of his recent death I think it right to put on record the words of Pastor Niemoller, who as you know was a U-boat captain in the First World War, then later was a Pastor in the Lutheran Church in Germany and then was arrested by Hitler.

> First they [the Nazis] came for the Communists, and I did not speak up because I wasn't a Communist. Next they came for the Trade Unionists and I did not speak up because I wasn't a Trade Unionist, next they came for the Catholics, but I didn't speak up because I was a Protestant. Finally they came for me and, by then, there was no one left to speak up for me.

Dissenters must be protected. They must be protected from the witch-hunters, from the book burners, from the Thought Police, from the Ecclesiastical Courts, from the mass media, from the KGB, from the CIA, from MI5 and the Special Branch who, in this country as in any country in the world, are always looking for difficult men and women who may be saying something that in some way undermines their authority in society and thus keep them under close surveillance.

Most of us have to work within the social and political, economic and religious structures of conventional wisdom.

But we have a special duty to understand, to cherish, to defend, and above all to *listen* to those who choose to challenge our structures and our opinions; those who assert higher values from the inner voice of conscience. Positive dissent and positive political and religious dissent is to be found throughout the whole of human history.

It is in all religions. It is in all societies. It is in all faiths and it is, I believe, if we look for it, in each of us.

Today, I believe, it speaks mainly through those who are campaigning for the right to think for themselves, for peace and development, for human rights and greater equality and greater democracy, and those voices may be our greatest hope for the future.

Thomas Paine

Thomas Paine was one of the very greatest figures in the history of popular struggle, and in celebrating the 250th anniversary of his birth this year his words come to us across the centuries with all their original freshness.

Paine was committed to free thought, to human rights, to morality in public affairs, to democracy, to internationalism and to the promotion of welfare, and it is for those very reasons that he is still hated and feared by the British Establishment because he still represents a direct threat to their power and influence.

I cite one example of this which gives an amusing insight into the way the Establishment thinks in unexpected ways. On 3 February last year I wrote to the Chairman of the Post Office Board, to ask for a postage stamp to be issued to commemorate the 250th anniversary of Thomas Paine's birth.

Sir Ronald Dearing replied, 'We considered this anniversary very fully and carefully when we were drawing up our 1987 programme, but I am sorry to tell you it was not among the subjects chosen.' He enclosed a list of the subjects that had been chosen: a stamp to commemorate the 150th anniversary of Queen Victoria's accession to the throne; and another to celebrate Scottish Heraldry (a matter of great concern), the tercentenary of the revival of the Order of the Thistle. If anyone thinks that is an unusual response, I must tell you that when I was Minister of Posts in 1975, I asked for a stamp to celebrate the bicentennial of the American Revolution. The reply came as follows:

Although the bicentenary of the Declaration of Independence by the American colonies has support from the Foreign and Commonwealth Office, it is our view this subject is not suitable for inclusion in our special stamp programme.

However it might be approached in design terms, there would be a danger that ordinary people would criticise the issue as celebrating a defeat.

Moreover, there could well be feeling in those former British colonies which did achieve their independence later, but without bloodshed, that whilst, for instance, we did not mark the centenary of the British North America Act of 1867, [that was the Canadian Act] we should seem to honour those who have rebelled.

That was 200 years later. And you know, if you blow on the embers of any old controversy the flames flicker again as they do around the name of Thomas Paine. Even today *The Rights of Man* is not allowed to be read by the prisoners in the Maze prison, although it is on the reading list for Open University courses.

It is a great thing to be controversial 200 years after you are dead and, I think, Thomas Paine ranks with the greatest of them all.

Thomas Paine was born in Thetford, son of a corset-maker. He became an excise man and came first to public attention by making the claim of the low-paid civil servants who worked in the Customs and Excise.

He went to America and played a leading part in inspiring the American Revolution, and was an advocate of free thought. He was a Republican and believed in the abolition of slavery – which did not make him very popular in America. He was a man who believed women should have equal rights with men which was as controversial then as it is today, and he supported the Irish cause.

Paine also put forward ideas about progressive taxation, about benefits, about family allowances, about hardship allowances, about the need for pensions, invalidity benefits, death grants and, of course, the proper funding of education – thus Paine can truthfully be said to have forecast the shape of the Welfare State. He supported the French Revolution, went over to France, was made an honorary citizen of the French Republic and an honorary member of the French Convention. Later, he was imprisoned by the French for his opposition to the death sentence on the King, and was very nearly executed himself only Robespierre, who wanted him executed, got executed first. His most famous book *The Rights of Man*, was in answer to Edmund Burke who was my predecessor as Member of Parliament for Bristol, a man who described the populace as 'the swinish multitude'.

Unable to return to Britain for fear of imprisonment here for seditious libel for the publication of *The Rights of Man*, Paine went back to America where his free thinking about religion and his continued opposition to slavery earned him a great deal of public disapproval, and he died there, a somewhat lonely man.

In Britain today we are witnessing an attempt to put the clock back – not just to Victorian times but to a much earlier period – and this is one reason why Paine is still so relevant.

Millions in this country now experience unemployment, low wages and poverty and we have seen enacted new Combination Acts which make effective trade unionism virtually illegal.

Democracy itself is under attack as with the abolition of the Greater London Council, ratecapping and the disqualification and possible bankruptcy of elected councillors, and the use of the Official Secrets Act to prosecute public servants who dared to speak the truth while the Security Services defy the law with impunity.

We see repression in Ireland, rampant racism, attacks upon the rights of women and the surrender of our own self-determination to a foreign army, however friendly, encamped in over a hundred bases in our country.

We see the police and the courts used to enforce a particular political view, all justified in the name of national security and law and order.

British industry is in decline and the institutions under which we live are corrupted by patronage and exercise their power at the top, in secret, inefficiently and bureaucratically, to repress dissent and protect a powerful clique who dominate the military and Civil Service, the banks, the multinationals and the mass media which dispense opium to the people on a daily basis, with the exception of the *Morning Star*.

This – almost medieval – system, for so it is, conceals its barbarity and brutality behind the glittering facade surrounding the Crown, so that the rich and the powerful, and their international allies, can despoil our land with nuclear bases and nuclear power, steal our property by privatisation and take away our liberties.

If we are to respond to this situation we shall need to go back to Thomas Paine and all the others who contributed by their struggle and their words to the traditions of radicalism which has enriched our history and inspired generations of our people.

Every society must determine which moral values it espouses and if we go on accepting the philosophy of the jungle, we shall make no change in our condition whichever government is in power. And, unless we rediscover the meaning of solidarity, we have no chance of mobilising a majority for change, since it is the prime purpose of the Establishment to confuse and divide us so that there is no effective challenge to their power.

For the poor and the disinherited throughout history, and for all those who depend for their income upon their labour, collective action, whether through trade unions or the ballot box, offers the best prospect of advance: that is why the rebuilding of a popular movement is of such central importance now.

If capitalism in Britain depended on 400 Conservative Members of Parliament, it would disappear tomorrow morning. Capitalism in Britain is entrenched in all the organisations that I have mentioned and if we don't have a popular movement – as strong as theirs – then we shall find it very hard to defeat their power.

Thomas Paine understood all this and by building on the concept of inherent rights he added a new dimension to the political argument, giving people hope that it could be done and thus overcoming the apathy and despair which has such a paralysing effect in entrenching the status quo by making it appear that there is no effective alternative.

Paine gave us hope just as President Roosevelt did when he assumed office in the USA in the middle of a financial crisis. He said to the American people in a famous speech: 'We have nothing to fear but fear itself.'

And it is important to remember that of all the capitalist countries in the 1930s, the only one that swung in a progressive direction as distinct from going towards fascism was the United States. That is perhaps a hope we should keep in our mind at this moment.

What we need in Britain now, I believe, is a break out from all the negative ideas which imprison us and the structures and patterns of ownership and control that confer no benefit on the overwhelming majority but are necessary to keep the Establishment in power.

There are many people – and I am one of them – who think the time is ripe for a relaunching of socialist and democratic ideas in Britain. For just as I referred to the power of capitalism lying in its organisations outside, so the power of the Conservative Party (and one must recognise this) lies in the fact that they have taken the incidents with which they had to deal, dealt with them and taught from them. And we have long ago, it seems to me, abandoned the role of socialist education as part of the daily business of political work.

If we want change, we have got to do it ourselves, and not plead with people at the top to do it for us.

Thomas Paine, were he alive today, would, I am sure, take up the cause of a 'British Revolution by Consent' with the same enthusiasm as he invested in the revolutions in America and France 200 years ago.

If we are to take up this task, we shall, I think, need to begin by making clear demands upon the system, as Paine did in *The Rights of Man*.

History always begins to change when large bodies of people say 'No' and refuse to accept the fate that has been allocated to them. For 'No' is still the most powerful preliminary word in the political vocabulary, and if it is followed by positive claims for justice those with power have to take account of it.

But we must also seek to re-establish morality, solidarity, democracy, equality and internationalism as the foundations of our political life and to build a popular movement to secure that those demands are met.

In speaking of morality as the necessary foundation for any advance, let me be clear that I am referring to the urgent necessity to challenge the idea that life must be a competitive rat-race in which the strongest actually deserve to run away with all the prizes.

It is very evident to anyone who reads Paine's writings or studies his life, that the concept of inherent rights, that everybody possesses when they are born, whether they are rich or poor, men or women, black or white, is central.

Until we re-establish the principle of inherent rights, we shall make no progress, whoever sits in No 10 Downing Street.

For without the concept of inherent rights, you cannot achieve democracy, and without democracy in the trade unions and through the ballot box, working people will find it very hard to achieve anything.

The key question that has to be asked of people who come forward with a desire to represent us is a very simple one: it is 'whose side are you on?'

Anyone can make marvellous speeches and write excellent pamphlets, and I assure you it is very easy to be a Right Honourable, and carry a red box, and have a ministerial car, but if you are not on the right side when it matters, you are not much use to the movement.

The Democracy of Here and Now

Democracy draws its legitimacy too from the idea of inherent rights; for if all men and women are brothers and sisters, then they must have equal rights in respect of their government.

And the idea of solidarity stems from the same roots, for if we are brothers and sisters, we have a duty to defend each other all the time, including Liverpool and Lambeth councillors, gays and lesbians, and women who are at Greenham Common and those who are being persecuted for their opinions.

Historically some bishops and priests used to try and avoid that imperative by saying, something like this: 'Well it's a very unfair world. We know that. But if only the rich are kind and the poor are patient, it will be all right when we are dead, and the angels will bring you a cup of tea in the morning and eternal life will be more tolerable than the present life.' Socialists replied to that argument by demanding justice here and now while we are still alive to enjoy it.

But before we laugh too loud at the bishops, we must recognise there is now an electoral version of the same argument which goes like this, 'All right, life's very hard but if you don't rock the boat, it will be all right when Labour gets into power.' And that too is a diversion from the central question because it is not an adequate argument either, for democracy is what we do here and now, and not what somebody else does for us, later, when they get into the seats of power.

It is very easy for any Labour minister to confuse his or her own arrival in his or her ministerial office with the dawn of socialism when all that has actually happened is that he or she personally has arrived at the top of the ladder. If we accept that view, then we do become spectators of what others do for us and the essential element of democracy of which Paine spoke virtually disappears. Politics becomes like the Eurovision Song Contest, or the award of an Oscar in Hollywood, which we are allowed to watch on television, but the outcome of which we cannot expect to influence.

The day we allow democracy to become a spectator sport, we shall have abandoned our basic rights. This, in my opinion, is why they are spending so much time now trying to make us do precisely that.

The British Establishment is afraid of democracy. It is the challenge to their power that frightens them and sometimes frightens off the leaders of our own movement. I think that the pressure for democracy explains a great deal of the crisis and debate that is now occurring in the socialist countries of Eastern Europe, and also in the bureaucracies of Social Democratic parties in the West.

For the more I reflect on this, the more I think that Morrisonian views of common ownership and some of the features of the Soviet system had a lot in common. They were both rather centralised and secretive and bureaucratic and both have now to be re-examined in the light of a popular demand for greater democratic rights since you cannot maintain socialism without consent and that means that without democracy you cannot carry people with you. And that is why there is this great debate about democracy within the socialist countries which I regard as one of the most hopeful things that has happened in the last forty years, and which has got such relevance for us as well.

But before we recommend our own brand of parliamentary democracy to others we had better recognise that under our system we are not really allowed to change the system but only to change the management, and that offers a fairly limited range of choice.

When Julius Nyerere set up a one-party state in Tanzania, an American journalist criticised him and Julius replied, 'Well even in America, you have a one-party state. But with typical American extravagence, you have two of them.' And I think it is important that we should retain a proper element of self-criticism when we talk about the 'Mother of Parliaments'.

What we need in Britain now is an absolutely major, democratic, constitutional change. But if we are to put democracy back upon the agenda we shall also have to re-examine the role of class in our society and here we come to an area of great controversy within the Left.

What, precisely, is the role of class, and why today, even on the Left, is it so controversial?

One could understand it from the point of view of the old rulers of this country. In early Victorian times, there was quite open discussion about class and the little rhyme 'God bless the squire and his relations and keep us in our proper stations' was a way of commenting upon the natural order of things. The upper classes were in charge and the middle classes bowed to the upper classes and sat on the lower classes, and that was the way God meant it to be.

However, class disappeared from polite conversation when Karl Marx, who had been working away at the British Museum, discovered that there was a conflict (and I am putting it very mildly to avoid sensibilities), a marginal difference of interest between those who created the wealth and those who owned it, and he therefore developed the idea of a struggle between the two.

Marx also argued – and this was what made the term 'class' quite unacceptable from that moment almost till today – that if the working class got together, there were enough of them to overwhelm the ruling class and they could change things. After that it became not at all acceptable for any respectable person to mention class at all.

Unfortunately there is a theory now, among some people on the Left, that class has ceased to be a relevant factor in understanding our society. This is a strange conclusion to reach at a time when the Government is pursuing the most vicious class policies for over half a century and when the explanations offered to us as an alternative to class, like North versus South, imply that the working class in Hackney is busy exploiting the working class in Liverpool. Or that somehow the issue of class, which is at the heart of apartheid in South Africa, has actually got nothing to do with class at all.

It is true, and always has been, that the composition of the working class changes. In the early days, they were all agricultural workers, then they became industrial workers, then you got craft unions, then you got general unions. Today you have got more women workers, you have got black workers, you have got part-time workers. But to seek to extend democracy without linking it to a class analysis seems to me to be utterly unrealistic.

Some people on the Left come along and say, quite properly, there is discrimination against women. There is great discrimination against women. But you can't actually use that argument as a case for dropping class, because exploitation by gender very often operates to deepen exploitation by class.

Similarly, the discrimination against black people is horrific still; the level of unemployment among black people is much higher than among white people, but it is the working-class blacks who suffer that discrimination. You cannot eliminate that factor and anyone who tries to do so is, I think, going back to an early and ignorant analysis of the nature of society and how it works.

We must bring together all those who want to see socialism in Britain to discuss and draw up a programme for the liberation of our people and to devise ways of bringing us closer to working people world-wide.

We need a common programme based upon a realistic analysis of the present dangers and the opportunities that exist. We need both to formulate clear and specific demands and to prepare workmanlike plans to show how they can be met. We must banish fear and encourage a vision of a future we can build together; and we must inspire the hope and confidence we shall need to do it.

As Thomas Paine himself wrote:

We have it in our power to begin the world over again. The birth day of a new world is at hand.

Karl Marx

A hundred years ago, in 1833, Karl Marx, one of the greatest thinkers in human history, died in London where he had spent the last thirty-four years of his life, working and writing.

Marx's influence on world events has been immense. Hundreds of millions of people now live in societies influenced by socialism and shaped, however imperfectly, by those who claim their inspiration from his writings. Most of those governments which describe themselves as Marxist came to power in countries which never enjoyed a democratic system which would have permitted change by consent.

For those who live in capitalist countries – including Britain, America, Germany and Japan – Marx has exerted an almost equal influence. He has come to be feared and hated by those who wield economic and political power, many of whom could not, correctly, repeat a single one of his ideas. So violent is the reaction that Marx's ideas produce that no known Marxist would stand a chance of being appointed to any senior post in the Civil Service or armed forces in Britain, and indeed would be likely to be removed if he or she admitted to being a Marxist. The security services will keep a file on almost everyone of any importance who comes to their attention, and is thought to be a Marxist.

So what is it about the man and his philosophy that produces such a situation, or, perhaps more accurately, what is it about a country that feels so unsure of itself that it cannot look at these ideas objectively?

One reason could be that Marx, and his close collaborator, Fredrich Engels, developed such a powerful critique of capitalism that anyone who knows and understands what they were saying is believed to be a danger to those who wield power.

To guard against this risk the ideas of Marx are censored or

distorted and the term Marxist is used by the media as a term
of abuse comparable to subversive, spy, terrorist or guerilla,
anyone who threatens our freedom and our survival, abuse
of the same kind as, in earlier societies, has been hurled at
Christians.

For these reasons alone Marx deserves serious study and
close attention, for anyone whose writings retain their vitality
and power a century after his death must have been saying
something of considerable importance.

What, then, was Marx saying, and what interest should it
have for us?

There are many answers to that question but the main one
is that Marx gave his life to the study of modern society and
especially of capitalism, and he offers us an explanation of how
it works and why – not in a dry academic way but with the
intention of showing working people how they can create, out
of the injustice and the inequalities of capitalism, a new and
different society that is more democratic and equal. Marx made
it clear that working people could do it themselves. For that
reason Marx ranks with the very greatest philosophers and
scientists who studied nature and explained how it works.

If we do not understand Copernicus, Darwin, Marx or Freud,
we cannot understand the world we live in. Like primitive
peoples we are forced back onto fables and myths as the only
explanation of our past history, our present life and the future.

The importance of Marx lies in the fact that he studied human
history in its varying stages of development including feudalism
and capitalism, and laid bare its essential nature with clinical
precision, so that we can better understand how our society
works. He was the founder of the social sciences as we know
them today.

But unlike many philosophers who tried to create a complete
theory of society in their own minds and then apply that theory
to the real world, Marx began by a deep study of the real world
itself in order to understand how it worked and why, and then
drew his own conclusions. What was different about Marx was
that he did not do this out of academic curiosity but in order
to discover how society could be transformed.

In doing so, he was drawn to the inescapable conclusion that
it was the technology available at different periods of history
which largely determined the way in which people related to
nature – the means by which they earned their living – but that
it was also the key factor in shaping their social relationships
to each other and the struggles which these released, and that

the whole structure of ideas and values which flowed from that relationship also was founded in technological development.

Thus primitive societies, living at subsistence level, developed their structures and attitudes from that very fact. Marx saw that feudal societies built up on more advanced methods of agriculture allowed a ruling class to live on a foundation of serfdom and the accumulation of power through landlordism. He recognised the creative role of early capitalism in developing the new technologies free from feudal constraints and explained the more liberal political structures which emerged as being a part of a package of institutional measures necessary to sustain a system of wage slavery. He also saw that that system reduced labour to the level of a commodity to be traded like any other and thus alienated workers from their work.

Then he argued that this new working class like every oppressed group was bound to organise to overthrow their oppressors and seek a transition to better social conditions, and eventually to socialism which he saw as a higher form of social organisation.

The model which Marx studied in the greatest depth was the model of British capitalism, since this country is the oldest industrial country in the world; its development and social and economic conditions were described in minute detail in a mass of Blue Books and White Papers and reports by commissions of inquiry of every sort and kind in the nineteenth century, and *Kapital* was written in the British Museum.

It is for this reason, if for no other, so strange that Marx should still be largely ignored by the very people upon whose economy he worked so hard.

The idea of class was not a new one and Victorians wrote openly of the upper classes, the middle classes and the labouring classes – but they did so as if they were describing an unchanging order of society that must necessarily be maintained in the interests of law and order. Many philosophers have described society in a similar way. Marx saw society differently and argued that the upper classes – or the bourgeoisie – drew their wealth and power from the labour of the working class and from no-one else, and that it was in their interest to exploit the lower classes. If there was any trouble they could use the apparatus of the state with its laws, its courts, its military and police forces, which the capitalists, and the ruling class, controlled, to enforce their interests.

Against such injustice Marx saw resistance as inevitable – hence his concept of the class struggle. Moreover in tracing capitalism out of its origins Marx argued that it was a transient phase in human development and looked towards a classless society, brought about by the emancipation of the working class through their own combined efforts, on the basis of international action.

When we look at the world today, with all its poverty, exploitation and hunger for millions, we may conclude that this dream is a long way off.

At one and the same time, Marx offered an explanation of what was happening that accorded to the daily experience of working people everywhere – certainly to many millions worldwide today – and seems to them to provide an answer that raises their hopes that change is coming, thus generating a vision for the future that liberates them from the apathy and defeatism which held them imprisoned in their own minds, thus paralysing all effort to struggle for justice and equality.

Even this brief description of the central message of Karl Marx should be enough to explain the repercussions which his thinking has had upon the world since the news of it spread.

Most people in this country are not taught about Marx or Marxism at school and those who come across his work have done so through a desire to understand their own situation more fully. They have often been very surprised to find what Marx really argued, as against the popular view of him as described in the media. That was my own experience too.

I was not introduced to socialism through a study of Marx and for that reason would not call myself a Marxist. The British Labour movement developed its own tradition of socialism over many centuries, long before Marx was born, and though Marx's contribution is recognised as having been massive – and there have always been Marxists in the party – the Labour Party is not a Marxist party.

Labour's origins lie more in the teachings of Jesus, who preached the brotherhood and sisterhood of men and women, and thus released into the world a radical and revolutionary message that still has echoes in every continent.

The campaigns for civil liberties, to legalise trade unions, to win the vote for working-class men and later for women, were not inspired by Marx, nor were the campaigns to end slavery – for these struggles have always gone on. What Marx did was to explain the pattern of these struggles, to chart the terrain through which these movements passed, to tell us where we had got to. He provided those who are travelling this route with a map to give us the lie of the land ahead.

He also reported on the nature of the opposing sides in all these conflicts and challenged us to choose which side we were on.

Without some understanding of what Marx was saying it is difficult for us to explain what is happening now.

Why do we have four million people unemployed in a rich industrial country with so many needs unmet? Is it because production geared to profit necessarily needs long dole queues to keep wages down and thus neglects real human needs of all kinds?

Why are millions in the Third World suffering poverty and destitution while the multinationals, protected by military dictatorships financed by the Western countries, make huge profits out of employing workers there at starvation wages, so much so that revolutions to overthrow the oppressors are almost inevitable? Could they be the result of capitalist exploitation in a bitter international class struggle?

Why is the arms race eating up resources we need for peaceful development? Is it because the West actually believes that the Soviet Union is planning a major attack on Western Europe? Or is it because every liberation group in the Third World that is struggling to free itself from exploitation looks to the socialist countries for moral and material help, and if they get it then the profits of Western bankers and industrialists and others who are trying to win new markets in the developing countries might be lost?

If the mass media does not present the news we read and hear and see every day objectively – as so many people suspect – is it that there is bias because the newspaper proprietors have a class interest of their own in choosing what they tell us and how they tell it?

But no explanation of the legacy of Karl Marx would be complete without looking at some of the arguments of those who regard him and his ideas as the embodiment of some modern Satan, an evil genius who has launched an unholy war against everything that is good and true, and which must be exterminated in a new crusade.

It is said that wherever Marxism is practised a hideous tyranny results, destroying all liberty. It is true that neither revolutionary nor post-revolutionary Russia or China have ever allowed political democracy and free speech as we embrace it here. But it must also be stated that neither the Russian nor the Chinese people enjoyed these rights under the Tsars or the Emperors which preceded the revolution, and in both countries socialism has brought great improvements for the mass of the people.

Nor should we forget that some of the most brutal and oppressive regimes in the history of the world were, and still are, officially Christian countries, many also now capitalist-armed and supported by Britain and America.

We might also recall that the British Empire in its heyday not so long ago maintained its power by military force under a Queen-Empress who was also the head of the Church of England.

It would be as absurd to blame Marx for the injustices carried out in his name, long after he was dead, as it would be to blame Jesus for every Catholic who kills a Protestant or every Protestant who kills a Catholic in Northern Ireland.

Marx must be judged by what he himself wrote and said and did, and we should use those parts of his inheritance which seem to us to offer a way to a fuller, freer, richer life and discard or oppose any part of his legacy which we believe to be wrong, dangerous or out of date.

But at least we should examine that experience carefully, and if we do so the tools of analysis that Marx has left us to use can be very useful so long as we do not regard them as offering a ready-made answer which we must accept completely or reject completely.

Perhaps the discussion that has been released by the centenary of Marx's death will encourage more people to read him, and about him, for themselves.

As a socialist brought up in the radical Christian and trade-union traditions that have so largely shaped the thinking of the British Labour movement, I believe that the ideas of democracy and socialism constitute a moral challenge to injustice, a hope for the future, and point to a higher order of society, helping us to understand how it can be achieved by consent in such a way as to enlarge our freedom, extend our rights and entrench democracy.

I have drawn six conclusions from my own study of Marxism:

1. No mature tradition of political democracy can survive today if it does not open itself to the influence of Marx and Marxism;

2. Communist societies cannot survive if they do not accept the demands of their own people for democratic rights upon which a secure foundation for socialism must ultimately rest, and that to continue to deny them amounts to a denial of Marxism itself;

3. World peace can only be maintained if we reject the idea that a holy war is both necessary and inevitable between Marxists and non-Marxists;
4. Moral values must be seen as an essential foundation for all societies and, in that context, Marxism must be recognised as a world faith and must be welcomed into a dialogue with other world faiths, including Christian and other religious beliefs;
5. Marxists, along with other socialists, should be prepared to learn from the women's movement, the ecological critique of capitalist industrialism, the movements for social justice and liberation by peoples in the Third World and from the socialist opposition inside the communist countries;
6. Socialism can only advance if we can develop, and sustain, a framework within which we can accept the full and rich diversity of our separate traditions and be ready to discuss the successes and failure of our own experience in socialist ideas and practice.

And in the long catalogue of people, known and unknown, who have contributed by their courage, and their intellect, to the advancement of humanity, Karl Marx must be listed among the greatest of them all.

Paul Robeson

After Paul Robeson's passport was withdrawn in 1950, a number of us (my father was one and I was another) were on a committee to try to get it restored. I wrote to the American Ambassador, and even on one occasion to the Congress of Cultural Freedom, which had been financed by the CIA, to ask why it was this great artist was denied the right to travel. Then on 15 July 1958 Paul Robeson came to have tea with my father and mother, myself and my wife at the Houses of Parliament. It was the first time I had met him personally and when this great towering man came into the House it was like a magnet passing through a pile of iron filings. Everybody detached themselves from the crowd where they were, and moved towards him, to get near him. And Herbert Morrison, not exactly the most progressive man of his period, positively scampered towards Paul Robeson as we went into the tea room. I had with me a very old aunt of mine who was in her late eighties – she'd been a nurse in mental hospitals all her life, a tiny little lady, under five feet tall – and she asked Paul, 'Will you sing?'. And in the tea room, so quietly you could hardly hear him, but so powerfully that it silenced the whole room, he sang 'Old Man River' to her.

Paul Robeson's life story is an amazing one. He was the son of a slave. His father became a Christian minister and throughout the whole of his life Paul Robeson felt very deeply about drawing upon the negro Christian tradition and the Christian tradition itself. He was a great scholar in his own right, a lawyer, a sportsman, an actor, and his film *Proud Valley* showed him with the Welsh miners who still remember him with affection. There have been other artists who have had successful artistic careers, and have appeared on progressive platforms. But in the case of Paul Robeson it was the uses to which he put his talent that makes him stand above so many of his contemporaries, because he devoted his life to the rights of American negroes, to the working class more generally, to internationalism, to the movement against fascism, to the anti-colonial movement, to peace and to socialism. But Robeson the political figure, a fully-fledged, fully committed, political figure, has often been suppressed because what he said, even today, ten years after his death, still represents a threat to some of the ideas that are gaining currency at this time. Indeed, he was so powerful a spirit, that the mighty United States, fearing his influence, took away his right to travel and banned him effectively from the public media in America. But anyone who has heard the cassette of his songs in Mother Zion Church will know that it begins with a reference by Robeson to the fact that, even during the years when the American television and radio would not broadcast him, and the press would not refer to him, he discovered other alternative media, which were the black churches of America, where he was able to sing his message across. The vitality of his legacy is a very important inheritance we have from the past.

He writes in his book, *Here I Stand*, of the rebellion of the oppressed against the discrimination which they experience in the US. And he speaks of his brother, Reid, who had died by the time this book was written, who was always in trouble with the police. He says of Reid, 'Reid is dead now. He won no honours in classroom, pulpit or platform yet I remember him with love. Restless, rebellious, scoffing at conventions, defiant of the white man's law, I've known many negroes like Reid, I see them every day. Blindly . . .', and I think this is the phrase that we should mark, 'Blindly in their own reckless manner, they seek a way out for themselves alone, they pound with their fists of fury against the walls that only the soldiers of the many can topple.' Now, that is a marvellous phrase in my opinion. 'Don't ever take blows, was the lesson Reid taught me. Stand up to them and hit back harder than they hit you. When the many have learnt that lesson, everything will be different. And then the fiery ones like Reid will be able to live out their lives in peace and no one will have cause to frown on them.' I think that is a perfect description of the difference between the personal rebellion and the collective transformation.

Robeson himself, of course, had to overcome the sense of inferiority which is imbued in all subject races by the institutions of the State. This is true in the colonial world and is the basis on which colonialism was maintained, it was true in the US with the negroes, it's true of the working class in Britain and all over the world and it is the power of institutional racism to which at long last we are beginning to turn our attention in Britain today. It was the power of institutional racism that Robeson himself had to overcome. And in order to do it he saw the need for positive policies. Robeson was at school under a director called Dr Appleby, who was very hostile to Robeson because he was black, and didn't think he was any good. This is what Robeson said when he won the scholarship to Rutgers University. 'I won the scholarship and here was a decisive point in my life. That I would go Rutgers was the least of it, because I was sure I would be happier at Lincoln.' The important thing was this. *'Deep in my heart from that day on was a conviction, which no one in America would be able to shake, that equality might be denied but I knew I was not inferior.'* Now for a man with such outstanding talent to have to tell himself that he was not inferior is an indication of what American blacks were up against and what so many people are up against all over the world. Indeed his first interest in the USSR was that there was no racism in the Soviet Union. He quotes an article written by William Reid who was the dean of the School of Agriculture from North Carolina, where his father had been a slave, on a visit he paid to the Soviet Union: 'I saw no signs of racial discrimination. I think it is fair to say that racial discrimination is non-existent in the USSR.' When Robeson was given an honorary degree in 1943 by Moorhouse College in Atlanta, he delivered a speech in which he observed that, and I am quoting him again, 'the tremendous strides of the various peoples in the Soviet Union have given the greatest proof of the latent abilities, not only of so-called agricultural peoples, presumably unfitted for intricate industrial techniques, but also of so-called backward peoples who have clearly demonstrated that they function like all others.' This awareness that you had to lift yourself above the institutional concept that you were inferior was a very important part of his life and a very important part of his lesson.

He lived for many years in London and he was very generous in saying that it was 'in Britain, among the English, Scottish, Welsh and Irish people of that land, that he learned that the essential character of a nation is determined not by the upper classes but by the common people. And that the common people of all nations are truly brothers in the great family of mankind.'

He went to South Wales and established a life-long friendship with the Welsh miners, which they still remember today. But he made 'that discovery which has influenced my life ever since, which made it clear that I would not live out my life as an adopted Englishman. I came to consider myself to be an African.' So here was a son of an American slave who came to Britain, found friendship among the British working class and, when he was here, discovered he was an African. While he was here, being a scholarly man, he went to the School of Oriental and African Studies and studied African culture, and he came to see that African culture was indeed a treasure store for the world. Those who had scorned the African languages, as so many barbarous dialects, could never know, of course, the richness of those languages and the great philosophy and ethics of poetry that have come down through the ages in these ancient tongues. Robeson was charged, part of the multiplicity of charges against him, that his friendship for Russia was part of a conspiracy. As he says, 'my views concerning the Soviet Union and my warmth and friendship for the peoples of that land and the friendly sentiments they have expressed towards me, have been pictured as something quite sinister by Washington officials and other spokesmen for the dominant white group of our country.' 'It has been alleged', said Robeson, 'that I am part of some kind of international conspiracy.' Now that's not unfamiliar today either. And he responds by saying, 'I have publicly expressed my belief in the principles of scientific socialism, my deep conviction that for all mankind a socialist society represents an advance to a higher stage of life, it is a form of society which is economically, socially, culturally and ethically superior to a system based upon production for profit. And history shows that the processes of social change have nothing in common with the silly notions of plots and conspiracies. The development of human society from tribalism to feudalism to capitalism to socialism, is brought about by the needs and aspirations of mankind for a better life.' You can see already why that man was feared. And so indeed he was because when he went to America, and was pulled up before the Un-American Activities Committee, Robeson said, 'I stand here struggling for the rights of my people to be full citizens of this country; they are not in Mississipi, they are not in Montgomery. That is why I am here today. You want to shut up every coloured person who wants to fight for the rights of his people.' One of his persecutors asked him, 'Why not stay in Russia?' This was his reply. 'Because my father was a slave, my people died to build this country and I am going to stay right here and have a part of it just like you and no fascist minded people will drive me from that, is that clear?' That was Robeson appearing before the might of the American Congress.

In the course of the action to take away his passport, his lawyer in Washington got hold of the State Department brief that had been put in the hands of State Department officials to deny him his passport, and found that the official government reason why his passport should be withdrawn was 'in view of the fact that the appellant's frank admission that he has for years been extremely active politically on behalf of the independence of the colonial people of Africa.' On those grounds, guilt would have been assigned to the great anti-imperialist America, which after all did break with George III, who was Queen Victoria's grandfather, just as the Russians broke with the Tsar Nicholas II, who was Queen Victoria's grandson. The very fact that the United States should be able to deny a passport to a black who was advocating freedom for another colony was amazing, and indeed one of the other charges made against Paul Robeson was that during his concert tours abroad had 'repeatedly criticised the conditions of the negroes in the United States of America.' So much for the freedom of which we hear a lot.

Robeson saw how important it was to develop the role of culture – in his case singing and song – in connection with peace and socialism. The importance of this becomes clear when you hear the records of Robeson singing the national songs of so many countries, working people's songs which he reflected, in the use of his talent. He refers, and I think it is very important we never forget this, to 'the simple beautiful songs of my childhood, heard every Sunday in church and everyday at home and in the community, the great poetic songs and sermons of the negro teacher and the congregation.' When he was prevented from leaving the US he found ways round those limitations. There was the very famous occasion on 18 May 1952 when he went to the Canadian border and thirty thousand Canadians moved towards him from the other side: he sang across the border to them without having a passport. In the autumn of 1957 he sang by telephone to the Welsh Eistedffod. And again in the Camden Town Hall on 26 May 1957 he sang over the telephone to a huge crowd of people, using technology to break down the limitations imposed on him by the American government.

Of fascism, Robeson spoke about the Civil War in Spain where Franco overthrew the Republicans; he spoke about the movement that paved the way for the bombing of Rotterdam and Warsaw, Coventry and Stalingrad, and finally Berlin itself, and he gave a very interesting reflection on the attitude of the English upper classes towards fascism. He once said that 'in the great country houses where I had often been welcomed as guest, having tea, and exchanging smiles with Lord and Lady this and that, a quiet serenity prevailed. Hitler and Mussolini might be bunglers, uncouth fellows really, and quite unacceptable socially, but upper class England was rather pleased by what the dictators were doing.' After all the Nazi-fascist partnership was based on the anti-communist pact which was to save all the great houses of Europe from the menace of Bolshevism. In Germany and Italy there was no longer any nonsense from labour, and business went ahead much better with no trade unions.

Robeson saw the need for organisation, he saw the power of organisation, and here he said something which has relevance for those who think that you can separate racism and sexism from the general class struggle. 'Let me point to a large group among this rank and file which is potentially the most powerful and effective force in our community, that two million negro men and women who are members of organised labour.' He said that negro trade unionists must increasingly exert influence in every aspect of our people's community life, 'No church, no fraternal civic or social organisation in our communities must be permitted to continue without the benefit of the knowledge of experience that you have gained through your struggles in the great American labour movement. You are called upon to provide the spirit, the determination, the organisational skill, the firm steel of unyielding militancy to the age old strivings of our people for equality and freedom.' And I think that today to try and separate colour off from class, and sex off from class, is to weaken the struggle, whereas he saw the necessity of one reinforcing the other. He said, too, that coordinated action will not come at once, it will develop in the grass roots and spread from community to community. It will grow from the bottom, it won't come from the top. Robeson saw the importance of campaigning with that objective and he spoke of the power of spirit – a spirit of steadfast determination, exultation in the face of trials, as the 'very soul of our people that is being formed through all the long and weary years of our march towards freedom.'

He also spoke about leadership in language that is wholly relevant. He said,

The term leadership is being used to express many different concepts and many of these meanings have nothing to do with what I'm concerned with here. Individuals attain prominence for a wide variety of reasons. The concept that I'm talking about has nothing to do with matters of headline prominence, personal achievement or popularity with the powers that be. The primary quality that negro leadership must possess, as I see it, is a single-minded dedication to their people's welfare. Any individual negro, like any other person, may have many varied interests in life, but the true leader must be subordinated to the interests of those whom he or she is leading.

He was a firm supporter of the anti-colonial movement, a supporter of China and passionate believer in the role of the United Nations and the way in which it would be transformed by the addition of new nations as they broke out of the colonial pattern. Above all he had two dreams. The dream of American freedom and the dream of co-existence. The dream of American freedom was this: ' . . . to walk on good American earth as equal citizens, to live without fear, to enjoy the fruits of our toil, to give our children every opportunity in life – that dream which we have held so long in our hearts is today the destiny we hold in our hands.' And his other dream was that the nations of the earth must find a way of peaceful co-existence, especially the US and the Union of Soviet Socialist Republics, whose friendship would guarantee the peace for all the world.'

R. H. Tawney

Political argument in Britain today is becoming more fundamental as the old consensus breaks down under the inherent
defects of capitalism. This breakdown is, in turn, dissolving the
modest welfare society which had been established and eroding
liberalism itself.

Never has democratic socialism been more necessary, but
never has its struggle to assert itself been more difficult, first
because it is constantly and maliciously misrepresented by a
mass media which increasingly acts as a propaganda machine
rather than an information service, and, secondly, because it
suffers from the experience of Labourism under the successive
Labour governments since the Second World War, which often
was not socialism, even though it was presented as such both
by its advocates and its opponents.

The price we have paid for failing to establish even a base for
socialism over the last thirty years is that a renewed and most
virulent strain of capitalism is now in the ascendancy.

The only 'opposition' being permitted to be heard by the
Establishment is a weak centralist liberalism which can, on
occasion, misappropriate the word 'socialism' behind which
authoritarian forces can muster and the trade union movement
can be broken.

It is at this very moment that the Labour Party is coming to
realise the price it has paid for its long neglect of socialism, as
a tool of analysis; as a set of moral values; and as the inspiration
for both political action and political education.

Fortunately, the Labour movement has its own tradition of
socialist writing upon which it can call, and none greater than
that from R. H. Tawney. The papers which he wrote are a part
of that inheritance, and will give a new generation of socialists
an insight into the unique nature of Tawney's mind, morality
and motivation.

His analysis will greatly encourage those in the movement who are now seeking to rediscover the socialist critique of capitalism and re-establish the socialist response to what is happening.

For some years Tawney has been quoted extensively by the right wing of the Labour Party, who have seemed to appropriate him as the father of their own school of thought.

The Social Democrats, whether they have left the party to fight against socialism from the outside, or whether they have stayed to fight socialism from within the party, have both laid claim to be Tawney's true disciples, and then to use his name to represent the socialist majority in the party as being a new breed of socialists who are outside the democratic tradition.

Yet Tawney identified many of the key political issues upon which socialists are now focusing; and he charted, well ahead of his time, the course which they are following.

In a chapter on 'The choice before the Labour Party', he referred to the 1929–31 Ramsey MacDonald Government in these terms: 'The degeneration of socialist parties on assuming office is now an old story . . . what was tried and found wanting was, in short, not merely two years of a Labour Cabinet but a decade of Labour politics.'

And again: 'The gravest weakness of British Labour is its lack of creed. The Labour Party is hesitant in action because it is divided in mind. It does not achieve what it could because it does not know what it wants.'

Tawney was clear about the meaning of a political creed. He saw it as 'a common conception of the ends of political action, and of the means of achieving them, based on a common view of the life proper to human beings, and of the steps required at any moment more nearly to attain it'.

He spells out his socialist objectives with great simplicity:

The fundamental question, as always, is: Who is to be master? Is the reality behind the decorous drapery of political democracy to continue to be the economic power wielded by a few thousand – or, if that be preferred, a few hundred thousand – bankers, industrialists and landowners?

Or shall a serious effort be made – as serious, for example, as was made, for other purposes, during the war – to create organs through which the nation can control, in co-operation with other nations, its economic destinies; plan its business as it deems most conducive to the general well-being; override, for the sake of economic efficiency, the obstruction of vested interests; and distribute the product of its labours in accordance with some generally recognised principles of justice?

Capitalist parties presumably accept the first alternative. A socialist party chooses the second. The nature of its business is determined by its choice.

Today, this statement has acquired a renewed significance, although in the light of our experience of state authorities in various forms, the democratic Left would want to emphasise self-management and the decentralisation of initiative and control to protect us from the abuses of central power.

Tawney accepted the 'existence of a class struggle' and argued for the 'transference of economic power to public hands' which in his view had to 'take precedence over the mere alleviation of distress.'

Thus, he placed himself firmly on the side of all those within the Labour Party who are now calling for socialism in place of the weak and woolly liberalism which so deeply penetrated Labour politics during the last thirty years.

One of the most scurrilous charges levelled by the right wing against socialists in the Labour Party is that our policies would endanger political liberty.

Tawney meets that charge head-on and rebuts it completely: ' . . . the suggestion that capitalism, at the present stage of its history is the guardian of any liberties but its own is an implausible affectation . . . it would more properly be described as the parent of a new feudalism.' He argued that the next Labour government should 'make its central objective to bring the key points of the economic system under public control; should have its measures for attacking that objective prepared in advance; . . . should introduce them at once, in the first months of taking office, while its prestige is still high; and should stand to its guns to the point, if necessary, of a Dissolution.'

Tawney places all this argument in its proper moral framework. As a convinced democrat and Christian socialist he saw Marx as being 'as saturated with ethics as a Hebrew prophet' and argues that 'Christianity and popular communism – though not, it appears, the official variety – are alike in holding the now unfashionable view that principles really matter.'

Tawney constantly reaffirms his commitment to socialism by consent. 'It is not certain, though it is probable, that socialism can, in England, be achieved by the methods proper to democracy. It is certain that it *cannot* be achieved by any other; nor, even if it could, should the supreme goals of civil and political liberty in whose absence no socialism worthy of the name can breathe, be part of the price.'

And these arguments have a direct relevance to our debates today. There is nothing in Tawney's work to support the Social Democrats or the Right of the Labour Party in their continuing attacks upon democratic socialism.

Tawney was a teacher, not a candidate for office, and he saw socialism coming up from the bottom, born out of experience, tested in struggle, inspired by moral values and its policies subjected to the rigid test of analysis and implemented by democratic means.

It is, in my judgement, highly significant that Tawney should have arrived at his conclusions after a lifetime in the adult education movement. He clearly learned as much from his students as he taught them.

His own teaching was obviously enriched by what had happened to them; and he saw clearly that the socialism he believed in could only be brought about if it was understood to be relevant to the lives of working people. Similarly he deeply believed that democracy itself depended for its survival and growth upon a clear commitment to it by those who needed democracy and who had to make it work.

At a moment in history when socialism is under attack and when our democratic liberties are being eroded, Tawney's teachings have a special relevance to the party, the movement and the world.

In Defence of British Dissidents

The rising clamour of vilification and abuse to which many of those who hold radical views are now being subjected, in Britain, has now reached such a point as to threaten the radical tradition itself. Those with power, who sense the depth of the developing social crisis, now seem bent on silencing the voices of dissent, and upon intimidating others who – if they could hear what the dissenters have to say – might agree with it.

The robust and vigorous presentation of arguments, and the equally robust and vigorous rebuttal have always been an integral part of the democratic process. But the personalisation of issues, and the attempts at character assassination of those who criticise the powerful, and thus earn their displeasure, represents a direct threat to democracy itself. This development marks a qualitative change in the character of our political life, and should be of concern to those, across the whole spectrum of opinion in this country, who value free speech and want to see it preserved.

The use of words like 'extremist', 'crank', 'loony', or 'subversive' is designed to prevent the views of those, thus labelled, from being heard or understood, and to set up a hue and cry against them with the intention of bringing about their destruction. This persecution of dissenters is now going on very widely, to isolate those whose views are not acceptable at the top.

Those who are now under attack are not confined to people who follow a particular brand of socialism, for the net has been cast far wider than that, and extends to many others outside the framework of party politics, including the peace movement, the women's movement, the black community, the Irish, gays and even some greens and supporters of animal rights.

It would appear that the whole radical, liberal, dissenting and moral tradition, of which the Labour and socialist movement is a part, is being identified as the 'Enemy Within', in the hope that it can be blotted out as an effective part of our on-going debate about the future.

Yet it has been that very radical tradition which has enriched our political debate over the centuries, and most of the gains that have been made over the years have been inspired and led by the very same sort of people who are now being vilified. Without the efforts of our radical forebears, who have always been honoured after their death, we would not, today, enjoy the limited rights we have to worship as we like, to organise trade unions or to vote, or even to hold rallies in support of the policies that we believe are needed to improve the lot of the people.

The time has come when everyone who believes in free speech, and upholds the parallel right to be heard, should stand up and be counted, and re-state our right to speak our minds without intimidation. In particular we should make it clear that to campaign for useful work, or essential services, does not make a person an extremist.

Nor are we subversives if we want peace, and believe that money wasted on weapons of war should be diverted to development. Favouring international co-operation is not the same as being a spy, nor do criticisms of the government of the day make anyone an enemy of society.

Efforts to protect our families or communities by working through the unions or advocating socialism and organising demonstrations does not constitute a threat to law and order.

Holding views that are unacceptable to the powerful, and believing that conscience must be above the law, is not the same as being a thug or a bully boy.

The British people have some big choices to make about the future of this country in the next few months, and we cannot discharge that task conscientiously unless we permit the debate to include every honest point of view, and treat each one with the respect which it deserves. I appeal to everyone who believes that democracy belongs to us all, and that it depends for much of its vitality on the acceptance of the legitimacy of dissent, to stand up against the present attempts to impose thought control in this country.

SOURCES

POSITIVE DISSENT
Extracts from speech to the Free Church Federal Council, March 1984

THOMAS PAINE
Marx Memorial Lecture, March 1987

KARL MARX
First broadcast on *Opinion*, Channel 4 Television, July 1983

PAUL ROBESON
Lecture to the inaugural meeting of the Paul Robeson Society,
April 1986

R. H. TAWNEY
Extracts from the introduction to *The Attack* by R. H. Tawney,
Spokesman Books, 1981

IN DEFENCE OF BRITISH DISSIDENTS
Extracts from speech given at City Hall, Sheffield, March 1987

3
FIGHTING BACK

The Falklands
War (April 1982)

Mr Tony Benn (Bristol, South-East): The major change that has occurred since the debate on Saturday is that a battle fleet is now under way towards the South Atlantic. We should make it quite clear that the Prime Minister herself has full responsibility for giving orders that that fleet should sail. Some hon Members have said that when our sailors are moving across the oceans towards a possible enemy we must unite around them. Let us be clear: they did not choose to sail to the Falklands; the Prime Minister has sent them. It would be absolutely improper for those who have sent them then to ask us to unite around those they have sent when the decision rests here. That is what parliamentary accountability is about.

The second point that I want to make is that now that a battle fleet has been sent with instructions, to which I shall come in a moment, events cease to be under the control of the Prime Minister. Having followed what was said by the Secretary of State for Defence, it seems that the Argentine Government are now in a position where they can take the initiative against the battle fleet. So this may well be the last occasion on which Parliament meets to discuss the matter before our troops are fired on. That is why I underline what my right hon Friend the Member for Leeds, East (Mr Healey) said: Parliament must not go away for Easter while this situation develops. We must at least be available to meet and keep the situation under control. [*Interruption.*]

Many hon Members wish to speak, but I want to make my comments absolutely clear. I am sure that the House agrees that we cannot leave our servicemen at risk and claim our full Easter holiday. I am sure that people outside the House would support that.

The House is united in saying that an act of aggression in international law has taken place. No one disputes that. No one has defended the junta or the Government of the Argentine, or has argued anything other than that we are faced with an aggressive fait accompli. The real question is quite different: what do we do now? It is to that question that the House should address itself, and I shall do so briefly.

The task force has been sent. Despite the exchanges between the Prime Minister and my right hon Friend the Member for Cardiff, South-East (Mr Callaghan), the Government's objectives are very unclear. There is all the difference in the world between saying that we are going to recover the sovereignty of the Falkland Islands under the British flag – which is what I thought the Prime Minister was hinting at – and saying that all that we want is an administration under anybody's sovereignty, where the Falkland Islands can be safe. The Prime Minister must be clear on that. She tried to get out of it. I do not wish to be personal but we must know what the task force will do. All that she said, when pressed, was 'We have always had sovereignty. It's all about allegiance.' The first question that must be answered tonight is: is the Prime Minister saying that the task force is there to restore sovereignty under the British flag to the position as it was before Friday?

Sir John Biggs-Davison rose –

Mr Benn: I am putting a question to the Prime Minister. If the Prime Minister calls, as no doubt she will, for a measure of support, people must know what they are supporting.

The second question is: what orders have been given to the fleet? No one expects the operational orders to be revealed, but the Secretary of State for Defence was asked a lot of questions on television on Sunday by Brian Walden. One was: 'Do you exclude an attack upon the mainland of Argentina?' The Secretary of State for Defence said – I speak from memory, but the sense of what I recall is correct – 'We do not exclude any option.' [*Interruption.*] That was what was coming out of the television interrogation – that we are sending a battle fleet to the Falklands with instructions that it may fire upon the mainland to restore—[*Interruption*]. That is what it is about – instructions that it may fire upon the mainland—[*Interruption.*] Before the House starts jeering, let it consider what effect this will have on world support, because that is my next point.

If the instructions are that we do not exclude an attack upon the mainland to recover the full sovereignty of the island, then, in effect, we are waiting for the fleet to engage this country in major war.

I sent a message to the Prime Minister's Office this morning to satisfy myself on one other question to which we are fully entitled to know the answer. Will she give a categorical assurance that there are no nuclear weapons of any kind in the task force that we have sent to the Falkland Islands? Not for one moment do I imagine that the Prime Minister has in mind the use of such weapons, but were a ship that carried such weapons to be sunk, that would be a major question too.

If the islanders are first blockaded and then bombarded, and then a landing is made, there may then be no islanders to consult. Therefore, to speak of this as a great military operation, with photographs in the newspapers of marines landing at the training camp on the South Coast, is to describe – in anticipation – the death sentence on those who live in the Falkland Islands and whose welfare must be our prime concern.

To commit servicemen in the Falkland Islands at this time of the year – it is winter there – in territory they do not know, against a fleet that is armed, with British weapons, the spares for which were supplied recently—

Mr Skinner: Thirteen days ago.

Mr Benn: Thirteen days ago. The Prime Minister may know the period more accurately. To submit our task force to attack by a navy that is well equipped with British ships and British weapons is to put it to a risk to which it should not be put.

There are also British interests and British citizens in the Argentine. When the memoirs are written, in my judgement – and I can only make a guess – Lord Carrington will be shown to have resigned in part because no responsible Foreign Secretary could put at risk so great a set of British interests, in pursuit of the objectives that the Prime Minister has set. But we shall have to wait to see that.

I wonder also whether it is conceivable – because no one has fought a naval battle of this character with the sort of weapons now available – that some military defeat might be inflicted upon us. If the Prime Minister knew about these events only last week, could the Chiefs of Staff really have favoured or advised the fitting of the ships for a task force within four days and then sending them off like some armada in medieval times?

I tell the Prime Minister that this is an ill-thought-out enterprise and will not achieve the purposes to which it is put. By acting in that way, she has lost the support that was carefully garnered for the Security Council resolution. Let no one think that, because the Security Council correctly opposed the aggression of the Argentine, that gives us a blank cheque to launch a major attack upon the Falklands – and perhaps upon the Argentine – because the Hispanic world will not support it.

The United Nations has been urging negotiations for ages. The Falkland Islanders were reluctant to have them, because they knew that the United Nations would want some settlement involving sovereignty.

Above all, the Prime Minister should make no mistake about the American interest in this matter. Like some hon. Members, I sat in this House during the Suez enterprise. I was here on 2 August 1956, when there was a debate not so dissimilar from last Saturday's debate. The whole House was up in arms in disgust at what Nasser had done. It was said to be in breach of international law. The Americans were most friendly. Dulles thought up the Canal Users Association. But by the time it came to the invasion, the Americans had withdrawn their support. It was Mr Harold Macmillan who had to tap the then Prime Minister on the shoulder and tell him that the game was up.

I tell the Prime Minister that President Reagan will not only be neutral, he will be bitterly hostile to any act of war against the Argentine, because American power rests on the rotten military dictatorships of Latin America. [*Interruption.*] Of course it does. For years it has rested on those rotten anti-Communist dictatorships. So long as they were anti-Communist, they could get United States weapons, but the weapons are not for fighting the Russians; they are for fighting their own domestic population.

I put to the Prime Minister this last parallel. President Carter was president of the most powerful country in the history of the world, with nuclear arsenals, with missiles, with aircraft, with fleets and with rapid deployment forces. Yet he sat paralysed in the White House when the Ayatollah Khomeini held the American hostages in the embassy in Tehran. The Prime Minister must have an astonishing view of her power if she thinks that she can bring 1,800 hostages out of the Falkland Islands with the British Fleet, operating 8,000 miles from home, when Carter had the humiliation of seeing the inauguration of his successor before the Ayatollah Khomeini would release the hostages.

We must be constructive today, because our people here at home, some of whose sons will be serving in that fleet, will want to know what we think should happen. I give three objectives to the Government. First, the safety of the islanders should be our prime concern. If we get it wrong, as I said, there will be no one to consult. That must mean seeking a local administration that will protect the islanders from the tyranny of their new, occupying proconsul. Alternatively, there must be resettlement, but do not threaten them with landing craft. Their little wooden houses would quickly be destroyed by either the invader or our assault troops.

Second, a United Nations peace-keeping force must be established in the Falkland Islands. [*Interruption*.] Every time the United Nations is mentioned hon Gentlemen jeer as if it was a direct attack upon our interests. If we want the world to support us and to help the Falkland Islanders, a United Nations peace-keeping force, that we have advocated elsewhere, has the only chance of assisting the islanders. If that proposal includes a United Nations mandate, the question of sovereignty could be merged into the United Nations and the world will support Britain against Argentina. It will not support us with the Prime Minister's strategy of threatened war, bluff, or both.

Third, previous Foreign Secretaries have tried to negotiate and we have little leaks about what might have been agreed such as a lease back and so on. Now is the time to come forward with concrete diplomatic proposals. One cannot be explicit about the Navy's plans and covert or secret about diplomatic proposals. Now is the time for the Prime Minister to say that we would be prepared to cede sovereignty to a condominium or to the United Nations. Sovereignty is not what we want, it is the welfare of the people. We must be prepared to contemplate a range of solutions provided the Falkland Islanders can live in peace.

None of those legitimate and constructive proposals require the task force. The task force involves enormous risks. I say as a neutral observer that it will cost this country a far greater humiliation than we have already suffered, and if history repeats itself, it will cost the Prime Minister her position. The attempt will fail. What would win world support and help the Falkland Islanders would be a decision not to send the task force. My advice, for what it is worth, is that the task force should be withdrawn.

The Falklands War
(April 1982)

Mr Tony Benn (Bristol, South-East): In seventeen hours from
now the total exclusion zone will come into effect. There is one
test by which this debate may be judged: How much interest
and relevance will today's debate have for those who will be
pitchforked into battle? When I hear the right hon Member for
Brighton Pavilion (Mr Amery) talk about a South Atlantic Treaty
Organisation and the right hon Member for Down, South (Mr
Powell) deliver a speech that would be more appropriate for
the naval cadets in Edwardian England, I wonder whether the
House of Commons has applied its mind to the main area of
responsibility which in some way – not directly, of course – it
shares with the Government.

I was also alarmed to hear so many people say that in
moments like this Parliament should, in effect, be shut down.
The strength of our democracy is that we respond to crises by
free discussion and we should not be told by *The Daily Telegraph*
that this debate should, in effect, be just a vote of confidence
in the Prime Minister or the Foreign Secretary; or to be told by
others today that we should respond to this tremendously
serious international situation by, in effect, saying nothing.

The reality is that there is unanimity in the House, on the
question of opposing the aggression of the junta. There is also
unanimity on the right of self-defence against aggression. I
deplore the odious hypocrisy of Tory Members who never
argued for force when Ian Smith seized a British colony and ran
it for fifteen years against the Crown and against the interests of
the African people there. I never remember the Tory Party
saying then that we should exercise the right to use force. I am
not reopening that debate and it may well not have been a
practical proposition. But do not let Tory Members pretend that
they have always stood for liberty and justice throughout the

world. They have supported some of the most rotten dictatorships.

The question is: should we now go to war with the Argentine? That may be determined in less than twenty-four hours. The second question associated with it is: what are our objectives in war and how do we secure them other than by war? If one analyses the speech of the right hon Member for Plymouth, Devonport (Dr Owen) very carefully—

Mr Bowen Wells (Hertford and Stevenage) *rose –*

Mr Benn: I shall not give way. I want to have a chance to develop this argument.

The right hon Member for Devonport uttered strong words in support of force. But, if one listened to his speech, he said that when we have won we will give it away in terms of sovereignty.

Mr J. Enoch Powell rose –

Mr Benn: I regarded the speech of the right hon Member for Down, South as an encrusted Edwardian lecture.

What I am asking the House to do is to face the reality of the situation and strongly support what the Leader of the Opposition said today: that the United Nations should be used; that it has been entirely ignored by the Foreign Secretary ever since resolution 502.

There are many people who are doubting now, and will doubt still further, whether it was wise to ask General Haig to be the man to handle peace negotiations. General Haig has a very powerful interest in the maintenance of American investment in and military links with the Argentine. The Argentine has been sending troops in to help pull America's irons out of the fire in El Salvador. I tell the Cabinet that the Foreign Secretary should have gone to the United Nations and not left it to General Haig. The Foreign Secretary has not gone – and everybody knows why he has not gone – to the General Assembly: the General Assembly would not support Britain on the question of sovereignty. That is also why General Haig will not go back to the General Assembly.

I support my right hon Friend the Member for Ebbw Vale (Mr Foot) most strongly, and so unanimously does the Labour Party, in saying that until the United Nations option is opened and discussed there should be no further escalation of military force. Let there be no doubt: any difference of emphasis that there may have been is over in the sense that the right hon Gentleman speaks for the whole Labour Party in saying that.

I now come to the key question. Is it possible for the Government to suspend military action? I pay little attention to the admiral's public statements. First, he says that it will be a walk-over. Then he gets a message saying that that was too aggressive and it does not help us win world opinion. Then he gives another direct interview. Is the admiral saying what he thinks? Is he misunderstanding the situation? Every speech the admiral [Woodward] makes has to be vetted and approved by the Government. The Government probably told him, first, to frighten the Argentine. When he was too tough he was told to speak a bit softer to reinforce the idea that the Government wanted diplomacy.

The truth is that the discussions going on between the admiral, the Secretary of State for Defence and No 10 are quite different in character. It does not require a great deal of imagination to understand what they are because the Prime Minister has outlined them word for word. In the first instance, the Prime Minister was in charge of operations. She told the Chiefs of Staff to put a task force together at breakneck speed and to send it to the South Atlantic.

Mr Peyton rose –

Mr Benn: No, I will not give way. [*Interruption.*]

Mr Speaker: Order. It is quite clear that the right hon Gentleman is not going to give way.

Mr Benn: In the first instance the Prime Minister was in charge of the operations. She told the military, whether they wanted it or not, to assemble a fleet: forty war ships and thirty-six requisitioned merchantmen now in the South Atlantic. But by sending them there she lost control of the situation because those men – God knows how many there are, some of them living in the *Canberra*, some of them living in sleeping bags on the flight decks of the aircraft carriers with forty feet waves, seventy-mph winds and freezing decks – and the Government are now being told that they must go into action because the admiral cannot keep them in those conditions for much longer.

The reality is that the Prime Minister is no longer in charge. She is now a prisoner of her policies, a spectator of the tragedy that she is about to impose on the country. If there is a war, it will I believe be because the Prime Minister has no time to wait. The Cabinet must be anxiously wondering for how long one can leave that fleet there doing nothing; for how long General Haig must be allowed to negotiate: and for how long they can wait to see what the United Nations might do.

The consequences of a war is now the dominant factor for us to consider. People say that we put lives at risk. We mean that people will be killed.

Mr Marlow: Tell that to the Argentines. They are making the war, not we.

Mr Benn: The hon Gentleman can shout as much as he likes, but he had better listen to the argument.

The men and women in the task force are there because the Prime Minister sent them. The Government are responsible for the lives of the service men and women and for the Falkland Islanders. If we are to represent those whom we are here to represent, many of whom are in the task force, we in this House must speak our minds about the consequences of Government action.

It does not require much imagination to realise that if the total exclusion zone means anything there will be shooting tomorrow, either against aircraft or against ships. The first thing that will happen is that British forces will be confronted by Argentine forces armed by Britain with British ships and missiles, with seamen trained in Britain. There is almost certain to be some serious loss of life.

I hope and believe, as all of us must, that such a loss will not occur, but even if the House does not consider it, we may be sure that the military is considering it and that the Cabinet is considering it. If there is the loss of a major vessel the pressure will grow, if the loss has been caused by a Mirage or Skyhawk from an Argentine base, to bomb the mainland of the Argentine. All those screaming Conservative hon Members who are jumping up and down with their *Boys' Own Paper* outlook will then be shouting for an attack by Vulcan bombers or the *Invincible* on the mainland of the Argentine.

I ask the House to consider before we go much further along that imaginary journey of Victorian imperialism what will happen if that occurs. World opinion will not support us. There is no question but that the House, if it is not serious at this moment, could well help to land this country in a situation in which we should be wholly isolated. That would have consequences for our interests in the Argentine. Our economic interests are many and varied in terms of British people throughout Latin America. It would be a betrayal of a very wide interest.

Of course, the Government have another interest, brought out by my hon Friend the Member for Preston, South (Mr Thorne). That is why they have the chairman of the Conservative Party in their Cabinet now. They see in this a diversion from the issues of unemployment and the destruction of the Welfare State. It is not only General Galtieri for whom the Falklands war is a diversion from domestic failure. There is no doubt that this is in the minds of many people in this country. Why else concentrate the expenditure of £500 million or £1,000 million on the Falklands, which have been ignored for years—

Viscount Cranborne (Dorset, South) *rose* –

Mr Tim Eggar (Enfield, North) *rose* –

Mr Speaker: Order. It is clear that the right hon Gentleman is not giving way to anyone.

Mr Foulkes: That is the Fascist junta over there, on the Conservative Benches.

Mr Speaker: Order. The hon Gentleman will lower the tone of the debate. We have had a very good debate. I hope that the House will continue with a good debate.

Mr Benn: Thank you for your intervention, Mr Speaker. I am trying to be brief, and I have my eye on the clock.

The Cabinet knows, but will not tell us, that no real victory can come out of this enterprise. There can be no permanent victory. That is what the right hon Member for Down, South senses. Once we return to the Falklands the first thing that will happen will be an attempt to get rid of the controversy by a transfer of sovereignty of some kind.

The reason is simple. I am surprised in a way that the Argentine Government, with their long claim, did not pursue another method. The Falklands are dependent on the Argentine. I read in the newspapers that 3,000 soldiers were being trained in Wales to be a permanent garrison, and the following thought occurred to me. Add to 1,800 Falkland islanders, minus those who leave, a permanent garrison of 3,000, if there is a military victory in that sense, and what happens afterwards? Is the Argentine to supply fuel, food, educational facilities, medical facilities and air facilities? Of course not. Those islands will have to be serviced for all those purposes by a permanent responsibility from London. It is an absurd illusion to suppose that even if the Falklands fell as bloodlessly as South Georgia that that would somehow resolve the problem.

Mr Eggar rose –

Mr Benn: I shall not give way to the hon Gentleman, whose contributions are without doubt some of the most absurd that I have heard. As the hon Gentleman's speeches are all in the *Official Report*, my words can be checked.

Let us invite the Government at this stage to define their objectives clearly. The first objective must be the safety and the future of the islanders. We must be concerned with their safety, their future and their right to be resettled. An amendment to the Tory British Nationality Act that would allow them to come here should be the first priority. I beg the Foreign Secretary not to mislead those 1,800 people into believing that in pursuit of their concept of self-determination there is a task force to be drawn from British ports at any time as far ahead as we can see to protect them. That cannot be the policy.

If China chose to take over Hong Kong, does anyone say that Admiral Woodward would be diverted into the Pacific to deal with 1,000 million Chinese? These are remnants of empire, outposts of empire, which we have neglected for years. If the public doubt the wisdom of war it is because they know that successive Governments would have loved to give them away if we could have done it without a humiliation imposed by Fleet Street or the local people. The House had better recognise that we have neither the means—

Mr Marlow: On a point of order, Mr Speaker. Is it in order for the right hon Gentleman to act as apologist for the Argentine junta?

Mr Speaker: Order. The hon Gentleman knows that that is not a point of order. I simply add that I have a long list of hon Members who wish to take part in the debate.

Mr Benn: I am no apologist for the junta. I have opposed the supply of arms to fascist dictatorships over the years, when we were in office and when we were out of office. [*Interruption.*] It was all public and on the record at the time.

It would be a gross act of self-deception to pretend to the British people that we have the power, the means or the will to defend outposts of empire that were left after the self-determination of the major colonies. Our interests in those people must now be redefined, associating ourselves with their interests as individuals. That has much more to do with our immigration rules than with the despatch of task forces.

When it comes to it, we shall have to make sovereignty negotiable, either by ceding it to the United Nations or arranging a transfer in some other way. The Foreign Secretary knows this better than most. He must have a file a foot thick listing attempts by the Foreign Office, under successive Governments, to get rid of sovereignty over the Falkland Islands. The right hon Gentleman knows it and the public sense it. Do not use that as an excuse for war. We cannot kill for flags today. It is time someone said so against the hysteria of the gutter press, which every day tries to speak as if a task force to restore the Union Jack is to be our purpose.

I believe that the Cabinet has lost control of the timetable. It has, in effect, been told 'You must use the fleet or withdraw it', which is what some of us said from the outset. We said 'If you are going to have doubts about using it, do not send it.' We foresaw the almost inevitable consequence.

The Government are negotiating without 100 per cent American support and time is running out. The British people would like to hear from this debate that a clear consensus is developing to prevent a war with Argentina, to put the United Nations in, in whatever form it might be, to protect lives and interests and to bring the fleet home. That is a message of hope that must and should emerge from the debate.

The Falklands War
(May 1982)

Mr Tony Benn (Bristol, South-East): One of the arguments given for the Government's reaction to the Argentine invasion of the Falkland Islands was that it took place during a period of negotiation between the British and Argentine Governments. I put it to the Prime Minister that if the interim agreement contained in the document had been made available to Argentina by this Government, or any Government in the past twenty years, the invasion would not have occurred.

Therefore, the task force has not played any part, because – as the right hon Member for Down, South (Mr Powell) said – the proposals involve the abandonment of the substance of sovereignty, which is the right to have troops on one's territory and to control its administration. By publishing this document – and hon Members should not think that a withdrawal makes any difference – the Government have published their readiness to abandon, in substance, British sovereignty over the islands.

The document says that the Government rejected a 'purely military policy'. I ask the House to consider whether that is true. What effort did the Government make to bring pressure to bear on the Argentine Government through the world bankers? Had they refused to reschedule the debts, they could have brought the Argentine Government to their knees. What effort did the Government make? None whatsoever.

I cannot anticipate the reason, but yesterday's edition of *The Times*, in conjunction with other recent articles, pointed out that if the Argentine Government had not had their debts rescheduled we might have seen something approaching the collapse of the world banking system as a result of the financial losses. To rational people it appears that the Prime Minister was prepared to protect the bankers and to send the soldiers in instead. The Government made no serious effort in that direction.

A massive task force has been sent. The Prime Minister allows and encourages the idea that a 'War Cabinet' meets every day. That is from a Government who say in their document that they have rejected a military policy. The briefings come every day not from the Foreign Office but from the Ministry of Defence. In various speeches the Prime Minister has encouraged what can only be described as war hysteria. I suspect that that is not like the spirit of 1940, but is expressed in a feeling among the people that a military solution is intended, should be supported and will be successful. The world certainly sees it that way, and that is why support for the Government abroad is eroding.

The Government's document states that Argentina has been playing for time. Of course it has. But who put the clock in its armoury? The task force gave it the clock as a weapon. It is impossible to leave the task force hanging about. Therefore, once the task force was dispatched, time was given to Buenos Aires—[*Interruption.*] Of course that was the reason.

The Prime Minister spoke about the weather conditions. Everyone can imagine the conditions faced by the troops. Events are in control. Whether Admiral Woodward is technically under political control is not the issue. The Prime Minister knows that even if she thought that negotiations would succeed in two or three weeks' time, the task force could not remain there for that time doing nothing. The very presence of the task force gave Argentina the right to dictate an ultimatum to us. Its ultimatum was fight, or withdraw. The Government have decided to fight. When they fight, world support will disappear.

I turn to the Government's negotiating position, as contained in the terms of the interim agreement. I invite those keenest on war on the Government benches to listen carefully. The document conveyed by Sir Anthony Parsons on Monday is a remarkable one. The offer made involved major concessions, and the war aims have thus been eroded by them. I want the House to understand the question of mutual withdrawal. The Government offered Argentina the concession that no British troops from the task force would land on the Falkland Islands. That is the meaning of mutual withdrawal. However, the essence of sovereignty and of the right to self-defence – to which much reference has been made – is that we have that right. Therefore, the Government conceded that.

Next, the Government conceded that if there were a ceasefire, economic sanctions would be abandoned at once. Thus the junta – which is properly denounced as representing a denial of human rights – would immediately be supported again. As soon as the ceasefire began, the junta would get back its money and trade. That was contained in the document, which I invite the House to consider.

The Government also conceded that a United Nations administrator would go to the Falkland Islands. Indeed, many of us urged that that should happen. However, the United Nations administrator would only consult the islanders and would take account only of their interests, not their views. So much for paramountcy! Argentine observers would be there to ensure that he took account only of their interests, not of their views. The Government said that they wanted that administration to continue indefinitely until they had obtained an agreed solution.

The essence of sovereignty is administration, but that was abandoned. Paramountcy was also abandoned. With the Government insisting on an indefinite agreement, there was no guarantee in the interim agreement offer made by Sir Anthony Parsons that British troops or a British administration would ever return to the Falkland Islands.

If such an offer had been made at any time over the past twenty years there would have been no invasion of the Falkland Islands.

Mr Rippon: Does the right hon Gentleman recall the terms of the draft Labour manifesto of 1980, which was published under the authority of the national executive – of which I believe the right hon Member is the chairman, or was at that time? Paragraph 28 reads:

> We reaffirm our commitment that under no circumstances will the inhabitants of the Falkland Islands be handed over to any Argentine regime which violates human and civil rights.

Does that still represent the right hon Gentleman's policy, or does he say it is different if Argentina takes them?

Mr Benn: I congratulate the right hon and learned Gentleman on reading our documents. There is nobody on the Labour Benches who supported the Argentine attack or who favours the handing over of the Falkland Islands. The point that I am making is that the right hon. and learned Gentleman's Government have been prepared to make an offer to keep British troops off the islands, and to have a United Nations administrator with Argentine observers. They made the offer and, although it is officially withdrawn, it is now in the public domain.

The task force was not needed. That offer could have been made at any time. With the whole British case conceded, what is the case for war? Why should people die for a pre-arranged abandonment of the paramountcy of the interests of the islanders to a United nations administration? This is what the debate is about. If we go on – and I am sure that the House knows that this is what is planned – to attempt to repossess the islands by force, there will be more deaths, there will be more killings, but for what?

We know the Government's furthest negotiation position. There will be escalation, because if we land troops they will be attacked, and Argentina must have some strategy for attacking our ships. When the ships, if any, are sunk – and God knows none of us wants to contemplate such a possibility – Tory Members will be demanding that we bomb the mainland. Some have already said it. Are we to bomb the mainland so that in the end we can give the Falklands to the United Nations and take our troops out? We shall be isolated if we do escalate the situation. Everyone knows that President Reagan will stop the present Prime Minister, as Eisenhower stopped Sir Anthony Eden, because the President cannot see the British bombing the mainland of a continent that he seeks to control. The costs, both direct and indirect, will be enormous.

I do not believe, in all conscience, that the House can support this policy. Those of us who opposed the sending of the task force from the outset, as my hon Friends and I did, have found all our warnings confirmed. We cannot support this policy. The Leader of the Opposition, who has urged on every occasion that the task force should be there but that there should be no escalation of the violence, cannot support a policy contemplating an invasion and then an abandonment. The Government's back benchers, who have urged war so strongly, cannot want war, only to prepare for abandonment.

Tonight I hope that hon Members from both sides of the House will go into the Lobby to vote against the Adjournment. I say against the Adjournment, because there is a special significance about the Adjournment. By voting against the Adjournment the House shows that it wishes to continue the debate so that these issues can be explored.

I finish with the points that have been made in earlier debates. We should go for an immediate and unconditional ceasefire. We should hand over to the United Nations the Falkland Islands administration in exactly the same way as the Government have conceded in the document. Far from abandoning sanctions at the moment when we unilaterally hand over responsibility for the administration to the United Nations, which the Government contemplate, we should step up the sanctions on Argentina. Financial and economic sanctions, combined with the transfer of the Islands to the UN responsibility, will almost certainly bring Galtieri down. Let us not forget that when Nixon wanted to bring down Allende he did not send a task force, he economically strangled President Allende. Reagan has the power to strangle Galtieri, provided that we do not make war upon him. Finally, we should bring the fleet home.

These proposals which are modest and to some extent build on what the Government are prepared to concede, will win widespread support throughout the country. At least tonight in the Division Lobby there will be those who will record their profound opposition to this war upon which we believe the Prime Minister has been determined from the outset.

Members voting against the Adjournment:

Abse, Leo
Allaun, Frank
Atkinson, N. (H'gey,)
Benn, Rt Hon Tony
Bennett, Andrew (St'kp'tN)
Brown, Hugh D. (Provan)
Canavan, Dennis
Cryer, Bob
Dalyell, Tam
Dubs, Alfred
Faulds, Andrew
Hart, Rt Hon Dame Judith
Holland, S. (L'b'th, Vauxh'll)
Huckfield, Les
Lambie, David
Lamond, James
McKelvey, William
McTaggart, Robert

Maxton, John
Maynard, Miss Joan
Meacher, Michael
Mikardo, Ian
Parry, Robert
Powell, Raymond (Ogmore)
Race, Reg
Richardson, Jo
Roberts, Allan (Bootle)
Roberts, Ernest (Hackney N)
Skinner, Dennis
Thomas, Dafydd (Merioneth)
Thorne, Stan (Preston South)
Tilley, John
Wigley, Dafydd

Teller for the Ayes:
Mr Martin Flannery and
    Mr Ernie Ross

The Falklands War
(December 1982)

Mr Tony Benn (Bristol, South-East): Millions of people in Britain
of many political allegiances, and of none, opposed the task
force and the Government's handling of the situation in the
Falklands from the beginning. It is right that our voice should
be heard in this debate.

The real lessons of this tragic and unnecessary war are not
dealt with in the White Paper, which is little more than part of
the campaign for a bigger defence budget. The Secretary of
State spoke of world affairs as if they could be thought of,
primarily, in military terms. In some cases, he spoke as if war
has already broken out.

The real lessons of the Falklands are political, not military.
The first lesson is that the future of the Falklands should have
been settled years ago by negotiations under the auspices of
the United Nations, as the United Nations decided it should be
on 16 December 1965. All Governments – two Conservative and
two Labour – since 1965 can be criticised for not taking those
negotiations seriously. For example, the Argentine claim and
its historical basis has never been presented to Parliament or to
the British people as having any serious basis. That is not the
view of the majority of the United Nations.

Second, Parliament and the public were never told of the
islands' dependence for their life support upon Argentina in
respect of trade, transport, education and health. The true cost
of replacing that support is only now becoming apparent.
Successive Governments have failed to think through the future
of those outposts of empire such as the Falklands, Hong Kong
and Gibraltar, which have been left as anachronisms in our
post-imperial circumstances. The real responsibility of the
House should be limited to the protection of the people who live
there not based on the protection of the territories themselves.

The armed invasion by Argentina, which was a clear breach

of international law and which the United Nations recognised as such, drew from the Government the first serious British peace proposals. These were published on 20 May and withdrawn on the same day. I have alluded to those proposals before.

If those proposals had been offered at any time since 1965, they would have settled the issue without bloodshed. They would have carried the full support of the United Nations and still would. The House should not forget that they will have to form the basis for any permanent settlement.

Instead of following that course, the Government deliberately chose a military solution. To justify the war, they adopted a policy that has brought discredit on the Government and on Britain.

Sir John Biggs-Davison: It was General Galtieri who chose a military solution.

Mr Benn: I am sorry, but the hon Gentleman has not been listening to what I have said. I was saying that if the Government's peace proposals of 20 May had been advanced at any time in the past seventeen years, the matter could have been settled without bloodshed. My right hon Friend the Member for Cardiff, South-East (Mr Callaghan) appears to be indicating support for that view.

Mr James Callaghan: My view is simply that, as long as Argentina insisted on absolute sovereignty, there was no chance of coming to any conclusion with her.

Mr Benn: The proposals that the Government issued on 20 May deliberately left the issue of sovereignty open. My right hon Friend the Member for Cardiff, South-East, who was once Foreign Secretary, will know, as will every other Foreign Secretary since 1965, that they would very much have liked an agreement with Argentina but that one of the factors involved was fear of public criticism if they were to come out openly with the Foreign Office plans under discussion.

I should like to deal with the way in which the Government justified the military action that they took. The first argument was that it was a war against fascism, but they armed the junta right up to the last moment. They supported a fascist junta in Chile, and a fascist government in Turkey and South Africa.

Even now, the Government appear to be assenting to a big bank loan to the Argentine Government. The Government pretended that the task force was sent to strengthen our hand in negotiations, but from the start it was intended to re-occupy the islands by force.

The third lesson is that the Government have isolated Britain in the world by their actions. There was full United Nations support for Britain on 3 April, but, after the 4 November debate in the United Nations, even the United States was on the other side. The Hispanic world has remained united against us, France and Germany, our major partners in the EEC, have renewed arms supplies to Argentina, and British communities all over Latin America have been in danger.

The fourth lesson is that, in the process, the Government have undermined the role of the United Nations as a peace maker, when our only real hope of avoiding a nuclear war is by international action under the United Nations.

The fifth lesson is that the Government committed hundreds of millions of pounds – probably billions of pounds – to an enterprise that is doomed to fail, in that Argentina will, in the end, acquire a leading position in the control of the Falklands. The figure now quoted – we have only been allowed the information in dribs and drabs – is £2 billion to £3 billion. Each year, £400 million – more than £1 million a day – is to be spent on the garrison. A further £20 million to £35 million has been allocated for development. Between £1 million and £2 million per Falkland islander has been spent on this enterprise, the lessons of which the retiring Secretary of State says are only military. The Government caused untold human suffering for those courageous men who died and for the families whose sons were killed or maimed in an enterprise that cannot achieve its prime purpose.

I shall go further and say what I know will not be popular among Conservative Members. I deeply feel, as do others, that the Government used the sacrifices of the dead and wounded to boost the political standing of the Conservative Party in general, and of the Prime Minister in particular. [Hon MEMBERS: 'Disgraceful.'] They invented and exploited the 'Falklands factor', and it has been paid for in blood and bereavement. That view is widely shared throughout the country.

The next charge that I level against the Cabinet is that it deliberately released the poison of militarism into our society. They praised war and killing and suggested that that dangerous virus was the best remedy for our national ills and that it would in some way restore our pride and self-confidence. In that campaign to reawaken militarism in Britain, Fleet Street, the

BBC and the ITN played a considerable part in spreading the poison.

I have made grave charges against the Government, but more and more people in Britain know that those charges are true, and the verdict of history will confirm them. After all that has happened, the Government have failed because everyone in the world knows that in the end the Falkland Islands will go to Argentina, just as China will recover Hong Kong and Spain will recover Gibraltar, however many warships and aircraft we build.

There are, however, two more hopeful lessons to be learnt for the future. First, nuclear weapons were unusable in this case and will be in any modern war because no country dares to use them. There is no doubt that there were nuclear weapons on board the ships, despite the Government's denials, but even if the Argentine army had secured a military success those weapons could not have been used.

The second point has a broader political bearing. If all the money, the human effort and the planning by Governments that now goes into war were devoted to fighting poverty, disease, ignorance and injustice, those scourges could be ended once and for all in Britain and throughout the world. That argument is well understood by many people who do not follow detailed defence debates. If the QE2 can be requisitioned to take troops to the South Atlantic, it can be used to take food to the starving peoples of Asia. The methods of war can be used to meet the underlying problems of people in this country and throughout the world.

Let anyone who doubts that recall that in 1945, after the horrors of the Second World War, the British people chose peace, reconstruction and social justice and rejected Mr Churchill, who was arguably the greatest war leader in our history. I believe that the British people will act in the same way when the real lessons of the Falklands tragedy sink in, and in so doing they will reject the leadership of the present Prime Minister, who has inflicted so much suffering on our people and so gravely damaged our national interest.

The Miners' Strike
(June 1984)

Mr Tony Benn (Chesterfield): We produce the cheapest deep-mine coal in the world. If subsidies in Britain were the same as those in the Common Market, the NCB would make a profit of £2 billion a year. Agriculture is subsidised up to the hilt. Indeed, the dairy farmers – including all the dairy farmers in the House – are up in arms if their subsidy is temporarily and momentarily eroded by a Government which has poured money into uneconomic land. Candidly, I am in favour of keeping our land in use for food production, just as I am in favour of keeping our pits in use for future energy for the nation.

People talk about cheaper South African coal. What about the wages of the South African miners? Mr Botha – that friend of Hitler who was invited to Chequers to celebrate, no doubt, the fortieth anniversary of D-Day – represents a coal industry which will not allow unions to exist and pays the miners a pittance. Yet we are told that we must be competitive with that industry.

Mr Marlow: What about Australian coal?

Mr Benn: When the present Secretary of State the right hon Member for Worcester (Mr Walker) was in charge of the industry in 1973, he ordered Australian coal. When we were in power in 1974, the Australian coal arrived. It was so expensive that the Central Electricity Generating Board sold it at a loss to Electricité de France, because it was more expensive than British coal. I remember that very well.

We are told about the necessity to be economic. What about nuclear power? No private financier has ever put a penny into nuclear power. It has been subsidised from the beginning. The reason why a pressurised water reactor is to be built and why the Government, in advance of the Layfield inquiry, have authorised the spending of £200 million is that the Americans want the plutonium for their cruise missile warheads. It has now been admitted in the newspapers, after reports in Congress, that the American Government cannot persuade their own people to build nuclear power stations and are therefore relying on British plutonium to maintain their warheads.

Those are the realities of the economics. The costs of the closures are greater than the costs of investment, and the cost of the strike makes economic nonsense of the Government's case.

The other argument is that the Government's policy is a continuation of Labour policy. Our investment programme under the 'Plan for Coal' was for 170 million to 200 million tonnes by the end of the century. The target is now to be under 100 million tonnes. Every item of policy, including closures, was discussed and agreed by us with the NUM. As Secretary of State for Energy, I offered the NUM executive a veto on all closures in order to be sure that the NUM, the NCB and the Government would be able to agree to produce the coal.

There has been a great deal of hypocrisy about the Government not intervening. They are deeply involved. The police are preventing peaceful picketing. They have set up road blocks, introduced curfews in the villages and provoked on the picket lines. There have been cavalry charges against unarmed pickets. That is a disgrace to the British police for the which the Government are responsible. This afternoon I asked in the House about the use of troops, and the Leader of the House was very evasive. At the beginning of the dispute, I asked the Leader of the House whether the armed forces had been alerted, and he gave a categorical assurance that they had not. Now the Prime Minister has written to me. I had asked her whether the troops were involved. She used a very skilful phrase. She said that there has been no authorisation. She did not say that the troops were not being used, and she admitted that the army and the armed forces are supplying facilities and transport as part of a joint police and military operation. Either the Leader of the House or the Prime Minister was misleading the House.

The magistrates have come in and introduced bail conditions that amount to a sentence – a sort of exclusion zone – for those who have been convicted of nothing. Much has been made of the crudity of the way in which the Government have turned off every source of funds, including social security, to starve the miners back to work. They have 'deemed' that the miners have been getting strike pay when in fact they have not, they have cut maternity grants and excluded from strike pay workers who have been only indirectly involved and were never employees of the NCB. One case that came to my attention was of the Government stopping a retired miner benefiting from the redundancy payment scheme because, for a short while, he was on the NCB's books before the strike began. The Government think that by starving the miners, or bribing them with thousands of pounds, the miners will respond.

The miners know that the large sums of money that are given to them is not real money. It is a lump sum payment for future social security benefits as they will not get those benefits until the redundancy pay has been spent. Neither the tightening of the screw through the Department of Health and Social Security nor the attempted bribery through redundancy pay will affect the miners.

The Miners' Strike
(September 1984)

When the Home Secretary said three days ago that miners convicted of picket offences might well serve life sentences, that was an indication of the desperation that the Government felt and they knew when they said that that they could never beat the National Union of Mineworkers.

We now know, not that Arthur Scargill ever doubted it, that the Government have planned this strike. Mr Lawson who was Energy Secretary said in the House of Commons in answer to a question of mine in July, 'I was Energy Secretary in 1981. I could have had a strike then.' Why didn't they have a strike in 1981? Because they were not ready in 1981. They had other things they wanted to do first.

They had to get the law changed so that they could starve the miners when the strike came. They had to recruit more police, and they had to pay the police more for the work the police would do when the strike came. They had to make allowance in their public expenditure for the cost of the strike and Lawson, who is now Chancellor of the Exchequer, said in the House of Commons two months ago 'The investment in this strike has been well worthwhile.'

I say all this because it must be obvious to everybody that this is a struggle between 'them' and 'us'. Nobody can separate themselves from this struggle. The miners are in the forefront now, just as a year or two ago, and still today NUPE is in the struggle in defence of the public services and the low-paid; just as Ray Buckton was in the struggle in the ASLEF strike to resist flexible rostering in the railway industry; just as the NGA was in the forefront of the struggle when Eddie Shah tried to break the trade union agreements in the printing industry; and just as the GCHQ workers at Cheltenham were in the forefront of the struggle earlier this year when trade unionism was banned from that particular communications centre. It is one big struggle.

Everything hinges now upon the support that the Labour movement, every trade unionist, every single member of the Labour Party, and millions of others, give to the miners now, because this struggle has been brought forward and made possible by the enormous courage and sacrifices of the mining community, and of young miners who are the finest there have ever been in the history of the NUM. The determination of the women's support groups has proved that women are capable of a contribution that many members of the trade union movement never dreamed possible, even six months ago. One of the most remarkable things, to me at any rate as a former Energy Secretary, is how little truth has been told about the real issues in the mining dispute. After all, the arguments about uneconomic pits are fraudulent arguments. It is wrong to close any pit while old people die of hypothermia in the winter because they cannot afford to keep warm. It is wrong to close down pits and disperse the most skilled mining community in the world in order to build up nuclear power when you and I know very well that nuclear power is primarily to build nuclear weapons and it is quite unsuitable for the long-term energy needs of the country.

We know now that the Government have been practising in Northern Ireland for years the police tactics that they are now preparing to use against the mining community. The Home Office has admitted that they have issued plastic bullets to some of the police forces in Britain. We have seen the cavalry charges by the police, banging the truncheons on the riot shields like a lot of Zulu warriors, trying to frighten people and intimidate them. We have witnessed the way the Magistrates have been manipulated, the way the judges have become tools in the hands of a Home Secretary who tells them that they have got to give life sentences to miners engaged in picketing pits.

It is one big struggle. And the reason we are going to win it is because so many people in Britain have now put their hopes behind the NUM. They know that if the miners were ever to be defeated, and they will never be defeated, that it would be giving a green light to Mrs Thatcher to ride over us with her jack boots and her tanks and millions of people would suffer. Therefore they are behind the NUM and they must express that support in positive action, as the railwaymen have done, and as the seamen have done and as we expect the steelworkers and others to do who can give practical industrial backing to the NUM cause.

When the history of the miners' strike of 1984 comes to be written I believe it will be seen to have been much more than an ordinary dispute. You can tell that when you go on the big demonstrations and you see housewives and youngsters and old people and people who would never come out on an ordinary miners' demonstration. They are coming out because they focus their hopes on your victory. In 1381, they called it the peasants' revolt, and I believe in 1984 this is a miners' revolt on behalf of everybody in Britain who is trying to build a decent society.

Let's look beyond this dispute. Let's look at what it is we want for Britain. We are a very rich country and one of the reasons we are rich is because we have got so much coal, a thousand years of coal. Why can't we build with our skill and our resources a society that is a socialist society worthy of our own people?

There are demands we have got to take up now and carry forward with the same determination that the NUM has shown in fighting for the mining industry. We want useful work for all. There is no justification for unemployment when you think of all the needs there are to be met. They tell us the microchip will mean permanent unemployment. If you have earlier retirement and a three-day working week, if you expand the public services that Rodney Bickerstaffe represents, if you provide twenty-four-hour-a-day care for old people, there is work for all. And we should *demand* work for all and devote the resources to it.

I read in the paper that 130,000 British troops are now on their way to Germany for war games, to please the Generals. That is costing millions and millions of pounds that ought to be devoted now to expanding our public services.

The second thing is homes for all people. There are enough bricks already on the ground to build a town the size of Derby and 400,000 building workers out of work. Why can't we put the building workers to work to build the homes that people need. I'll tell you why. It's not profitable: just like uneconomic pits.

The third demand is an educational policy. It is that we should raise the school-leaving age to 85 so that everybody can go in and out of education whenever they want. Our present education system is a rotten system. If you don't get an O Level or an A Level, you are shunted off into a Youth Training Scheme to teach you to accept the bosses' orders, while the boss is paid to exploit your labour and then hope you will never cause trouble when you are unemployed until the day you die.

We want a much better Health Service, even better than the one Aneurin Bevan gave us. And why can't we treat old people with dignity? That is not only about pensions. When a man or woman has worked through his or her life, maybe served in two world wars, suffered unemployment in the thirties – when they come to retire they should have dignity *with* free fuel, free television, free transport.

And what we want too is a bit more control over our own lives. Let's demand the election of our Magistrates instead of having them appointed by a Tory Lord Chancellor who wants them simply to provide some way of disciplining the working-class movement. And finally, let's go for peace. We have got here representatives from the French Labour movement, and we have got a film unit from Bulgaria. I will tell you that what is being said about the mining dispute in other countries on their mass media is much fairer than we are hearing from the BBC and ITN. We are an internationalist movement: we are at one with the German metal workers who were on strike for months for the thirty-five-hour week; we are at one with the black miners in South Africa under Mr Botha, Mrs Thatcher's friend, who are not allowed to organise proper trade unions; we are at one with the peace movement in America and the Civil Rights movement in America; we are at one with the Third World where millions die of starvation because we exploit them and then spend the profits on weapons of war. These are enormous objectives. Because what they are saying is what generations of working-class people have said throughout our history, that we want a society in which the people who create the wealth determine how it is used, in which we go back to the basic values of brotherhood and sisterhood, against the idea of profit and loss, that we believe in solidarity because an injury to one is an injury to all.

You have taken up a historic cause. It is the most important political event in my lifetime, superseding the General Strike, superseding anything that has happened before and the main weight and burden of it falls upon miners, their wives and families, and the communities in which they live. But the whole Labour movement has a moral obligation to support your struggle in every possible way. And we believe that victory for the miners will be victory for working people here and all over the world.

The Miners' Strike
(February 1985)

Mr Stanley Orme (Salford, East): I beg to move,

That this House condemns Her Majesty's Government for their
public and private activities to impede progress towards negotiations
in the mining dispute, despite the massive costs to the nation of
prolonging the strike; welcomes the decision of the National Union
of Mineworkers to seek an immediate resumption of negotiations
with the National Coal Board without preconditions; and demands
that the Government takes a positive approach by urging the
National Coal Board to settle this long and damaging dispute
forthwith.

Mr Tony Benn (Chesterfield): It is now quite clear that, far from
believing in the prerogative of management and in not intervening, the Secretary of State has masterminded the strike from
the beginning. The preparations were made long ago, as the
Ridley report proves. The police were equipped and trained to
work on picket lines. The whole strike was organised to break
the NUM.

If any Conservative Member wonders why Arthur Scargill is
so highly respected, he should realise that for five years – and
long before he was president of the NUM – Arthur Scargill went
to countless miners' meetings saying, 'Mind my words, the
Government have a hit list of pits.' Ministers and Coal Board
officials denied that, but miners have followed Arthur Scargill
because he has stayed loyal to them. No Conservative Member
or minister has taken that factor into account. Since no other
hon. Member has done so, I should like to place on record my
tribute to the 130,000 miners and their families who have
endured appalling hardship in the past, almost, twelve months
in order to defend the industry, their jobs, and their communities. I feel great pride for them.

It is a great tragedy that, because of many secondary issues, the real question has never been allowed to be properly discussed. That question involves the link between this country's economy and coal. I am very proud to have signed the 1977 'Plan For Coal'. I negotiated it with the NUM. The basis of it was that there would be a joint agreement on the industry's future. Much has been made of pit closures under the Labour Government. I am not saying that all of them were right—[HON MEMBERS: 'Ah!'] Of course I am not saying that, but when, as Secretary of State, I offered a veto to the NUM on pit closures, it represented a recognition that one cannot run the mining industry without the goodwill of the British miners. Any Government who try to convert the 'Enemy Within' to the 'Enemy Underground' by driving men back to work through hardship will destroy the industry and its prospects.

The NUM has never objected to pit closures when there is genuine exhaustion. I am not talking about being down to the last tonne of coal. Anyone who has had anything to do with the industry knows that generally the argument is whether a bit more investment would reveal more coal faces. The argument is not about the last tonne of coal, and to say that the NUM has said that is a blatant lie designed to deceive those who do not know the truth. If there are geological faults or dangerous conditions, the NUM insists on pit closures. It will not put its members at risk. The argument is whether the Government now have a case for closure on what are called harsh economic grounds. The plain truth is that they do not.

If a pit is denied investment, it can be turned into what is called an 'uneconomic' pit, just as, if the roof of a home or a burst pipe is not mended, or if broken windows are not replaced, that home will be turned into a slum. The charge that the NUM rightly makes is that the Government have deliberately starved pits that have great reserves of coal in order to feed money into the so-called high productivity pits with the intention of selling them off when the Government get the chance. Conservative Members should not shake their heads as if to suggest privatisation was a wicked smear against the Government. This Government would sell off the royal family if they could make a quick profit.

The second argument concerns the relative costs of nuclear power and coal. As the House knows, not a single penny of equity capital has ever been put into nuclear power anywhere in the world. Not a single penny has been put into it in the United States. The United States has cancelled ninety nuclear power stations, and has not ordered one since 1977. Nuclear power is financed for defence reasons. Therefore the argument that nuclear power is cheaper than coal is quite false.

We sell our oil from the North Sea to the CEGB at three times the cost of production, because OPEC fixes the price. There is no case for saying that coal is uneconomic compared with nuclear power or oil. The social cost to the Exchequer of closure where there is no other work is twice that of keeping the pit open. SDP Members with their fake statistics come along and try to pretend that they are presenting mathematical realities that others have to face, but in doing so they are just proving that they are on the Right wing of the Tory party. I think that that is clear.

Then, of course, it is said that there is no market for coal. But as coal is cheaper than nuclear power or oil, we should be converting from nuclear power and oil to coal, and providing free fuel to pensioners who die in their hundreds from hypothermia during the winter. Those old people cannot afford to keep warm in winter. But the miners who dig that coal could keep their jobs, save the country money and save the lives of the old.

Not for the first time in our history the NUM is defending the national interest—[Interruption]. Yes it is. When the oil runs out – and it is being depleted at a disgraceful rate – and when gas runs out, Britain will again depend on coal.

The Government have tried to bribe and starve the miners into giving up. They have put thousands of policemen on the picket lines who are trained in techniques perfected in Northern Ireland. The magistrates have abused bail conditions by taking away civil liberties without trial. The judges have sequestrated funds that the miners donated with the very aim of defending their jobs if the union was under attack. The mass media gathered up there in the Press Gallery have been pouring out propaganda against the miners. For example, when BBC television covered the Orgreave picket, it showed stones being thrown, and then cavalry charges being made by the police. I know from BBC editors who took part in that bulletin that there were three cavalry charges by the police before a single stone was thrown. But the BBC, pretending to be impartial, put out a bulletin designed to mislead the British people about the sources of violence.

Time is short, so I must be brief. There are 130,000 miners on strike. There have been some casualties – those who have gone back to work because they could not survive. But I tell the House that 90 per cent of the miners who have ever been on strike are still on strike. As one-third of miners never went on strike, it means that, even if the 51 per cent mark was achieved, all that money and propaganda and all the police would have shifted only 16 per cent of miners from their original view.

The cost of the strike has been enormous, but the miners have received massive support. They have received support from their communities, from women's action groups and from people and communities all over the country and the world. The public now know that what my right hon Friend the Member for Salford, East (Mr Orme) said is true – we are witnessing an attack on the jobs, living conditions, trade union rights and civil liberties of working people in Britain. The Government rely on cold and hunger to try to drive the miners back, but I do not believe that they will succeed. The other way to end the strike quickly is to follow the lead of the National Union of Railwaymen, the Association of Locomotive Engineers and Firemen and the National Union of Seamen and provide industrial support and further political action.

Ministers should study their history. After the 1926 General Strike, the Tory Government were swept from office in the following General Election. In 1974, when the present Secretary of State was making the same speeches, even though there had been a ballot, he was swept from office. The British people will never, never, never allow the Tory Party to destroy the miners, their families and their communities, because, given the choice of the ballot box, they prefer the quality, decency, dedication and loyalty of the miners to the get-rich-quick people who support the Tory Party and have contributed to the creation of this strike.

Gay Rights

Mr Tony Benn (Chesterfield): I have never spoken before in the House on this subject, but I am moved to do so by growing alarm at the effect that the clause would have upon millions of people and not only upon those who are gay or lesbian, for their relatives have a concern for them and know that this campaign has been whipped up by the gutter press which has done more to lower the standard of personal and public morality than any others in modern British society.

I believe that the pursuit of people who are gay and lesbian is as morbid as could be imagined. It is one thing for the popular press, the sewer press, to pursue such a campaign, but for a Government who have responsibility for the education of children to adopt that campaign and to make it part of the statute of the land can only be interpreted as the crudest opportunism for political purposes. That is my conviction. The effect of it is to scapegoat gays and lesbians. Whatever may be said in the House by ministers, the courts will not take into account assurances by ministers. The courts take account only of the wording of legislation.

This is the most blatantly and dishonestly worded clause that I have ever come across. I shall tell the House why. If the sense of the word 'promote' can be read across from 'describe', every murder play promotes murder, every war play promotes war, every drama involving the eternal triangle promotes adultery; and Mr Richard Branson's condom campaign promotes fornication. The House had better be very careful before it gives to judges, who come from a narrow section of society, the power to interpret 'promote'.

To identify homosexual and gay relationships specially as contributing to crime is to fly in the face of all the evidence that as there is more heterosexual sexual activity, more crime is associated with it than with gay and lesbian relationships.

Since the clause first appeared, I have received many letters from people who are gays and lesbians who are in genuine fear for their safety and for their lives. Any hon Member who is interested in civil liberties will be aware that the harassment of gays and lesbians, first initiated by the sewer press and now by the clause for which the Government are responsible, is a major problem. People are afraid of the legislation and of the effect of the Government's endorsement of this scapegoating.

I have decided to read to the House in full the resolution on lesbian and gay rights carried by the Labour party conference two and a half years ago by a majority of more than half a million.

This Conference opposes all discrimination against lesbians and gay men and recognises that this discrimination is institutionalised in society. Conference notes that existing Labour Party policy with regard to homosexuality fails to meet the legitimate demands of lesbians and gay men and that a consistent and principled campaign conducted over a number of years is necessary to reverse that failure. Conference therefore:

(1) instructs the NEC to draft a lesbian and gay rights policy which would specifically:

 (a) declare that lesbian and gay relationships and acts are not contrary to the public policy of the law and that judges must not use their discretion under Common Law to invent new and discriminatory offences;

 (b) repeal all criminal laws which discriminate against lesbians and gay men, and clarify and codify those sections of the Common Law which deal with public morality;

 (c) in this clarification they should be guided by the maxim that there should be no crimes without victims;

 (d) prohibit discrimination against lesbians and gay men in child custody cases;

 (e) prohibit discrimination and unfair dismissals on grounds in any way connected with lesbian and gay sexuality or life-style;

 (f) prevent police harassment of lesbians and gay men.

(2) Calls upon all Labour local authorities to adopt practices and policy to prevent discrimination against lesbians and gay men, and in particular:

 (a) adopt and enforce equal opportunities in relation to lesbians and gay men along the same lines as Islington, Hackney, GLC, Manchester, Brent and Nottingham;

 (b) end discrimination against single people and lesbians and gay men in housing policies;

 (c) support financially and otherwise special lesbian and gay phone lines, centres and youth groups;

 (d) publicise these anti-discrimination policies.

(3) Instructs the NEC to

(a) organise a campaign of education among Labour Party trade union membership on lesbian and gay oppression in conjunction with the Labour Campaign for Lesbian and Gay Rights;

(b) produce a leaflet for public campaign using the slogan 'the Labour Party support lesbian and gay rights—join the Labour Party'.

(4) Instructs the NEC to set up a sub-committee to organise the implementation of this policy.

The day will come when people will look back on this debate and be glad that there were hon Members on both sides of the House who stood against what is an incitement to harass decent people, who, in the course of their orientation, have adopted gay and lesbian practices, which are not contrary to the law of the land.

Fortress Wapping
(May 1986)

Mr Tony Benn (Chesterfield): I spent four or five hours at Wapping on Saturday night, and I saw scenes taking place within two miles of the House that I have never seen before in this country and that I hope not to live to see again. Ten thousand demonstrators were there in order to greet marches from Scotland. There were 1,700 police officers present. According to Home Office figures, there were 175 police casualties. As the Home Secretary knows, I have written to him, asking for four things: the names of the police officers injured at Wapping; the nature of their injuries; the names and addresses of the hospitals at which they were treated; and the dates on which each officer returned to duty. There were more than 80 casualties among those present at the meeting. I could list many of them, but they are recorded in the many photographs taken and in a video taken that night.

Whatever the Home Secretary may say, he is responsible for the Metropolitan police. He found it unnecessary to make a statement to the House, and has chosen instead to shield himself behind the Commissioner of Police of the Metropolis, Sir Kenneth Newman. If he thinks that the demand for control of the police by the London elected body is something new, I should tell him that in 1892 my grandfather moved that the police in London should be under the control of the new London County Council. The reason given for opposing it then was that the Home Secretary had to preserve control over the London police because of the risk of Irish terrorism. Thus, I hope that no one tells us that demands for the democratic control of the police are a product of the hard Left or of some new breed of extremism.

I was struck by the fact that running through the speech of the hon Member for Westminister, North (Mr Wheeler) was the fear that the people might have an opportunity to determine the nature of policing through the ballot box. I have always believed – and the GLC's abolition confirms it – that the Conservative Party is afraid not of the rhetoric that may be engaged in by Socialists at public meetings but of democracy.

Like every citizen in Britain, I want a strong and effective police force. I readily agreed to give lectures at the Derbyshire police college in Butterly Park, Ripley. Those who have attended the lectures will know that I turned my mind as best I could to the way in which an effective police force could enjoy the public's confidence. But it is impossible to preserve law and order if there is the sort of suspicion between the public and the police that was released by the events at Wapping.

The hon Member for Westminister, North seemed to think that he had just discovered that crime occurs on council estates. But I get many complaints from my constituents about the failure to provide proper local policing on council estates where there are problems of vandalism and mugging, or where young people are running round out of control.

One of the reasons why the police do not police these areas properly is that they are diverting their efforts to other matters. Another reason is that local police chiefs have no responsibility to the communities they police. They do not have to take a blind bit of notice of them. They are supported in that by the hon Member for Westminster, North, who believes that they should be wholly exempt from any democratic control. If one applied that to the Army and said, 'Surely no one will say that the Army should be under democratic control,' the next question would be, 'Why should the Government be under democratic control?'

In a democracy, the police are under democratic control. It is that control which does, or should, distinguish this country from a police state. It may be that, for practical reasons and sensibly so, operational responsibilities rest with the policeman on the spot, but the use made of that discretion must be as answerable afterwards as is the Army if, under the orders of the Ministry of Defence, it engages in conflict. Just as the Civil Service, the Treasury and any other department responsible to Parliament through a Ministry has to answer for what it does, so must the police. In the absence of that, the hon Member for Westminster, North is advocating nothing less than a police state.

Mr Wheeler: I am grateful to the right hon Gentleman for allowing me to respond. He has totally misrepresented my position. I believe, and the law at present believes, that the police are accountable. Ultimately, the police are accountable to the Chamber. They are accountable for their actions to the courts of law and the magistrates. The police should decide their operational priorities. It is that which divides the right hon Gentleman from me and other Conservative Members. He would wish to direct police operations.

Mr Benn: No, that is absolutely false. I have made it clear that, for the purpose of operational activities, the police have to take decisions, but they must be answerable for what they do and they must be answerable to the people over whom they exercise their powers. To put it in a nutshell, the police are there to protect us and not to control us, they are there to defend us and not to attack us. That is the issue I wish to deal with arising from the scenes at Wapping.

I must give the House the background to what happened on Saturday night. Mr Rupert Murdoch, who made £47 million out of News International in the past year, sacked 5,500 print workers, with no compensation whatever. Those print workers – I might add that over the years they have printed stories not very helpful to the causes which I espouse – have been treated in a shabby, rotten way. Since the decision to sack them, the print workers have been meeting outside the Wapping works. I have attended meetings there before and, on Saturday night, they planned to receive a group of marchers from all over the country who had marched through Britain telling people what Rupert Murdoch had done.

The members were given a civic send-off at Glasgow. They came through Chesterfield and I marched in with them. At Chesterfield, they were given a reception and there was a meeting in the market square the following day. The marchers arrived at Wapping on Saturday night with 10,000 people because the justice of their cause required it. When they reached Wapping they met the police.

I should like to say a word about the difference between this and the miners' strike. In the case of the miners' strike, ministers said that the police were there to guarantee the right of people to go to work. In Wapping, the police are there to prevent 5,500 people from going to work. In the miners' strike, we were told that the dismissals were due to the fact that the pits were uneconomic, but Murdoch has made £47 million out of the labour of those whom he has sacked. The relationship of the police to the print workers is totally different from that which existed with the miners. We now know one or two things about the police. The tactical operations manual was forced out of the police under cross-examination in the Orgreave trials. You will recall, Mr Speaker, that, on 22 July last year, I asked for your consent to place this manual in the Library, which you gave. From the manual we learn what instructions are given to the police, with the authority of the Home Secretary, although the instructions were drafted by the Association of Chief Police Officers. That body has no authority whatever in this country other than the fact that it is a sort of trade union or club for chief constables.

I have explained the background for the print workers and Murdoch's background, but what was the background for the police who attended in Wapping on Saturday night? They had the tactical operations manual. Sub-heading e deals with the functions of the mounted police which concern: 'Dispersing a crowd using impetus to create fear and a scatter effect.'

Manoeuvre No 10 states: 'Mounted officers advance on a crowd in a way indicating that they do not intend to stop.'

Let us not be told that these scenes were necessarily triggered by missiles being thrown. Manoeuvre No 10 states the instructions given to the police and we could see the police lined up outside the plant ready to follow them. Manoeuvre No 6 refers to the short shield baton team deployed into the crowd. It states: 'They disperse the crowd and incapacitate missile throwers and ring leaders by striking in a controlled manner with batons about the arms and legs or torso so as not to cause serious injury.'

Manoeuvre No 7 states: 'This unit will initially be protected by long-shield officers or personnel carriers and on the command will run at the crowd in pairs to disperse and/or incapacitate.'

These are the police instructions. There is no question about it. They were prepared by the police. The ordinary decent constables – many of whom I know – thoroughly dislike what they are asked or ordered to do. We must not let anyone say that those instructions, which were given to the police, were necessarily the wishes of the constables at Wapping on Saturday night.

When the incidents at Wapping were raised in the House on Tuesday, the Leader of the House said that it proved the value of trade union legislation. What has trade union legislation got to do with releasing mounted police into those who attend a public meeting? From the Home Secretary's language today it is implied that those people were rioting. The question of riot came up at the Orgreave trials and I saw some of that riot on television. Every one of those accused were acquitted. Why? When the police video was shown, it was seen that there were six cavalry charges before the stones were thrown.

The BBC bears a heavy responsibility in this. I heard from one of the newsroom people that the director of news on BBC television ordered those preparing that film for the night bulletin to transpose the order of the film to show the missiles and then the police charging. The police video, which was consecutive, showed a very different picture.

I saw what I saw with my hon Friends the Members for Newham, North-East (Mr Leighton) and for Newham, North-West (Mr Banks) – my hon Friend the Member for Hammersmith was on site – and Rodney Bickerstaffe, the general secretary of the National Union of Public Employees and Brenda Dean were also there.

I appealed to the crowd to write to me, and I received seventy letters this morning, which I have not had time to analyse in detail. I also have pictures showing the injuries that were sustained. One is of a photographer who was battered by the police. I have others, and I shall send them to the Home Secretary. Last night, I received a video recording taken by a unit which was on the spot. The matter must be taken seriously.

I went to chief superintendent Goodall and appealed to him to withdraw his men. I appealed to the crowd to stay calm. I was on the platform and relatively safe but there was great anxiety among the people who saw the casualties and how the police were behaving. Two ITN men were hospitalised. Why did ITN not report that? Can hon Members imagine another incident in the world when a cameraman is hospitalised trying to film a demonstration because he is attacked by the police which is not even referred to on the news bulletin? No wonder Sir Alastair Burnet got his knighthood! A BBC unit had its lights smashed by the police because it was filming what they were doing. That did not appear on the BBC news either. No wonder MI5 vets those who run the major news bulletins and administration on the BBC.

This is a matter which must be dealt with other than by an exchange in the House. If this had occurred in South Africa, Poland or any other country, it would have dominated the headlines and the news bulletins for days and days. I can understand the newspaper proprietors not wanting it to be reported because they hope that Murdoch will beat the print workers so that they can beat their own print workers, but that public service broadcasting stations should deny the public the truth about what happened that night is an utter disgrace and the matter should be raised in the House.

Sir Eldon Griffiths: To prevent the right hon Gentleman from making more of a fool of himself, may I tell him that there is an objective video recording of the incident?

Mr Dennis Skinner (Bolsover): The hon Gentleman is paid to say this.

Sir Eldon Griffiths: Although I can understand that, from one vantage point, the right hon Gentleman may have formed certain impressions, which he has described, the objective video of the entire operation is available, timed and does not coincide with his description of events.

Mr Benn: I believe that the hon Gentleman is a paid employee of the Police Federation. He is entitled to come here and earn his money supporting the Police Federation if he chooses to do so. I have no objection to that because there have always been trade union representatives in the House. I shall quote some of the letters that I have received. One comes from Chelsfield in Kent and says:

> Printers who bring their mothers, fathers, wives and children to a rally to meet colleagues who had marched from Glasgow and Newcastle, do not use the occasion to attack the police. The riot squad entered the enclosed area from all sides attacking anyone in their path. Within yards of me a man was felled and had a heart attack. He was one of the marchers from Glasgow. We appealed to the police to retreat, but they showed no regard to any of the injured. About thirty minutes passed before an ambulance was able to get through.

A woman from Orpington writes:

> I am the wife of an ex-*Sun* employee . . . The shocking behaviour of the riot police who constantly attacked the crowd, many of whom were women and children, was nothing short of barbaric. They were completely out of control and seemed to enjoy what they were doing. The impression that this will leave on the minds of young children is unthinkable.

A woman from Shepperton wrote:

> On Saturday night the BBC lost its camera, knocked out by the riot squad before the horses charged. This is not the first camera they have lost. This also applied to ITN. These are planned attacks by

the police. On the second charge of the night – and there were many – that I happened to be involved in, the pickets, including a TV cameraman and his crew from Western Germany, were chased by screaming abusive police into a side road which may have been Dock Street.

Some people might say that not all of those who went were print workers. I know that that is true. I have here a letter which runs:

> I am not a print worker, but a middle-aged deputy head teacher of a primary school, who now finds it very difficult to instil into children a respect of the police after my experiences at Wapping.
> Last Saturday I was not at the main entrance, but at Glamis Road. Everything was calm until about midnight, when with no warning, the police horses were ridden like a cavalry charge from Glamis Road into the crowd. Even when the demonstrators rushed to the pavements for safety, the horses charged on to the pavements knocking people over and against walls.

It is no good Conservative Members trying to pretend that it did not happen. It did happen. I was not present, but that deputy head teacher has evidence which should go to a public inquiry.

All of this results from a deliberate attempt by the Government to criminalise dissent in Britain. It has happened at Greenham Common, although not as badly. It has happened to the black community. It happened to the miners. It is happening to the print workers. I believe that the Government are guilty of a gross misuse of the police in support of their own political policies. It is a serious threat to civil liberties.

There should be a public inquiry, but I am encouraged by the Home Secretary saying that it is all the responsibility of the Commissioner of Police of the Metropolis, to ask the House and the Government to suspend Sir Kenneth Newman as he is responsible for what happened on Saturday night and Sunday morning. We must have elected police authorities.

Police constables are under no obligation to obey unlawful orders. I saw a man with a helmet and a few pips on his shoulder – I do not know whether he was an inspector – instructing them to go into the crowd where they wrought such havoc among innocent people. I believe that that was an unlawful order.

After the Nuremberg trials, police constables should know – they will know better than me – that it is not lawful to be told to attack people and to incapacitate them, when they are simply there to attend a meeting. If somebody can be found throwing stones, they are arrested, charged and tried, but they are not incapacitated. One does not use police horses against innocent people. I advised the crowd that night and I advise them again to follow methods of non-violence. Non-violence practised by Mr Gandhi got the British out of India and non-violence in this country is the best answer. Having said that, I must also say that innocent people, unlawfully attacked, whether by police or anybody else, are entitled to the right of self-defence.

People who are now thinking of organising demonstrations should have doctors present, because they will need them. They should also have nurses and lawyers present. I took a lawyer with me when I tried to see Chief Superintendent Goodall. He said that he did not want to speak to me because I had someone with me. I told him that I was going to raise this matter in the House and I insisted that a lawyer be present. People who are organising demonstrations should also have video cameras there because one will not see the truth on the BBC or ITN and one should have photographers there to know what really happened and have independent witnesses.

The media black-out makes it difficult for those who are not present to understand what I have said, the detail that will be in the letters, which I hope will all be published, and the passion with which I have spoken. Never in my life have I seen anything like that happen in this country.

I believe that the cause of the print workers is just. I believe that people should not buy the *Sun*, *The Times*, the *Sunday Times* or the *News of the World* or distribute them. If people go to listen to those who have marched the length and breadth of the country, like the Jarrow marchers, to alert people to what is happening, and they gather for a peaceful meeting to be addressed by five people, three of whom are Members of the House, they ought not to be attacked in such a way and systematically batoned by the police. The responsibility ultimately rests with the Home Secretary. Since I do not expect any satisfactory answer, I appeal from this House to the public to see that there is such a wave of protest that such a thing can never happen again.

Fortress Wapping
(January 1987)

Mr Tony Benn (Chesterfield): Is the right hon Gentleman aware that the many tens of thousands of men, women and children from all over the country who have been to Wapping over the past year will understand perfectly why the Home Secretary does not wish an inquiry. It is because an inquiry would reveal what I and others who have been there could confirm from our own eyes – occasions when there have been savage and brutal baton charges by the police against those who were present, as last Saturday when the legal observer, John Bowden, had his face smashed in by a police baton, when a photographer of a national newspaper was trampled on by a horse, when one of the television units there had its lights smashed deliberately by the police and when the police broke the windows of the bus which has been used as a first-aid station since 3 May. Is the Home Secretary aware that those who were there understand perfectly that the Government need Rupert Murdoch and are giving him free police for the purpose of denying work to those who used to work for him?

The Irish Struggle
for Freedom

I was brought up to believe in Indian independence and Irish independence. It was talked about constantly at home, and the argument entered my bloodstream.

After the Government of Ireland Act of 1949 when the guarantees to the Unionists were enshrined in legislation, the Irish question (although I prefer to think of it as the British question in Ireland), didn't really begin to surface again publicly in Britain until the civil rights movement and the election of Bernadette Devlin. I followed it with keen interest, but had no direct involvement.

I was in the Cabinet in 1969 when the troops were sent in, listened very intently and participated in the discussion. I remember recording in my diary at the time that this was no real solution, but the current wisdom was that the Catholics needed protection from the B-Specials and there was no real challenge to that policy. Next time Labour was in power, we had the Ulster Workers' Council strike in 1974. It was the only successful example of industrial action being brought to bear for political purposes. Certainly it worked and the Labour Government capitulated.

The strange thing was that Ireland was hardly ever discussed in Cabinet. I wrote to Callaghan around the end of 1978 saying that we ought to have a proper discussion, but we never did. Ireland came up in the Ulster Workers' Council strike and again after the bombings in Birmingham when the Prevention of Terrorism Act was rushed through, but there was never any review of the policy fundamentals.

There was an Irish Committee of the Cabinet, but that was concentrating on masterminding the security operation. It became clearer and clearer that policy was failing. You couldn't push Ireland aside, it was the dominant domestic issue in the United Kingdom, yet nobody thought we needed that discussion. I mustn't mislead you, it took me a long time to realise the extent and depth of bipartisanship on the issue.

In 1979, Ireland came up during the discussion of the Labour Manifesto, and when it was suggested we include a commitment to ultimate unity and independence; the response of the leadership was almost hysterical: 'You can't do that, people will die.' Indeed, when anybody said anything, it was the same: 'All this will lead to violence.' But of course the violence was mounting all the time.

So whereas before when I was asked about Ireland I used to refer to what my Dad had said about how partition was a crime against the Irish people, from then on I started being much more explicit. The Bill that Ernie Roberts MP is now sponsoring, calling for an end to British jurisdiction, is the end-product of that process of political development. It's not a very glorious record I admit, but it shows you how things developed over a period.

I'm now absolutely certain that the reason Britain is in Ireland has nothing to do with the reasons given to the public. Britain is there for military purposes. When no longer useful, Zimbabwe and Hong Kong were handed over. I think the Tories are prepared to hand over Gibraltar. In the end we'll probably hand over the Falklands. No one is ever going to convince me that there is some deep commitment in the Conservative Cabinet to the maintenance of the rights of the Protestants in the North. From the very beginning, and certainly after the First World War, it was the defence argument that was dominant.

When I read that during the Second World War, Churchill had offered De Valera Irish unity in exchange for their neutrality without bothering to tell Northern Ireland leaders. I began to think afresh. If Ireland is merely wanted as a base, then the peace argument becomes paramount. Is Ireland entitled to be united, independent and also neutral, or is it to be a military colony of the Western Alliance, even if it is 'free'? Now when you put it that way, you begin to see the need for an alliance between the peace movement and the Irish.

The twelve-month miners' strike in Britain also convinced a lot of people that police and army activity in Northern Ireland was a preparation for its domestic application. I see that following the Brighton bombing, the RUC are going to be used to train the British police on techniques of searching and surveillance. Our police have already got riot shields, plastic bullets and Sir Kenneth Newman. Gradually we are seeing a complete transfer of the whole apparatus of repression from Northern

Ireland to Britain. It creates a real convergence of interest between the British and Irish working-class movements for a withdrawal of the British presence from the North.

I think co-operation between the working-class movements will take a huge step forward once British occupation and repression is halted and once the military integration of Northern Ireland into NATO is ended.

I think that it's useful for everybody to examine the background of their own thinking. It gives you a certain depth and strength, and means that you don't get diverted by arguments that are suddenly thrown in in some current controversy about a particular act of violence which is almost inevitable in the present situation.

The loyalist veto is a very clever technique. Keeping the loyalists on a string means that sectarian divisions can always be whipped up. At the same time, knowing that there is a loyalist majority, the government can shield behind it, claiming that its policies represent the majority. The veto would have been brushed aside by Churchill's wartime offer. If the Republic decided to join NATO, I think it would be brushed aside again today. That veto has no constitutional validity whatsoever, and it restricts the rights of the British Parliament as much as it does the Irish. Supposing we had a vote in the House of Commons in favour of British withdrawal from Ireland. The fictional veto would mean we could not activate that policy, that it would be subject to a veto by a majority of a minority in Ireland. The exposure of this wholly undemocratic concept is essential.

I don't think anyone on the Left believes that the problem in Northern Ireland has anything to do with religion. We must now take in the idea that the loyalist veto is also a deadly threat to the Protestants because it creates and continues instability in Ireland. The debate should begin to shift so that people think beyond withdrawal.

If it were clear to the Protestants and the Catholics in the North, to the people of the Republic and the people of Britain that there was to be a date after which there would be a termination of British jurisdiction, then I think this would release into the debate a whole range of arguments that are now held back. For one thing, the whole 'security' argument would assume quite a different aspect; it would release a great deal of money at present being spent on the 'emergency' into potential projects that are not now available. In this context, the trade unions would be bound to feel they could begin to play a new role. A lot of the tension would go out of the situation. I'm also sure that after a declaration of this kind, the military activities and energies of the nationalist movement might well be directed into more constructive purposes.

I personally find it very hard to accept the argument that you can't act for fear of a bloodbath triggered off by the loyalists. If we lived in a fair world, this threat of violence to prevent a political settlement would earn the same denunciations as the nationalist violence has. But where would the loyalists have to go? They would be living in an Ireland in which they were required to play some part, not in one from which they were excluded. I think that calling the 'Carson bluff' or however you might describe it is an absolutely integral part of any successful negotiations.

There's no doubt that there are difficulties which may continue after a settlement has been reached. There may be threats to the structure of the state in the process of changing from an undemocratic South and an undemocratic North to a more democratic united Ireland. But it is for the Irish people to decide how to deal with it. I'm allowed, I hope, to observe, as a friend across the water, that it is something which to be confident that they are capable of doing. I have absolute confidence in that. Contacts across the water would obviously continue, but they would be on the basis of comradeship and equality, free from any constitutional 'responsibilty' and all the other illusions that have been deliberately fostered to justify our continued occupation of a part of Ireland.

We should support the fullest possible expression of sovereignty to an independent Ireland. Sovereign nations bound by the political and economic dictates of others are not uncommon throughout the world.

Geographically, Ireland is placed in a position of great significance in the Atlantic between the USA and her Western allies. The more I thought about this, the more I understood why it was that, despite the anti-British imperialist tradition of American politics and despite their both being of Irish stock, Kennedy and Reagan were not really supporters of Irish independence. In a funny way, Britain is also an island separating the USA from its western-European base. The pressures that would be brought to bear upon a united Ireland would be very similar to the ones brought to bear upon a Britain that decided that it was not going to be in the Common Market or NATO.

As both parts of Ireland are at the moment in the EEC, it would present no particular problem if Ireland decided to remain in; it would just be a matter of reclassifying those elected

MEPs from the North as part of a united Irish delegation. But a British withdrawal would involve Northern Ireland's ceasing to be part of NATO. The relationship with NATO might have to be renegotiated with a new Ireland. There would be enormous pressure both from the Americans and the British military attempting to retain a base. They see neutrality as a threat.

There would be other pressures on Ireland – from the bankers and the International Monetary Fund, just as Britain is under pressure from them. You might discover, if you look ahead, an enormous common interest between the Irish and British people which at the moment is obscured by this unhealthy imperial relationship.

As to the actual modalities of the arrangement and what would be the eventual form of the state: there is endless scope for skill in constitution-drawing around what the exact relationships would be, whether there would be a federal, bi-polar or unitary legal system and so on. All that could be the subject of discussion once it was absolutely clear that the old status quo was definitely going. That is why the intent to persist in withdrawals is so important. I cannot see how it could possibly be in the interests of anybody to intensify the violence when the one thing that is known for certain is that it would not produce the return of the British troops.

When the nature of the conflict changed from being conflict with Britain to being a potential conflict internally, then the whole security argument would be transformed. Both the Republic, which seems to be a military state in some ways, and the North, which *is* a military state, would be faced with a wholly different situation. I think the argument would increasingly become a class argument, and the trade unions would get involved. With the border question removed by an external unilateral decision, the possibility of some class politics emerging in the unions is much more likely. There are some most formidable questions that have been suppressed because the British occupation has made them secondary – about unemployment, housing and so on. I don't think that it is unreasonable to look forward to what might emerge with some optimism.

In speeches from Labour platforms, you are guaranteed to get a good response if you say what a grand thing it would be if we had a Labour movement that defended our class with the same commitment as the Tories defend theirs. I forget who said that the Tories were too busy waging the class war to talk about it, but they do have a much clearer idea of where their interests lie.

In the early days, at the time of Carson, there was an economic interest in retaining control of Ireland; I don't think there is now. There is a certain crudity about monetarism whereby you might expect merchant bankers to argue that too much money is being spent hanging on to Northern Ireland, it is time to get out. The exception to their strictly financial view of the world is defence. The overall defence of Western capitalism from the threat of socialism, whether it is an external, or even more an internal threat, is something they are prepared to pay through the nose for. You are left with the defence argument.

I believe that Enoch Powell has spotted this – if the government could get the Republic to join NATO and satisfy the requirements to defend Western capitalism, then all the guarantees to the Unionists wouldn't be worth tuppence. Britain would just pull out.

The strange thing is that if the Tories were left in power, they would, on present showing, be more likely to get out of Northern Ireland than Labour. The Labour Party leadership has in the past used the language of imperialist paternalism which goes right back to the Fabian Colonial and Commonwealth Bureau. Liberal imperialism has found its home in those sections of the Labour Party which believe all the myths that the Tories have used to justify their oppression of other peoples.

If the Tories decided to make the break, it would be a Churchillian break – painful and brutal, but frank. They would say, 'We are happy now that this or the other guarantee has been given, we think the time has come to leave', and they would set a date just like that. They would of course use all their influence to see that what followed was not just an Ireland in NATO, but a united Ireland that had its internal security system so tight that socialism didn't stand a chance. It would be the very opposite of what we would want to do, but British occupation would end.

There are times in politics when you have to be crystal clear. When you're crystal clear, a lot of other things will make sense. If you fudge your way through, then you don't know where you are. What has to come out of this discussion is an absolute certainty of intent to end jurisdiction. There will be difficulties, yes. But I don't believe that they would be anywhere near as big as is being made out. There is a very large element of bluff. It used to be Carson; now it is a military interest dressed up as a great concern for the loyalist community. The certainty, that it is our intention to withdraw and that we mean to go through with it would, I believe, release a lot of constructive forces. The future is for Irish people to decide, not us, but I am optimistic.

After Eniskillen

People were shocked by what happened at Eniskillen; but also by the response to it. For a while we were told it was not possible to discuss the question of Ireland. Ken Livingstone was given the full media treatment. I know what it's like. The media used this treatment to avoid discussing the issues. They didn't want to discuss Ireland – they wanted to discuss Ken Livingstone.

Another purpose of this treatment is to distract people's attention from the long historical background, without which it is quite impossible to understand what has happened. If we're going to make progress – and I think we are – we must excavate some of the background to the struggle.

One of the things missing in modern British politics is the radical tradition that goes back to before the birth of socialism; the opposition to militarism, the opposition to imperialism, the opposition to the dictatorship of the mind. This is readily apparent when discussing the 'Irish Question', as it is called.

In 1892 my grandfather stood as a Liberal and a Home Ruler against the Tory President of the Local Government Board, as it was then called – the Nicholas Ridley of the day. In response the Tory, Ritchie, said: 'To vote against the government of the day would be a vote for civil war, for anarchy'. That was in 1892. And when the London County Council was set up the Home Secretary, Sir William Harcourt, refused it control of the police on the grounds of 'Irish terrorism'.

This argument has gone on and on. At the time of the Black and Tans in the 1920s, my father moved an amendment to the King's Speech condemning the coalition government for having 'handed over to the military authorities an unrestricted discretion in the definition of punishment of offences and frustrating the prospects of an agreed settlement to the problem of Irish self-government'.

I think that it's important to root this in history. Those who forget history are condemned to repeat the mistakes of history.

The continued British occupation of Ireland takes away the liberties of the British people as well as those of the Irish people – their rights to live a full life in independence and unity. We therefore have a common interest in finding a way to end this mutual tragedy as soon as possible.

Public opinion in Britain is well ahead of the political leadership on this matter as on so many others. Millions of people realise that if there is ever to be peace there must be a negotiated settlement to the war – after the decision to withdraw has been taken. The violence in Northern Ireland indicates the urgency for a negotiated settlement.

The partition of Ireland was itself the product of a British Government policy of the ballot and the bullet under which the Black and Tans were sent in to undermine the clear majority vote for Irish independence after the First World War – a policy opposed by Labour then as it should be now.

The question we have to face is not whether, but when, how soon and under what conditions British withdrawal takes place. The starting point must therefore be the setting of a fixed date for that withdrawal to which we would adhere and for discussion to begin with everyone in the North to work out what will happen once Britain has withdrawn.

That is why the Campaign Group of Labour MPs has decided to present a Bill in the House of Commons to terminate British jurisdiction in Northern Ireland, to campaign around that Bill with working people in both our countries so we can all liberate ourselves to build a decent and fair society in Britain and Ireland.

That's a summary of our position. Now let's look at some of the objections we will face when advocating this view. The first problem is that there is a basic contradiction in the position of those who say we are there because we are involved and it is part of the UK. There's an awful lot of ignorance in Britain about Ireland, encouraged by the media. And it's an awful thing to say but when there's no violence, there is no discussion – and when there is violence, you can't discuss it. If anyone tries, they're greeted with a yawn or a broadside.

Another argument used by Labour people is the argument about democracy. That the republican movement in the North is a denial of democracy. Of course, the reality is that Lloyd George denied the democratic vote by the use of enforced partition.

There has been no vote, and none is contemplated, in which the Irish people as a whole would be involved – or the British people for that matter.

We are told that there should be no talks with republican leaders, but everyone knows that even the Conservatives have had talks with republican leaders. A recent PLP meeting was designed to be a drum head court martial to deal with Mr Ken Livingstone. Yet Clive Soley, our former front-bench spokesperson met Sinn Fein, Merlyn Rees met Sinn Fein. We are misled into assuming that there have never been talks – it's an important point to make.

Then there is the argument that you cannot talk to terrorists. The word 'terrorists' is a term of abuse to describe those with whom you disagree. According to Mrs Thatcher the ANC are terrorists. According to President Reagan the Contras are freedom fighters. According to the British Establishment the people in Afghanistan are freedom fighters. Our history has it that that the Free French in the Second World War who blew up restaurants with German soldiers in them were freedom fighters. The term doesn't stand up as an argument.

If you want to get rid of violence you have to deal with the political problem that underpins it. To argue that anyone who wants to hold talks with republicans is stimulating violence is to speak an absolute untruth. That is doing the opposite of what has to be done – to seek a political solution.

The other argument is that Dublin doesn't want unity. But, of course, partition creates two states whose structures depend on the border. The politics based on the border lie at the root of many of the problems which face Ireland.

Then there's the argument that there would be bloodshed if Britain withdrew. The fact is that there has been bloodshed for many centuries. When the troops went in in 1969 there was a proposal from Dublin that a UN peace-keeping force be sent in.

Then we come to the Anglo-Irish Agreement, which I voted against. It was a fraudulent agreement which pretended to be all things to all people. It hinted that it recognised an all-Irish dimension and at the same time recognised the veto. My opinion is that, although I opposed it and think it won't work, it confirms the recognition by this Government of a special position there. But also, it was done to win the support of the US and the EEC to the partition of Ireland and the fact that this was thought to be necessary is an indication of the weakness of Britain's international position. I think the deal will soon be shunted into the long list of failures on Ireland.

Now I come to the position of the Labour Party itself on Ireland and right back at the beginning we had a position of outright opposition. After a war we got dragged into a bipartisan position on Ireland. Many efforts were made to drag us out of that position and we did make a move towards a break with bipartisanship but now with support for the Anglo-Irish Agreement we're back in a bipartisan posture.

It is time for us to renew the campaign for British withdrawal. We've always been told you can't raise the Irish question because it is difficult and divisive, but if we had adopted a clear position a long time ago we would have made some real progress.

We must remember that Northern Ireland has been a testing ground for weapons and methods of repression that we've seen employed in the UK. About ten years ago *Time* magazine had an interview with a British officer who said that all British soldiers must be brought here to prepare them for what must be done on the mainland.

The military's minds are now on the instruments of domestic control. We saw that in the miners' strike. It is only when this is made clear to people that we will make progress.

What we need now is a clear decision to withdraw. Some want this done immediately. Personally I think we need to set a date and adhere to it. The Bill we are going to propose is based on the Palestine Act of 1947. That is the only precedent where a British government unilaterally decided to terminate its interest in Palestine. There was a date fixed and it was adhered to. The terms of the Bill are based on those of 1947, designed by the best parliamentary draughtsmen of the time to be most appropriate for the protection of British servicemen during withdrawal.

I don't doubt for a moment that there would be problems in pursuing such a course. But I think that is what we should go for. I think the reaction would in general be a positive one, but if there were peace-keeping problems the one army in the world least equipped to deal with them would be the British Army whose withdrawal we would be announcing.

In campaigning for this we should see it as a joint enterprise. We are campaigning for the liberation of Ireland/Britain and of Britain/Ireland. We should get away from the bloodshed which has characterised our relationship and move to one of co-operation for the development of a decent society there and here.

I'm absolutely certain that whatever the reaction of the media and the Establishment, before the end of this century we shall see that withdrawal take place.

Privatisation of Gas

Mr Tony Benn (Chesterfield): One could not have a clearer description of the difference of opinion that divides the two sides of the House. Like a vulture, the Conservative Party is already beginning to hover around the British Gas Corporation to see what rich pickings it can make for its own people.

So far there has been no mention of the fact that many people look to gas for security of supply, high levels of maintenance and repair and high levels of safety at a price that they can afford. During this winter, as with every other, many people will be wondering whether they will be able to pay their gas bill when it arrives later in the year. As is well known, people die every winter from hypothermia simply because they cannot afford to pay the price of fuel. Therefore, to look to this industry as a way of making more profit, rather then of meeting a need, shows the real motivation behind the introduction of the Bill.

The Secretary of State was totally unconvincing. His arguments for privatisation were not valid, and he never mentioned the real reason for this measure. In 1969/70 and from 1975 to 1979, I was the sponsoring Minister for the British Gas Corporation. Since the public ownership of gas there has been major investment, higher safety standards and a very good repair and maintenance record. The industry has bought British equipment, which has maintained employment, and there has been a sense of service. Successive Governments have taxed the industry, but one can also tax an industry in private ownership. For example, we tax petrol. Anyone who thinks that once gas is in private ownership it will be free from a predatory Chancellor does not understand how this works. For various reasons, any Chancellor will from time to time look at ways of raising revenue, and private gas could be taxed as easily as public gas. The only difference is that gas is now being taxed for a different reason – to make it more profitable to sell it off.

I happened to be Secretary of State when North Sea gas was brought ashore. Because British Gas was a monopoly buyer, it was able to get a good price from the oil companies because the oil companies could not play one customer off against the other. British Gas was able to say, 'If you want to sell gas in Britain, you must sell it at the price that we offer.' One reason why gas prices have been so low – in some ways too low, to make it easy for electricity and coal – is that British Gas was able to force oil companies to sell gas at a low price.

Massive investment in a new distribution network was set up and a programme to convert appliances was successfully established. The case for the common ownership of gas is unanswerable. It was not always and only in private ownership before nationalisation. Hon Members might remember the phrase, 'Gas and Water Socialism.' There was a proud municipal record of running town gas before nationalisation.

Gas is a vital national asset. Energy policy under any Government is bound to take account of depletion policy. It would have been possible for British Gas, if it had so chosen and if the Government had allowed it, to deplete at a massive rate and bring the gas ashore so that people converted to gas when it was cheap, only to be caught with equipment that they could not afford to use when more expensive gas came in because ours was starting to run out. Energy pricing as between gas, electricity and coal is a central part of national policy.

I should like to mention one consideration that has not come out so far, unless the Secretary of State dropped a hint. Once gas is taken out of public ownership, British Gas will be under the complete control of the Common Market Commission. I have warned the House about this before, and am speaking from knowledge. When I was Secretary of State, it tried to argue in Brussels that the continental shelf was under the Treaty of Rome. We said that it was not and were able to enforce our will because we owned the gas fields there. The Commission wanted the pipelines to take the gas straight to Europe rather than come through our system to the continent. We were able to say, 'No, we do not accept that the continental shelf comes under the Treaty of Rome.' Privatisation will enable the Commission to enforce its will under the competition articles of the treaty. Moreover, the record of buying British equipment will dissolve because the EEC requirement to put orders out to tender will be enforceable with a private gas corporation, whereas it was not when it was public, when we were able to have regard to the long-term security of supply of equipment.

The Bill hands over North Sea gas to Common Market control by the act of privatisation. It will lead to higher prices, greater fuel poverty, lower safety, a weakening of regulation, poorer maintenance, loss of control to the EEC and reduced demand for British equipment.

The real motivation for the Bill should be spelt out with absolute clarity, as the Secretary of State did not touch on it. It is to sell assets, which the Government do not own, to their business friends, who will buy the assets at knock-down prices. It is to pay City institutions enormous fees to sell the assets and to use the proceeds for a once-and-for-all tax cut to buy support at the next General Election. It is important that we make it clear that business firms put up money to pay for Saatchi and Saatchi advertising to get a Tory Cabinet elected, knowing that a Tory Cabinet will put on the market, below their real price, assets the value of which comes from the labour of those who work in the industry concerned and from public investment. They will buy them, make a large killing and support the Tory Party again. It is corruption. There is no question about it.

I have been here for thirty-five years and I have never seen a measure which so reeks of corruption as this one. We should consider the figures. British Gas is valued at £16 billion. The Government have already sold £4.7 billion of public assets and lost £1.4 billion by underpricing. That is statistically established. British Telecom shares, for example, rose 93 per cent in value before night fell and the Government lost £1.3 billion in a single day – money that would have solved the problem of inner cities, made the Archbishop of Canterbury happy and ended the tragedy in the Broadwater Farm estate or in Brixton or in Liverpool or in Sheffield.

That money could have been used to meet needs, but it was used to pay an electoral debt incurred by the Government, who gained support from business companies. If the House doubts that assertion, the figures are public. The City institutions received getting on for £300 million in fees for selling assets. That is four or five times as much as Band Aid and Live Aid raised in one year of concerts for the starving of Ethiopia. The City of London was rewarded with six times as much as the generosity of the public could provide for the starving of Ethiopia. But here is the rub. Of the City underwriters, thirty-three of the fifty-five who got the business contributed to Tory Party funds. I have some figures to prove it. Baring Brothers gave £25,000 to the Tory Party in 1983 and shared in fees of £5 million to sell off Cable and Wireless. Kleinwort, Benson paid £30,000 to the Tory Party and shared in more than £5.5 million for selling British Aerospace, £190 million for selling British Telecom, more than £5 million for selling Cable and Wireless and £9 million for selling Enterprise Oil. That investment of £30,000 in Tory Party funds was pretty good. Hill Samuel paid £28,000 to the Tory Party and shared in £5.5 million of fees for the sale of Jaguar. Lazards put in £20,000 and shared in £1.75 million for the sale of Wytch farm. Morgan Grenfell put in £30,000 and got a share of £3 million for the sale of Amersham International and Sealink.

When I think of the district auditor chasing councillors in Lambeth on the ground that they were a bit late fixing a rate and compare that with the massive sums of money given, in effect, in return for political support to City institutions that have contributed nothing to raise the quality of service of British Gas or to provide safety for those who use it, I can only call it corruption. The public should know how it all works.

I am glad that my right hon Friend the Member for Salford, East Mr Orme said that an incoming Labour Government would deal with this matter. The precedents for legislation set by the Tory Party are many. I have gone through the legislation of the 1970 to 1974 Tory Government who took powers under the Counter-Inflation (Temporary Provisions) Act 1972 to control prices, to demand information, to amend statutes, to control profits, to vet investment and to control multinationals. They introduced the Insurance Companies (Amendment) Act 1973 which gave powers to veto directors, to inspect books, to issue directives and to define unfair practices. The fair trading legislation gave powers which included entry and seizure. The classic case was the one-clause Rolls-Royce (Purchase) Act 1971. Through one clause, they brought Rolls-Royce into public ownership. My right hon Friend need have no fear that he will not be sustained by Tory precedents when dealing with this abuse of public trust, which is a denial of the fiduciary responsibility to taxpayers and the public of whom the judges are so ready to speak when they criticise Labour councillors.

There will need to be changes in the nature of public ownership. Over the years, for my sins, as Postmaster General and as an Energy Minister I have been responsible for many public corporations. There must be real accountability to Parliament. I have never believed it right for the Secretary of State of the day – I had many years experience of this – to have no explicit authority over a chairman such as Sir Denis Rooke, but always to have to twist the chairman's arm and then not be accountable to Parliament. There should be explicit powers of direction subject to parliamentary approval.

We should get away from the crude patronage of appointments. Parliament should have to approve the chairpersons appointed to our public corporations so that people can give evidence about them before they are confirmed.

A final precedent from the Tory Party is the Trade Union Act 1984. Many ministers have talked about the need to restore the power of union members over the unions. A minor amendment to the Government's own Act would allow workers in industry to choose by ballot the boards of directors of the companies for which they work. The alteration of one word – from 'union' to 'company' – would secure a measure of power for those who have invested their lives in the gas industry comparable with the power now supposedly enjoyed by those who have invested their money in it.

The party of which I am honoured to be a member, which still lives under the shadow of and perhaps affection for the Herbert Morrison legislation after the war, must look again at these matters. There must be accountability to Parliament. There has never been proper accountability. Parliament must be able to vet the chairmen of these great corporations. There must be accountability to elected local authorities to see that the big bosses in the public sector do not ride roughshod over local needs. Those who work in the industry must have powers over their own industrial management – based, perhaps, on the legislation introduced by the Conservatives to deal with trade union democracy.

I have long urged those changes. When the history of all this comes to be written, for this privatisation will not last long, it may be that by breaking the Morrison mould the Government will be remembered for having paved the way to a form of common ownership which entrenches service to the public and not the pursuit of profit which is the Government's sole interest in introducing this measure.

Legal Reform

Neil Kinnock's government will face three major obstacles in its work for peace and social justice. The first is the American Government who want to dominate our foreign and defence policies. The second is the world bankers who want to control Britain's economic and industrial policy. And the third are the British Establishment who want to protect their privileges, property and power by using their laws to deny justice to our people. There are three aspects of the problem that have been brought out in the debate. First is the need for access to the law by millions of people for whom the law is remote. It is expensive, and legal aid is now effectively being rate-capped under a legal system which is lengthy, full of mystification and riddled with restrictive practices at which the profession has always excelled.

As every councillor, trade union official and Member of Parliament knows from casework, there is a massive unmet demand for justice. The Citizen's Advice Bureaux handle 6 million cases a year. The law centres have been cut down to 57 – one law centre for every million of the population – and even now some are threatened with closure. The unemployed centres are overwhelmed with work they cannot cope with and so are the voluntary agencies.

Therefore, when the delegate from Wythenshawe argued, as did others, that we must strengthen the facilities and open up the system, that must mean the central funding of resources to provide law centres for everyone who needs them. And do not let us forget that, if that need, like so many other needs, was met, then it would also create jobs. This argument applies also to the provision of family courts which could deal with greater sensitivity in some of the matters which come before the courts today.

The second issue relates to the role of the magistrates. I would like to pay tribute, as many would, to the good Labour magistrates who do their best in very difficult circumstances. But we all know that the magistrates are appointed in secret by a secret committee the names of which are not allowed ever to be published. And we also know that, in many areas, there are politically biased Tory magistrates who use their power against our people.

Let me give some very clear examples. What about the Tory magistrates who in effect punished the miners through bail conditions being applied before there had ever been a case. What about the peace women at Greenham Common – I was in Newbury Magistrates' Court when, unbelievably, the women speaking for peace were convicted of action likely to cause a breach of the peace when inside the camp were enough nuclear weapons to destroy the whole of humanity.

Comrades, we must open up the magistracy and establish real accountability. I am asked this question, perhaps others are too: if we elect councillors and MPs and we are to have statutory ballots for trade unionists, why cannot we elect magistrates too because they are people who are supposed to defend our local interests?

The third problem is that of the judiciary itself, of which Tony Gifford spoke – nobody is better qualified than him. He linked it with an idea of a Ministry of Justice. The problem of the judiciary is complex, not made easier by the fact that judges come from one narrow social class. Though we often talk about the vicious Tory laws which must be repealed, how do we deal with judges who interpret those laws and the common law in a way that is biased against justice and against our people? Let me give some examples of that too. There was the scandalous sequestration of trade union funds by judges in judgements that were wholly unfair; the savage sentencing like that on Terry French, the Kent miner, which was wholly unjustified; the treatment of women as in some notable rape cases; and the tendency which the police begin, and the courts sometimes continue, of criminalising the black community in a way which makes them feel properly alienated.

What about the local authorities? Would you believe it that – in a country which boasts of justice – to build homes and provide services in Liverpool or Lambeth is now described as 'wilful misconduct' by judges who have never depended on any of those services themselves. Nor should we forget Northern Ireland, where the Diplock Courts sit without juries and the supergrass trials convict on the basis of uncorroborated informer evidence; nor the ten people convicted for the Birmingham,

Guildford and Woolwich pub bombing cases where there is a grave doubt as to their guilt and those cases must be re-opened.

Comrades, none of these matters should surprise socialists because we know in a capitalist society the law protects property at the expense of the people. But the next Labour Government, democratically elected, must use its majority in Parliament to put it right. The Tories have changed the law to protect their privileges. The Labour movement will demand from the next Labour Government that it enacts just laws that offer justice to our people and to all people.

SOURCES

THE FALKLANDS WAR
Extracts taken from the House of Commons Official Report (*Hansard*) of proceedings on 7 April, 29 April, 20 May and 21 December, 1982

THE MINERS' STRIKE
Extracts taken from the House of Commons Official Report (*Hansard*) of proceedings on 7 June 1984 and 4 February 1985; Extract from speech to National Union of Miners Rally, Barnsley, September 1984

GAY RIGHTS
Extracts from the House of Commons Official Report (*Hansard*) of proceedings on 9 March 1988

FORTRESS WAPPING
Extracts taken from the House of Commons Official Report (*Hansard*) of proceedings on 8 May 1986 and 26 January 1987

THE IRISH STRUGGLE FOR FREEDOM
First published in *Ireland After Britain*, ed Martin Collins, Pluto Press, 1985

AFTER ENISKILLEN
Extracts from the Miriam James Memorial Lecture, 1987

PRIVATISATION OF GAS
Extracts taken from the House of Commons Official Report (*Hansard*) of proceedings on 10 December 1985

LEGAL REFORM
Extracts taken from a speech on behalf of the NEC to the 1986 Labour Party Conference, Blackpool

4
BRITISH FOREIGN AND DEFENCE POLICY

The Case for Non-Alignment

I want to examine some of the interests and assumptions which now underly Western foreign and defence policies, and to consider whether it would not be better for Britain to move towards a more non-aligned position which might allow us to play a more constructive role, with others, in the search for world peace, development and human rights, and in the process restore self-government to Britain itself.

My main purpose is to get that debate going in this country, rather than to argue for one specific alternative. One of the most dangerous effects of present policy is that it has effectively blanked out any serious discussion of alternatives. The present argument about nuclear weapons has become rather narrow since defence policy must be set against the background of foreign policy and a clear analysis of the world situation. British policy is, in effect, conditioned by our relationship with the USA, and has been fashioned in response to certain assumptions about the intentions of the Soviet Union.

Two key questions therefore need to be asked at the outset: does the USSR really want war, and does the USA really want peace? The official answer to both these questions is a resounding 'Yes'.

If, therefore, after closer examination, it turns out that these answers represent at best a gross over-simplification of the truth, or are actually wrong, then we are bound to look again at the policies that flow from them.

The conventional wisdom of the Western and British establishments is that world peace has been maintained since 1945 by the fact that the West has had nuclear weapons and that these weapons have deterred the USSR from attacking us. It is this assumption that lies behind the current arguments for the deployment of a further generation of nuclear weapons in

Europe, and for the regular increase, in real terms, of Western defence spending.

The Russians see it differently having been invaded three times this century; by the Kaiser in 1914, by the British in 1920 to overturn the Revolution, and by Hitler in 1941, involving them in the loss of over twenty million of their own people.

It is much more likely that the real reason that we have had nearly forty years free from war in Europe is that neither side wanted war.

The USSR was over-run and ravaged by the invaders, an experience from which the USA and the UK were happily spared and, because the Soviet Union bore the brunt of the Nazi attack, we in Britain enjoyed a breathing space – in which we were able to re-build our forces, defeated after Dunkirk – which carried through until after the Japanese attack on Pearl Harbour brought the USA into the war. It is important for Americans to be reminded of this sequence of events since the older generation of British people have never forgotten that the Russians were our allies before the Americans came into the war, and that some of us believe that our liberties were saved, in part, by the sacrifice of millions of Russian lives, lost in the defence of their own homeland.

The advocates of the Western alliance have always feared a return to isolationism in the USA and have concluded that the best way to prevent it is to maintain a continuing presence of American troops in Europe, to make available the necessary bases and facilities for that purpose so that the US is physically locked into our continent and its security.

Others have drawn the very opposite conclusion: that we could never rely upon the US to put its own people and cities at risk, simply to defend us, and that one American motivation for retaining a presence in Europe is to be sure that if another war does break out it will be fought here and not there.

But the central question remains to be answered and that is whether the USSR, is planning, or has ever planned, to over-run Western Europe. No firm evidence to suggest that this is their strategy has ever been produced in a form that carries conviction. It is true that the Soviet Union has maintained a tight grip over the countries of Eastern Europe, and sent its forces to Afghanistan to protect its southern flank. It is no part of my purpose to defend these actions but they do not, of themselves, tell us much more than that the USSR is behaving like all great powers in history, including Britain in the past, and the USA today, in using its military supremacy to protect its own borders and seek to secure the maintenance of governments friendly to itself in neighbouring countries.

These Soviet policies cannot, of themselves, be held to prove that the USSR is preparing military action to occupy other countries, least of all the immensely powerful countries of Europe.

Nor are the moral arguments used against the USSR very credible when they come from another super-power. There is no evidence to suggest that those parts of the world that are under US influence or control have any better record in maintaining political freedom, civil liberties or democracy than those in the Soviet sphere of influence.

Some of the most corrupt and rotten military dictatorships to be found anywhere, as in Turkey, the Philippines, South Korea and Central and Latin America are backed to the hilt by Washington and supplied with arms specifically to hold down their own populations, who might otherwise demand democracy and social justice, and elect governments which would threaten US economic and military interests.

This was exactly how the British behaved when we had an Empire, and boasted of our Imperialism, at a time when great powers did not have to pretend that they had troops all over the world to protect democracy. They were known to be there to protect British Imperial interests as when Britain invaded Afghanistan, which we did four times over the last century to protect our interests in India. Nor were there any comparable sustained campaigns, by Western governments, in favour of democracy or civil liberties in Russia at the time of the Tsars before 1917, against the denial of civil liberties by fascist dictatorships in Europe before 1939 or after 1945 in Spain, Portugal, Greece or Turkey, or in respect of the non-communist nations that still oppress their own peoples.

It is important to put these facts upon the record because the Western alliance has got very little to do with the defence of freedom and a great deal to do with the defence of Western, and in particular American, global economic and political interests. These interests are to a great extent the interests of Capital, rather than the interests of Labour, and it should surprise no one that Labour is rediscovering its own internationalism in response to this pressure.

It would also be quite wrong to interpret the views that I am seeking to develop as being in any way anti-American, for the same arguments are being put forward, in very similar language, by many of those who work in the American peace and Labour movements. Indeed it is now becoming clear that the peace movements in the West and the national liberation movements in the Third World, constitute an identifiable voice for working people against oppression. Such peace movements are, in no sense, seeking to substitute Soviet, for American, domination in their own countries, but they are not prepared to suffer from domestic tyranny solely on the grounds that this tyranny proclaims itself to be anti-communist and is committed to protect US and Western economic influence.

The peace movement represents a potentiality for social change, which may best explain the bitter opposition to it amongst many leaders of the Western alliance and their political supporters, who see it as threatening their own position. And it may well be the fear that the peace movements could prove to be a wider focus of political opposition in their own countries, rather than any genuine anxiety about the risk of a Soviet invasion, which explains the policies which they are now following.

Indeed, from the time of the Russian Revolution in 1917 it may always have been the fear of internal repercussions, rather than the fear of direct expansionism by the Kremlin, which has pre-occupied the leaders of the West. That was certainly the view of Hitler, Mussolini and Franco who made hostility to the Soviet Union the centrepiece of their propaganda, and it looks very much as if those anti-Soviet fears are being stimulated again, and for similar reasons.

Cold War–Detente–Cold War

The pattern of pre-war Western thinking about the USSR was resumed after 1945.

Indeed the decision to use the Atomic Bomb on Japan seems likely to have been motivated at least partially by the desire to warn the USSR, since the readiness of the Japanese to surrender was known to President Truman well before those bombs were dropped. West Germany was re-armed, NATO was formed and permanent bases were offered to the USA on the continent, and in the United Kingdom.

It is true that after the death of Stalin, and when the Western economies were growing fast and bringing self-confidence with that growth, some progress was made with disarmament, as with the signature of the partial Nuclear Test-Ban Treaty. Detente opened up dialogue and co-operation, and East–West trade and contacts developed on a more normal basis. That period of relative peace has long since passed, and we are back in a new Cold War that is infinitely more dangerous – because of the growth of the nuclear armouries on both sides – than we experienced at the time of the Berlin blockade.

Conventional Western wisdom attributes this deterioration entirely to Soviet actions, in Poland, Afghanistan or elsewhere and to their own arms build-up. But that is not the whole story and we would be very foolish to ignore the impact upon Western policy-makers of other events which have made them feel very insecure.

For in the years of detente the advance of national liberation movements in Asia, the Middle East, Africa and Latin America undoubtedly weakened the power of the West, and was often attributed to Soviet intervention or Marxist influence (though here it must be noted that Marxism is no barrier to Western support provided that, as in the case of Yugoslavia and China, the Marxist governments are anti-Russian). Thus the victory of Fidel Castro against Batista, the American defeat in Vietnam, the election of Allende in Chile, the overthrow of the Somoza dictatorship in Nicaragua, the ousting of the Shah of Iran and the holding of the American hostages, and the victory of the liberation movements in Angola and Mozambique seem to have been interpreted in the Pentagon as proof of a world plot, organised in the Kremlin.

Meanwhile the Western economies were badly hit by the OPEC price increases of 1973 and began to slide into depression. The result is that the sense of insecurity in Western capitals has intensified ten-fold, more from fear of what may happen to their own societies, and their own systems, than because there is any particular evidence to support their widely proclaimed view that the Soviet Union has launched into a new and more aggressive policy against the west.

Indeed it is certainly arguable that Soviet policy has been exceptionally cautious in its responses to recent world crises which they might well have exploited to their own advantage – as in Iran, the Lebanon, the Falklands or Central America.

The election of President Reagan in 1980 helped to create a completely different climate of opinion in Britain about the nature of our links with Washington. There is widespread anxiety in Britain about the negative attitude adopted by President Reagan towards the current round of arms control talks, and a genuine fear that there may be a new school of thought within the White House that believes that the arms race could actually be used to bankrupt the Soviet Union, and hence destabilize its governments, force it out of Eastern Europe and that, as a last resort, the West could fight and win a limited nuclear war in Europe, and should be prepared to do so.

Such policies, or anything like them, would run absolutely counter to the professed peace aims of NATO itself, and would be deeply damaging and dangerous for Britain. The American people might well reflect on the fact that President Reagan, despite his military build-up, has actually undermined much political support for the USA around the world.

What matters to us is how we, in this country, should react to what is happening, and what options are open to us. There is a school of thought that shares some of these fears, but believes that the answer lies in a bigger build-up of the European end of the NATO alliance, both to give Europe a stronger voice in seeking to influence the American President, and to allow a move away from over-dependence on nuclear weapons.

Somewhere in the background lies the dream that the European Community itself might develop its own armed forces as part of a full-scale European Federation, which would, so it is argued, produce a real counterweight to Washington, guard against any return to American isolationism, and offer permanent security against any threat from the East. Such a policy may also contain within itself the idea that these troops along with others in what is called 'Civil Defence' would also be available for internal use in Europe, should that ever prove necessary.

Labour Attitudes to Foreign Policy

The Labour Party has always contained a strong strand of opinion which has analysed world developments and British policy along the lines that I have described, welcoming the events of 1917, opposing the war of intervention in 1920 to overthrow the Russian Revolution, arguing for an understanding with Moscow to defeat Hitler and Mussolini, and believing that 'Left could speak to Left' in the post-war world.

This section of the party – the Third Force movement – was opposed both to the foreign policy pursued by Ernest Bevin in the Attlee Government and to Stalinism. Instead we looked for a different and more independent policy that would allow Britain to work more closely with the United Nations and all those countries that were trying to throw off the yoke of foreign domination, and move towards democracy and the planned development of their own resources.

But the Cold War, and the commitment of all post-war governments – including Labour governments – to the Atlantic Alliance, prevailed against all its critics, and it looked for a time as if the debate about British foreign policy had been effectively stifled.

When it did surface again it was in the form of CND and opposition to American policy in Vietnam. But since the election of President Reagan I would hazard a guess that distrust of the USA, and uneasiness in Britain about our apparent subordination to America, may be far more widespread than we know.

The ties that bind Britain to the USA are, in fact, very much closer and more intricate than has ever been made public. One starting point must be the war-time arrangements reached on nuclear co-operation, at the heart of the special relationship, which began during the war. Britain agreed to put is own work on the Atomic Bomb into an Anglo-American project, on the clear understanding that the technology would be shared after the war was over. Even though the Congress passed legislation that made that impossible, the links remained very close, so close indeed that the old US Atomic Energy Commission enjoyed virtually supervisory powers over British nuclear developments, and was able, through its own advanced capability, to make it a condition of future exchanges that they should also be able to satisfy themselves upon all matters involving security in Britain.

The fact that, for twenty years, Britain was supplying plutonium from our own civil nuclear power stations for the American weapons programme, without telling Parliament, or for that matter – as far as I can make out – the responsible ministers, gives some indication of the closeness of this part of the Alliance.

More generally there is no doubt that almost all British intelligence material is made available to US intelligence agencies who are also allowed to operate here and to vet our services, in return for which some of their intelligence information is made available to the British Government.

The links binding us to the US became much tighter with the arrival in the UK of the first US aircraft which was presented to the public as a mere training visit, and the secret agreements under which these aircraft, and later the bases and missiles, are controlled have never been shown either to the Cabinet or to Parliament. In addition to these arrangements, which lock

Britain into a very subordinate role in the Anglo-American relationship, the USA has enormous economic, industrial, cultural and political influence in Britain, the full weight of which is hard to assess because it is so all-pervasive, and it extends to the IMF, which is itself under a great deal of American influence.

It is clear that if any British Government were to wish to distance itself however slightly from Washington and its policies the task of disentangling us from these arrangements would be both long and difficult. The American President would have plenty of time in which to apply pressure, or to take action to see that that British Government's re-election was jeopardised. This has to be said plainly because those who favour some measure of disengagement have a duty to explain just what it would be likely to mean if it was attempted.

Those who would oppose any disengagement warn us of the danger that it would make us liable to pressure from Moscow, whereas the truth is that the really heavy pressure would be coming from Washington.

For those who would like to see a measure of disengagement from the present subordination of the United Kingdom to the United States of America there are a number of clear options.

The 1983 Labour manifesto went some way along that road by pledging the complete closure of all US nuclear bases in Britain, the removal of all the nuclear weapons themselves and implied the termination of all Anglo-American co-operation in nuclear weapons technology, as part of a completely non-nuclear defence strategy for Britain.

Though these proposals would, in fact, have made necessary a major change in NATO, it is also true that within NATO there are already a wide range of different policies on nuclear weapons and their deployment.

De Gaulle, while building his own Force de Frappe, refused to allow US bases to remain in France, and no Cruise or Pershing missiles are to be sent there this time round. West Germany is not permitted to have its own nuclear weapons but allows the US to deploy its own missiles there. Canada, itself a member of NATO, neither has its own nuclear weapons, nor will it permit the US to station its missiles on Canadian territory.

It might thus be that only if the US or NATO were unwilling to accommodate a change of British policy along the lines that I have been discussing would the issue of our formal membership come up – although a Conference resolution rejected British membership of any alliance which was based upon the possibility that it might engage in the first use of nuclear weapons.

The fact that an American President whom we do not elect, do not control and cannot remove has the power to make war from our territory, and hence make us a prime target, should never be underestimated as a permanent source of fear and resentment.

In this context the defence issues must always be seen to hinge upon the democratic control of our own foreign policy, and any change of British policy must begin with a fresh analysis of what is really happening in the world, and how we should respond.

I am arguing that the real world is very different from the one we are told about and that we should start to think things out for ourselves again. Above all we must stop being bemused by the present fears which are being so skilfully built up, and exploited, by those who have a vested interest in escalating arms budgets and associated military apparatus. And if we do so we shall find that Britain's most useful role would be in working for detente, for a nuclear-free and more united Europe of fully self-governing states, for the UN and for the freedom and development of all countries.

Who Is Our Enemy?

The foreign policy of the British Government is very closely linked to the oppression of people at home who are seeking social justice. The concept of the *'Enemy Within'* which has been developed since the Falklands War and was in particular related to the miners, is a concept that has a very strong resemblance to what Hitler and Mussolini did in the inter-war years. The peace movement as well as the miners are now thought of as the *'Enemy Within'*.

I was at Greenham Common last year the day they evicted the peace women who were not at all like miners on the picket line. But they were treated by the police with similar brutality. Or consider what happened at Molesworth where they chased out that little group of campaigners and drove them from the little peace chapel they have built. Consider also what happened at Stonehenge in June where the police arrested four or five hundred people and many of them were badly beaten up.

Defending Democracy

The Government intend to create in the public mind the idea that those who defend their jobs, those who defend peace, or in the case of Ireland those who are seeking Irish unity and independence are all part of a subversive domestic element against which military preparations have to be made. The Public Order Acts which are going to be strengthened as a result of all this rhetoric are primarily motivated, not by the situation which might arise in the football grounds or by any other similar matters, but because the Government want greater power in their hands to deal with the growing discontent that their own policies are creating.

Let me quote from a letter written by the Chief Executive of

Sedgmoor District Council to the Chief Constable of Avon, dated the 17 August 1982. It related to civil defence, and this is what it said:

> In Somerset there has recently been tremendous activity at parish level and the emergency planning team have been working like Trojans to set up self help emergency committees in the villages to get advice, bring local relief, and generally assist the District Controllers in wartime. The best laid plans of mice and men come to naught, however, should lawlessness be rife, and I am sure Controllers designate would welcome some indication from the Chief Constable on the likely level of Police support and protection that would be available to controllers aiming to execute their war plans effectively – requisitioning, rationing of fuel and food, guarding of essential supplies, *shooting looters or the gravely injured*.

Here was a civil servant asking the police to give an assurance that they should shoot *'looters or the gravely injured'*. Now what sort of civil defence is that? All this is presented to us as a necessary part of the responsible role of citizens in the event of a crisis.

We have got to dig a bit more deeply into it if we are to make sense of what has happened.

A New Agenda for the International Labour and Socialist Movements

I am most grateful for this invitation to come to Poland. I would like to take this opportunity to discuss, personally and informally, some of the issues that concern the international Labour, socialist, trade union and peace movements, and their relevance to our two countries.

The time has come when the International Labour and Socialist movement, as a whole, in Europe and worldwide, should begin taking the initiative, at every level, to end the Cold War and the arms race, and start to build a new international order, based on the UN Charter, providing for real co-operation and development in the interests of working people, and the diversion of resources to make that possible.

I am certain that both the Polish and the British people have a significant role to play in such an undertaking.

Britain is now paying a very high price for the Cold War, with heavy military expenditure that absorbs well over 5 per cent of our gross domestic product, which in real terms is 20 per cent above what it was in 1979, when Mrs Thatcher became Prime Minister.

This is by far the highest percentage for any country in NATO, except the USA, and contrasts with just over 1 per cent spent by the Japanese.

The real danger lies in the continuing poison of Cold War propaganda which prepares people psychologically for the possibility that nuclear weapons may one day have to be used.

Inevitably such a huge military budget means that we have a powerful military establishment, living off the money provided by the State, but actually more interested in retaining its power against the possibility of domestic opposition to the Government than to the likelihood of a Soviet military attack.

This military, and especially nuclear, role has played some part in the suppression of civil liberties, in that neither Parliament nor the public are told the truth. This makes it hard to exercise even the most basic rights of electors under our parliamentary system.

With 30,000 US troops permanently stationed in Britain and 125 American bases, of various kinds, it is, in part, the function of the Army, together with the police, now being re-equipped as a para-military force, to guard against those who engage in direct action in the peace movement. Such people are liable to arrest and imprisonment.

British membership of NATO means that over 90 per cent of our military budget is committed to that alliance, dominated by the Americans, but, as proved by the recent bombing of Libya by US aircraft from bases in Britain, our subordination to US global strategy allows them to use our territory for purposes that have nothing to do with NATO. Indeed one of the reasons why the American Government supports the British occupation of Northern Ireland, where a long-fought civil war is in progress, is that the Republic of Ireland is neutral, and the US does not wish the re-unification of Ireland, for fear that a British withdrawal would also mean that NATO lost its foothold in a united Ireland. And similar military and economic interests best explain why the US and British Governments do not want to take effective action against apartheid in South Africa, which, in strategic terms, they see as a reliable ally, and where there are billions of dollars and pounds invested.

US policies, after the Libyan bombing, the threats to Nicaragua, and the denunciation of the SALT agreement, are becoming increasingly unpopular with the British people. Recent public opinion polls put support for President Reagan's America at around only 25 per cent, with the rest expressing varying degrees of hostility.

The tragedy at the Chernobyl reactor should have taught us all that nuclear weapons used anywhere would carry dangers of a deadly kind to the rest of the world. In particular the Star Wars project is seen as a gross waste of scarce world resources, a threat to escalate the arms race, an attempt to bankrupt the USSR and a means of injecting high technology into American industry, via the Pentagon, to compete with the Japanese.

By contrast there is growing sympathy for the recent initiatives taken by Mr Gorbachev. Many people find his appeals for an end to the arms race to be credible, in part because they are so obviously in the interests of the people in the socialist countries, and would benefit us all.

The Recent History of Britain

It was the fact that Britain was the first country to experience the industrial revolution that has shaped our history most recently, and that revolution gave birth to all three of the dominant political philosophies which now compete for world supremacy.

The first was capitalism itself, explained and advocated in *The Wealth of Nations* by Adam Smith. The second was co-operative socialism and political trade unionism, associated with the name of Robert Owen. The third was communism, developed by Karl Marx as a direct result of his studies of British capitalism.

Initially British trade unions, like the medieval guilds which preceded them, were strictly non-political craft organisations, but they were politicised through the struggle for recognition, came to be associated with the campaigns for the extension of the franchise to working-class men, and then formed the labour representation committees, out of which the Labour Party was born.

It was in 1918, in the year following the Russian Revolution, when Europe was in ferment, that the Labour Party adopted an explicitly socialist constitution and programme. However, as the experience of the intervening years has shown only too clearly, the existence of a strong trade union party officially committed to socialism has, despite many years in office, never secured anything approaching any sort of socialist transformation of British society, which remains a subtle blend of feudalism, capitalism and corporate paternalism, scarred by gross inequalities of wealth and power.

There are many reasons why successive British Labour governments have followed policies comparable to those other social democrats in the rest of Western Europe and failed to achieve the objectives which the early socialists wished. First there is a grave weakness in the electoralist politics which made parliamentarianism central to its operation, limiting democratic rights to the cross on the ballot paper. Second, the nature of the planning mechanisms adopted, and the structure of the publicly owned industries that were nationalised, became hopelessly bureaucratic in their structures and methods. Third, the trade unions, despite their formal affiliation to the party, remained essentially non-political, negotiating for the best deal that they could from capital, and hoping that their leaders could become a part of a new tripartite corporatist ruling class with government and employers in a consensus devoted to making capitalism work more efficiently. Fourth, this corporatist pattern seemed to decapitate both the political and industrial wings of the movement, in that their leaders entered the governing classes and left their constituents in the working-class movement without the independent spokespersons that they needed to defend their interests. Fifth, there was an overall failure to develop and extend democracy at the grass-roots level, or even to consolidate it at the national level, both of which are essential if the formidable power of new technology is to be made to serve us and not to enslave us. Sixth, there was a serious failure to develop any sort of international working-class links that were greatly needed if the international power of capital was to be contained and prevented from establishing a new imperialism of the market place.

A major factor which has dominated much of the official thinking of a succession of British Labour leaders, has been hostility to Marx and Marxism and the socialist governments which came to power by revolution.

The arguments used to build hostility to these states, and these ideas, have rotated around the question of human rights, the different concepts of what constitutes democracy, and the theory that the USSR was planning a war to extend its power, worldwide, by military aggression.

After the Russian Revolution, the capitalist governments in the West became very alarmed at the effect that that Revolution might have upon their own economic interests and the power structures which they sustained in their European empires and in their own societies. In its most acute form fascism, particularly Nazism, was an expression of these policies. They grew out of the inter-war crises of the capitalist system, and attracted a lot of support from Western governments.

It is important to remember that the only capitalist country that did not move to the Right during the 1930s was the USA which, under President Roosevelt, made use of Keynesian ideas to save capitalism by methods that had some progressive elements, especially in respect to the role of Labour. But the guiding principles that united all those right-wing regimes in Europe were nationalism, imperialism and militarism; state support for capital; hostility to trade unionism and socialism; anti-Soviet propaganda; and repression of civil liberties.

These were the ideas which underpinned Appeasement, and blocked off the possibility of an agreement with the USSR to stop Hitler, at a time when war might have been averted.

It could even be argued that some Western governments

believed that they were being drawn in to fight 'the wrong war, with the wrong enemy and the wrong allies', and that ever since 1945 there has been an attempt to 'correct that error'.

Certainly the Cold War policies advocated by the right-wing forces in the West, since 1945, have revealed some of the attitudes held before the Second World War. At its worst there has been talk of the 'Liberation' of Eastern Europe, as by John Foster Dulles, or the subtler idea of 'destabilising' the socialist countries by subversion as was done in Chile, or more crudely the possibility of creating civil discontent by a competitive arms programme designed to bankrupt those same socialist countries.

The establishment of the EEC was largely motivated by the desire to extend and hence strengthen capitalism in Western Europe. Similarly the NATO alliance was intended to act as a *cordon sanitaire* to prevent the spread of socialism. But meanwhile, this system also provided a cover for the growth of a formidable American Empire, sustaining, with the help of 3,000 US bases across the world, the huge economic, industrial and political interests of the USA, and of the multinationals and the banks which the US government regard as its special concern.

It is a tragedy that so many social democratic parties have gone along with the United States in its anti-Soviet policies, however sharp their criticisms may have been of some of the other policies pursued by Washington.

But now, at last, attitudes are beginning to alter, at least in Britain, as we experience more clearly the nature of our subservience to US policy, as the impact of the arms race on world poverty becomes clearer, and as we realise that working people everywhere are becoming prisoners in a conflict that it is not in their interests to maintain.

In this connection we are severely handicapped by the absence of an effective labour or socialist international, the split in the trade union movement, the division of Europe and restrictions on contact.

If we are to make progress we must build up the confidence of working people everywhere. We must try to establish a new internationalism of labour to counter, and replace, the powerful internationalism of capital which operates against the interests of those we have to represent.

Amongst the items we should consider for a new International Agenda are:

1. The extension of direct links, at every level, between the Labour, socialist, peace and other progressive movements.

2. The re-unification of the world trade union movement, to bring the WFTU and ICFTU together.

3. The establishment of regular forums for the open discussion of our experience of socialism, so as to learn from both our succcesses and our failures.

4. The adoption of specific policies to strengthen confidence in Europe by developing the Helsinki accords, moving towards the acceptance of nuclear-free zones, and working to replace the military blocs by a pan-European security system, that safeguards the interests of all the countries involved and allows general disarmament.

5. The launching of campaigns for a cut in arms expenditure within our own countries, to allow the diversion of resources to urgent development at home, and worldwide, in support of the non-aligned countries with their demands for a new world economic order and an enhanced role for the the United Nations.

These five items are, I believe, both simple and realisable – if seen as part of a long term perspective for the twenty-first century.

We cannot accept that we must live forever under the shadow of a divided Europe, and a divided world, which was the legacy of imperialism, fascism and the Second World War.

It is not too soon to be looking towards a new and different world in which our children and grandchildren may live in peace.

The danger posed by the splitting of the atom can only be contained by the power of uniting peoples in every country and we should never forget that humanity now has in its hands the power to solve most of the problems of poverty, ignorance and disease that exist in the world.

Above all we need to have confidence in ourselves to take the initiative where we live and work, drawing upon the widely differing traditions of which we are all heirs, and act together to realise the possibilities that now exist.

Many philosophers have studied the world – the point, however, is to change it.

Some Facts About Defence

In 1986 the world's military expenditure is going to top £634 billion – that is £1.2 million a minute – and at the present levels of world arms' spending the average individual can expect to give up three or four years of his or her working life to pay for it.

With only 11 per cent of the world's population, the Superpowers account for 60 per cent of overall military expenditure, 80 per cent of weapons' research and 97 per cent of all nuclear weapons. In the United States, which accounts for 30 per cent of the world's military expenditure, defence spending rose more than any other component in its budget.

At constant prices the world total spent on defence is now two and a quarter times greater than it was in 1960, the first year records were kept. And for those who think conventional weapons are safer, 20 million people have been killed by conventional weapons since the Second World War and the world stockpile of nuclear weapons, which was three in 1945, is now over 60,000. Today's arsenals contain the equivalent of 1,000,000 Hiroshimas.

I regard this as a highly important Conference. Not a very big one, but it is the beginning of a serious long-term campaign, which may take a decade, to bring about a change in British foreign policy. This is an attempt to penetrate beyond the sort of normal horizons of British politics: What is going to happen in next week's public opinion poll? What will happen in the budget on 17 March? What will the outcome be of the Greenwich by-election? Or, if you are a visionary and prophetic figure, What will happen in the borough elections in May? We are trying to look beyond that because one of the victims of electoral politics is serious long-term thinking.

As a Labour candidate I shall have honestly to explain to the people of Chesterfield that if a Labour Government is elected we shall stop making, or rather servicing and maintaining, Polaris weapons; that we shall ask the United States to remove their nuclear bases, though we now understand that is to be done by agreement with them – whatever that may mean; that American ships with nuclear weapons will be allowed to visit British ports, even though they cannot in New Zealand; that we are firmly committed to NATO membership; that we are not aiming to make any savings whatever from the shift from nuclear weapons in our general defence budget – every penny of it will go on to other conventional weapons; and, more than that, we are going to inflation-proof the present defence budget so that, if prices rise, the defence spending in cash terms will increase, even though it is now 20 per cent above what it was in 1979 when we left office.

This policy is a gain, I suppose, in terms of the commitment to remove our own nuclear weapons programme and seek to remove American nuclear bases. But there is no questioning whatever of the assumption that the Soviet Union is a military threat to Britain, or that the United States is the friend of freedom all over the world. In this connection, I was sent a book the other day by a man, a retired education officer, which included some of the captured German Foreign Office documents released by the Soviet Foreign Ministry. I will just read from a couple to give a little bit of historical background.

On 19 November 1937, Lord Halifax visited Hitler. Lord Halifax began by saying he 'welcomed the opportunity to achieve a better understanding between England and Germany. It was the opinion in England that the existing misunderstandings could be completely removed. The great services the Führer had rendered in the rebuilding of Germany were fully and completely recognised and if British public opinion was sometimes taking a critical attitude towards certain German problems, the reason might be, in part, that people in England were not fully informed.'

He then went on to say that in spite of the difficulties, he, Lord Halifax, and other members of the British Government 'were fully aware the Führer had not only achieved a great deal inside Germany but that, by destroying communism in that country, he had barred its road to Western Europe and Germany could rightly be regarded as a bulwark of the West against Bolshevism.'

Now, a little later, in March 1938, the British ambassador also visited Hitler and Hitler said that the British press stood in the way of Germany and was conducting a campaign of calumny against her. He went on to say there were 'continuous attempts at interference from the English side by Bishops, by certain Members of Parliament and by others.' In this connection the British ambassador mentioned in confidence that Lord Halifax had appointed a Press Conference of responsible newspaper editors and had also had a talk with the President of the Newspaper Proprietors' Association and leading officials of the BBC – that is interesting – in the course of which he emphasised their responsibility for the maintenance of peace. Halifax, Foreign Secretary by 1938, had already exercised his influence very considerably on the basis of his talks in Germany by means of the British way of personal contact. Today the pressure on the BBC is identical; like the pressure in news management during the Falklands War; like the fact that Sir Ian Jacob, the Director-General of the BBC, was spoken to by Eden during the Suez War; like Norman Tebbit is doing now in the same typical British way of personal contact.

So what we are doing is trying to set a new agenda and start a new initiative, primarily in foreign policy: and it is important to remember that the main objectives of this campaign will be to confirm the giving up of nuclear weapons; the unilateral proposals to remove all American bases, not just nuclear bases; to work with the non-aligned countries, which are very active and strong in the world, though very little is reported about them in the British press; to disengage from the NATO Alliance and to re-allocate defence expenditure to meet the needs of development at home and abroad.

One of the arguments that will be put to us, of course, is that we are out of tune with public opinion. That is a criticism shared by all pioneers throughout British history. I doubt whether Karl Marx, when he was writing in the British Museum, could have got a single public opinion poll to confirm the existence of a class struggle, because they had never heard of it. I doubt, actually, at the time whether the Tolpuddle Martyrs would have got a very clear majority on the Mori poll on the desirability of an agricultural workers' union.

This is a very urgent matter because, although we may seem like fringe speakers at this meeting today, if there is a Labour Government, as I hope there is by the end of the year, the first thing that will happen is that the US will not let us remove their bases and we will be told we have got to make a choice between staying in NATO or following the manifesto commitment. At that point we will have to make a decision and it will then be seen that those of us who raised this question now will, in fact, have been – as always happens on the Left – a little bit ahead of the time.

There is, of course, a big Anglo-American crisis with the trade war and a lot of other things coming up, and I personally find that rather distressing and disturbing, because I do not want to see an anti-American Europe. An anti-American Europe and an anti-Russian Europe will be getting much too close to what Hitler was all about anyway.

We have got to have an internationalism of Labour with the Left in America, the Left in Europe, the Left in the Third World, and we have got to see that we take up seriously the changes that are manifestly occurring in the Soviet Union and in Eastern European countries. We have got to look beyond the legacy of Hitler, which left a Europe divided, to a Europe united by its people in the twentieth century.

Towards a Permanent
New Forum

It is sometimes hard for people in this country to realise what an immense number of scholars there are in the Soviet Union who study our internal politics, or to appreciate the honest self-criticism now taking place of their own earlier stance on many matters, or to take on board their constructive approach to the future.

A recent expedition to Moscow provided me with an opportunity to compare the atmosphere with that which prevailed on my first visit in 1960, just after the U2 incident had wrecked the Summit that year, and on a number of ministerial visits in the 1960s and 1970s.

The old Soviet political and economic system with its centralised control of the economy – and ideas – had never had any appeal to me as a model for development in this country, even though it was easy to understand that the trauma of war, revolution, counter-revolution and the ravages of Hitler's invasion made possible some of the things which had happened.

Since the election of Mikhail Gorbachev there has been a sea change in two areas: disarmament policy and internal reform, and hence in the perception of the Soviet Union abroad – especially in Britain.

There is no doubt that *perestroika* – the restructuring of their planning systems – is an urgent and inescapable priority, given the grave limitations of the *gosplan* method of planning everything from the top. The old methods had denied them the opportunity to develop the economy, using the skills and talents of their people to meet the legitimate demands of the population for a better quality of life under socialism. But it would be a mistake to suppose, as some Western commentators have done, that this will lead them towards capitalism, via the adoption of a cost-accounting system and a reliance on market forces.

Those with whom I spoke saw their problems as being more

political than strictly economic, and the extension of democracy in industry, with its emphasis upon decentralisation and industrial democracy, is seen to offer the best chance of achieving the growth they need.

It was interesting to hear them put forward these ideas with the sense of urgency that might have characterised the Chartists or the Suffragettes when campaigning for the political franchise.

Nothing could have less resembled the present assertion of 'management's right to manage', which now goes almost unchallenged in the British Establishment, than to their insistence that the directors of their enterprises must, in future, be elected by those whom they manage.

It was pointed out to me that, in this way, they intend to outflank the West in its own limited acceptance of the role of the ballot box in five-yearly elections for Parliament or Congress, and yet they could also see a possible role for their citizens in choosing between alternative candidates when picking their own political representatives.

It occurred to me, listening to all this, that since, in Britain, the effective choice in our parliamentary elections seems to be between alternative political parties each committed to the maintenace of capitalism in some form, maybe the Soviet leadership could also perceive a genuinely free election between alternative candidates, all committed to the development of socialism.

It is for these reasons, and to allow us to learn from each other, that we need to establish some permanent forum which, being free of the old rigidities of earlier socialist internationals, might allow progressives from East and West and the Third World to meet on a regular basis. I put this idea forward in Moscow, and received a generally positive response.

I also found some interest in the idea of renewing the Anglo-Soviet Treaty of 1942, which, when the war-time clauses are removed, would provide a new and firmer basis for our relations in the future.

Finally I urged that the UN, to which they attach great importance, might play a more active role in promoting disarmament by bringing some of the leaders of the non-aligned countries to Europe and the US to influence public opinion.

The time has come when we should be turning our minds to the possibilities of closer relations with the Soviet Union, especially in the field of disarmament, development and peace, and also begin thinking about the need for reform in Britain –

including a bit of *perestroika* and *glasnost*, just as urgent here as they are in the Soviet Union.

Paying for Apartheid

What is at stake in South Africa is not simply, or even mainly, a question of racial discrimination, but an economic question. Apartheid uses the excuse of race to force the black majority into doing the manual work necessary to sustain the privileges of the whites and the employers.

This is not a conflict confined to South Africa in which we are merely spectators, for the British economy is closely tied up with South Africa, with whom we do a great deal of trade and from whom we receive a number of important raw materials.

For example, the uranium which we use in our nuclear power stations comes from Namibia which South Africa occupies, and British power stations turn that uranium into plutonium which is then sent to America where it is used to make the warheads for the US Cruise missiles that are stationed here.

Apartheid also benefits those American and British companies which have invested so massively in South Africa because that system keeps wages low, and profits high, by suppressing black trade unions and civil rights.

And all the millions of pounds of British capital which is exported to South Africa goes there just because low wages under apartheid make it financially attractive to invest in that country, rather than here, in our own industries, which would create jobs in Britain.

Thus many of the unemployed in Britain are themselves paying a price for apartheid, too.

The arguments we hear about international competitiveness which are used to justify factory closures here are, in reality, another way of saying that wages and conditions in Britain must be reduced to South African levels – and the trade unions must be defeated – before it will be financially attractive for businessmen to start investing here.

It may have been the protection of those profits, by British companies, which led the Prime Minister to invite Botha to visit her at Chequers last year and which now leads her to oppose economic sanctions, and order the metropolitan police to arrest those anti-apartheid demonstrators outside the South African embassy in London.

The fact is that international capital is very happy to invest in apartheid so long as there is no threat of revolution that might endanger their profits. This, in its turn, explains why the US and Britain are so interested in the defence of South Africa against the possibility of a real change that might usher in a regime hostile to American or British commercial interests.

President Botha's recent speech holds out no hope that the African majority will ever be able to achieve their full rights peacefully, and they will draw their own conclusions as to what they will need to do to win those rights for themselves.

There must be a limit to the acceptance of brutality, and that limit has been reached as the South African Government systematically uses troops and police, and torture, to suppress all those who oppose it.

Thus South Africa seems headed for a full-scale civil war, and, if it does come, it could spread and will have repercussions all over the world.

President Botha tells us that he is defending Western civilisation and Christian values against a bunch of communists and terrorists who are trying to destroy them, which are very similar to the arguments that Hitler used before, and during, the last world war.

We shall each have to make up our minds whose side we are on, and consider how to bring pressure to bear on our own Government, and what actual support we can give to the Africans.

Certainly a complete boycott of all South African goods, including coal and uranium imports, and an ending of all sports and other contacts, would help, but unless that is backed up by the tightest possible Government ban on all trade and investment, preferably as part of a United Nations blockade, it will be little more than a gesture.

There should also be a complete break in diplomatic relations, the British ambassador should be recalled and our embassy there closed at once.

But we must be ready to go further than that, and if the Africans need weapons to pursue their struggle for democracy, as they will, Britain should be ready to supply them.

For once the conflagration starts, as it will, it will be for the

Africans themselves to win their own freedom, since no-one else can do it for them, but we can shorten the agony by giving all the practical and political help that we can.

This is not only a moral duty because the struggles of the South African workers – white as well as black – are indivisible from our interests here.

Justice and peace are indivisible and we cannot escape from the consequences of our own involvement in the repression that now exists there.

SOURCES

THE CASE FOR NON-ALIGNMENT
Extracts taken from a lecture to the Royal Institute of International Affairs, October 1983

WHO IS OUR ENEMY?
Extracts taken from the George Caborn Memorial Lecture, Sheffield, June 1985

A NEW AGENDA FOR THE INTERNATIONL LABOUR AND SOCIALIST MOVEMENTS
Extracts taken from a lecture given at the Polish Institute of International Affairs, Warsaw, July 1986

SOME FACTS ABOUT DEFENCE
Extracts from a speech to the Conference on Non-Alignment, January 1987

TOWARDS A PERMANENT NEW FORUM
First published in the *Guardian*, 7 December 1987

PAYING FOR APARTHEID
First published in the *Chesterfield Star*, 21 August 1985

5
WORK AND WEALTH IN A GREEN AND PLEASANT LAND

The Unemployment Tragedy

Mr Tony Benn (Chesterfield): I should like to talk about the problems we would face if we tried to restore full employment in Britain. It has not been touched on by any Government speaker because the restoration of full employment has never even been a Government objective. [An hon Member: 'Rubbish.'] It is not a Government objective and no minister has ever spoken about the restoration of full employment. The problem of unemployment is a wide one and goes well beyond an economic debate. There is the tragedy of young people in Liverpool who have not worked since they left school and have no prospect of work, and women who are doing part-time low-paid jobs and who will be affected for the worse by the change in Sunday trading.

Unemployment has an impact on the amount of money available for the public services and on the amount of money available for local government. There is also the effect of unemployment on the ethnic communities. But there is another aspect of unemployment and that is the cost. It is very simply costed, because the Government spend £7.5 billion a year on unemployment pay. The loss of taxation and national insurance as a result of 4 million unemployed is another £12.5 billion. That is £20 billion basic, but then there is a loss of production by the people who are unemployed.

If we take as a reasonable assumption that people in work could have at least 80 per cent of their production matched by those out of work, we are talking about another £52 billion of production if we had full employment. With so much suffering and so much cost, why have this Government abandoned the objective of full employment?

When I first came into the House thirty-five years ago this month, the idea of maintaining full employment was a consensus point. Harold Macmillan has now appeared in the House of Lords commenting again, but of course all Conservative leaders – Churchill, Eden, right through to the noble Lord – accepted that the maintenance of full employment was one of the central points of policy. It is fair to say that the policies pursued by the consensus Governments that followed one another did not succeed. That is why I do not listen with enthusiasm to Harold Macmillan while others do.

That was the objective and now that objective has been dropped. The fact that it has been dropped is not an accident. I have never accepted the idea of what is sometimes called Thatcherism. I do not believe that it is about monetarism, and I do not believe that political decisions are taken by going into a room with a cold towel round one's head and looking at a calculator to find out what the PSBR will be. After looking at the experience of the consensus years, the Government decided that they needed the dole to discipline the work force. That is what it is about.

What has happened is that the fear of unemployment has given management a power that it has not had since the 1920s or Victorian times.

Unemployment performs vital economic functions. It keeps wages down. If a worker goes to his employer and says, 'I cannot live on the money', the employer will say that there are 4 million people on the dole who will be happy to do the job. For the same reason, unemployment weakens the unions. It undermines the public services, which are costly. The Government do not want to finance them. Unemployment justifies rate capping and, of course, it boosts profits. If wages are kept down, marvellous profit figures can be produced, and it is the profit figures that make the Cabinet confident, because they do not intend to go back to full employment and do not believe in doing so.

To restore full employment, it would be necessary, with 4 million unemployed and a five-year Parliament, to create 1 million new jobs a year. That is what it would take to get back to what was the consensus of all parties in Parliament for forty years.

Twice in my lifetime we have created 1 million new jobs a year, all funded by public expenditure. The first time was from 1938 to 1942. It was public expenditure on rearmament at the end of the 1930s that gave us 1 million new jobs a year. That was when the PSBR was 27 per cent of the national output – ten times what it is today. If people are taken off the dole, put into armaments factories and taxed on their earnings, the project finances itself. It was done by very strong central direction and by public expenditure.

I do not need to stress to the House that rearmament was not done by private expenditure. Granny did not buy a Bren gun, mother did not have a tank, and father did not buy a Spitfire with an A registration. It was all done by the Government. People say that Government cannot create jobs. Of course they can, if they wish to do so.

The second example was from 1945 to 1948, when we brought 3 million servicemen out of the armed Forces and put them back to work. It was the biggest example of defence conversion that there has ever been. Compared with it, the problems of defence conversion that an incoming Labour Government would face would be simple. In Bristol, my old constituency, the Bristol Aeroplane Company, as it used to be, stopped sending out trucks with Blenheim bombers and a few months later it was producing prefabricated houses. That was done by having a central control over the economy. The powers were there and the objective was clear. The powers were used. If we want to restore full employment, it will not be done by tinkering about with the PSBR.

I did not hear the whole of the speech of the right hon Member for Glasgow, Hillhead (Mr Jenkins), but anyone who thinks that joining the European monetary system and going back to an incomes policy will get us back to full employment is absolutely wrong, because those actions are simply tinkering on the margin. If we want to get back to full employment – the objective that we should set ourselves in Britain for a range of social, political and economic reasons – we shall have to do more than that. We must re-equip and re-establish British manufacturing industry by direct methods. It is no good speaking about industry as if it is an optional extra, and that if it loses it can be closed down, as if manufacturing is like white side-walled tyres – one has them if one can afford it. We have got to have industry.

One of the reasons why the Japanese are so successful is that they look ahead for ten or twenty years. Any sensible planning of a modern society would include the planning of investment in high technology industries and in the maintenance of what are now called the smoke-stack industries, mainly to justify closing them.

Next, we would have to refurbish and develop the infrastructure. I am often amazed when I see industrialists whose whole market depends on public expenditure calling for cuts in public expenditure. Hon Members will know the old joke in the construction industry that sewage is their bread and butter. When sewers are renewed and when bridges are built, there are jobs for the construction industry, and we need a modern infrastructure, but that would involve public expenditure.

Next, we would have to expand the public services. If it is said that now that we have the microchip there is no demand, I could take any Member of this House, as other hon. Members could, to hundreds of houses where there are old people. In the modern jargon, they are now called the psycho-geriatrics. They are simply a bit old and confused. They need homes to live in; they need twenty-four-hours a day care. To meet their needs would create jobs. We need day centres. We need creches so that women can be released to work or to college. No one can persuade me that Britain is not full of things that need to be done. Just as rearmament brought us back to full employment, the expansion of the public services can bring us back to full employment.

If technology allows us to achieve the necessary national output without seven days a week of back-breaking work, let us have earlier retirement and a shorter working week. Let us raise the school-leaving age, and enable adults to go in and out of education. If we wish to do those things, we shall have to plan our trade, for if we reflate the economy when we don't have a manufacturing base we shall be flooded, not with imports of the raw materials of engineering products which will be needed, but with consumer products.

If people had to wait a little longer for a Honda but could get a hip operation a bit sooner, what would be wrong with that? That is the sort of priority we would have to set. Unemployment is a form of import control. An unemployed person cannot afford a Japanese video, French wine or American tobacco. The Government have import controls, but they apply only to the unemployed, the low-paid and the people living on supplementary benefits.

We would have to stop the export of capital. Since the Government came to power, for every family of four, £4,300 has left Britain. The Chancellor of the Exchequer says that we must tighten our belts because that is the way to solve the problem. But if a worker tightens his belt, the employer sends the money to South Africa, where the wages are lower still, because Botha's police will not allow the unions to organise. The export of capital could not continue if we wished to solve the unemployment problem.

We would also have to ease the arms burden. I have already mentioned Japan, but people do not often talk openly of the fact that the Japanese spend only 1 per cent of a much bigger national income on defence. We spend 6 per cent. Why are the shops in Britain full of Japanese videos, cameras and motor-cycles? It is because that is what the Japanese produce. Our Government's hopes are based on tourism and selling battlefield communications systems to the Americans. We have abandoned the serious intent of being a major manufacturing nation. That policy would have to change.

The Secretary of State for Defence comes to every household every week and takes £24 off a family of four to finance the defence burden.

We would have to deal with the Treaty of Rome. We could not solve any of the problems under a constitution which makes it illegal to intervene with market forces.

We would have to have a major expansion of public responsibility and control over our economy.

I do not believe that anything less than the measures I have outlined would bring us anywhere near the achievement of full employment. The Government do not want it. The wets could not get it, although they tried. The SDP–Liberal alliance thinks that if we squeeze the wages in Whitehall, join the European monetary system and have a federal Europe, full employment will come automatically.

The Mitterrand dash for growth came a cropper because he did not really deal with the power structure. His economy zoomed up and fell flat. Mitterrand's policy failed because, apart from anything else, he could not escape from the Treaty of Rome. The Treaty of Rome and the way in which it operated brought down the French economy.

To achieve full employment, we need fundamental changes in our policy and in our thinking. If this House is to be a forum for the nation, one of its functions is to tell the people outside that we cannot have full employment simply by tinkering with the economy. If we want full employment again, we have to set the objective and take the powers to bring it about. We must have the courage to implement it. That is what the choice will be when the General Election comes. It will not be much influenced by whether there are a few tax cuts, purchased by selling off public assets. The choice will be a basic one. I have a feeling that, after their experience with this Government, the British people will be ready to take it.

Trade Unionism in
the Eighties

It is an honour to be asked to deliver this Lecture in memory of George Woodcock. In his own Lecture, in 1968, he surveyed the achievements of the trade union movement at the end of two decades of full employment brought about by the war and the post-war boom.

His Lecture came just before the conflict over *In Place of Strife* had surfaced, when monetarism was seen as a weird Chicago cult and before the Conservative leadership had gathered at Selsdon Park to plan their counter-revolution, which ended with Mr Heath's removal from office after a battle with the miners.

In the last fifteen years, a great deal has happened to the trade union movement which calls for a fresh analysis of the strategies open to it. Trade unionism grew out of the need to protect working people from exploitation by their employers and from oppression imposed on them by unjust laws passed by parliaments from which the working class was excluded by the narrow franchise.

The Combination Acts made trade unionism illegal and its pioneers liable to prosecution, conviction and imprisonment. These particular legal restraints have of course been repealed. But, we should not fall into the trap of supposing that the threat posed by the law to trade unionism or trade unionists has disappeared. Quite the reverse.

The new employment legislation recently enacted, though skilfully drafted, was intended to make practices necessary to maintain effective trade unionism illegal – for example, in restricting some forms of picketing and sympathetic action.

I have deliberately interposed this contemporary reference into an historical account because it is important to realise that the struggles to legitimise trade unionism are now going to have to be fought all over again. We can no longer afford the luxury of liberal illusions that the bad old days are over and progress is inevitable, however slow.

The bad old days are not over. They are coming back again and progress, far from being inevitable, is now being put into reverse.

To resume the nineteenth-century story, we know that the right to organise industrially was soon seen by the leaders of the trade union movement to require a parallel development in parliamentary representation, which explains the support given to the Chartists.

This struggle for the vote, first fought for by men, and later by women through the Suffragettes, took a very long time before it reached its final success, with the extension of the franchise to every man and woman at 18 a mere thirteen years ago in the June 1970 General Election. But this sovereignty of the electors through Parliament and a complete adult suffrage to make and unmake the laws under which we are governed, and to impose or repeal the taxation which we pay, actually lasted less than three years from the date when it came into full effect. For on 1 January 1973 Britain became a Member of the Common Market under the control of a Commission operating under the Treaty of Rome, which makes and unmakes laws and imposes taxation without the authority of the Members of Parliament we elect.

In short, within months of winning the full franchise, some of the crucial powers that made that franchise worth having were subtly spirited away to others who are not subject to our ballot box democracy.

Now to return to the history. The trade unions, when armed with legal status, and having achieved a vote for their members, set up a Labour representation committee in 1900. This committee secured the election of Labour men as Members of Parliament and in 1906 the Labour Party itself was formed to consolidate that work. At that time MPs received no salaries and the early Labour MPs were sponsored financially by some unions, which made it possible for them to give up their normal employment and serve in the House of Commons.

Again we can see an interruption to the illusion of continual progress which is so widely propagated by the Establishment, because the next stage of Government legislation against the trade unions seems likely to be a counter-attack upon the financing arrangements under which the unions affiliated to the Labour Party collect and disburse a political levy raised from the membership.

There is, of course, a provision under which members may contract out if they wish to do so. Unlike business companies which are free to make unlimited donations to the Conservative Party, or other right-wing organisations without providing any facilities for contracting out to their shareholders or customers who are conscripted to pay for the political activities of the Right, the unions are now likely to be required to substitute a contracting-in provision which the Government hopes and believes will strangle the political work of the unions through the Labour Party.

Another achievement of the trade unions was to adopt a socialist perspective for their political work through the adoption of socialist aims in many of their own rule-books and the acceptance of socialist objectives as set out in Clause Four of the 1918 Labour Party Constitution.

But these aims which inspired successful campaigns for full employment and the welfare state, and which brought the unions into partnership with successive governments as a recognised estate of the realm, are also being reversed by the policies of mass unemployment, the erosion of the public services and the whole-scale policy of privatisation.

The Trade Unions Today – Fighting for Survival

I have set out this history of gains and losses in this form because it is a necessary background against which the future work of the trade union movement has to be seen.

In describing the setbacks I do not intend to suggest that no progress has been made, for that would be wholly wrong too.

The trade union movement is immeasurably stronger than it was fifty or a hundred years ago. It is well organised and well financed. It has many members in the white collar, technical, scientific and managerial grades, as well as the old skilled, semi-skilled and manual grades. It is still involved directly in many aspects of public policy making and policy implementation. It has valuable international links and important educational programmes.

But it is also true that the trade union movement today is fighting for its survival in the most hostile economic and political environment it has faced for many decades, and none of its past achievements are free from a direct counterattack which, were they all to succeed, could seriously harm, if not actually cripple the unions in their task of representing working people.

Before turning to the strategies which are now open to the unions to recover the position, it may be helpful to consider how it was that these setbacks came about.

In 1940 when the General Secretary of the Transport and General Workers Union, Ernest Bevin, became a member of Mr Churchill's wartime Cabinet as Minister of Labour, the trade union movement, as a whole, entered into a close partnership with that Government and became, in that sense, a part of the British Establishment, both feeding in the aspirations of its members at the highest levels in the State; and helping to see that those coalition policies were carried into effect.

Churchill, the old Liberal, found nothing strange in that relationship, nor did anyone seriously question its continuation into the post-war Labour Government headed by Mr Attlee.

The success of the coalition policies in the formulation of which Keynes and Beveridge had played a significant part, brought Britain through the years of reconstruction with full employment, the health service, comprehensive social services, and a large public sector which secured massive investment in our basic industries.

The defeat of that Government in 1951 and its replacement, first by Churchill and then by Eden and Macmillan, did not involve any major departure from the consensus policies of the wartime and post-war Governments.

Indeed, so successful were these consensus policies that in the 1959 General Election Harold Macmillan won a landslide victory under the slogan 'You have never had it so good', implying that welfare capitalism was working so well that a trade unionism aspiring to socialism was out of date and could be consigned to the museum.

As a Conservative slogan it was brilliantly successful, but that sort of thinking was not confined to the Conservatives. The Labour Party under Hugh Gaitskell accepted a great deal of that political analysis, and so did many of his contemporaries in the TUC leadership. Thus, a praetorian guard of right-wing union leaders rallied round a right-wing parliamentary Labour leadership to suppress socialist activities within the movement.

With a revisionist party leadership and an increasingly non-political trade union leadership, the stage was set for a retreat from socialism.

The union leaders were invited to join the NEDC and many

were appointed to the boards of the nationalised industries and other government bodies.

The television screens showed them going in and out of ministerial offices and No 10 Downing Street to be consulted about how the economy should be run. Labour, under Harold Wilson, was elected to power on the basis of a National Plan with which the trade union leaders were intimately involved. For a time it seemed that the Labour movement had at last come into its own inheritance and further advances were certain to be made in the future.

But the high hopes of 1964 did not last for long. Despite a huge parliamentary majority of almost a hundred, secured in March 1966, the honeymoon was short. A seamen's strike and an economic crisis followed, the National Plan was dropped and a statutory incomes policy was introduced.

'Stop' followed 'Go' and *In Place of Strife*, which was published early in 1969, led to a head-on collision between the Government and the TUC.

Industrial militancy on the shopfloor would have made TUC cooperation unworkable even if it had been forthcoming and the following year Wilson was defeated by Heath who sought to solve the problem by an Industrial Relations Act and a further statutory pay policy upon which he, in turn, foundered in February 1974.

Again Labour returned to power, this time with a 'social contract' which, within eighteen months, had evolved into another pay restraint policy, culminating in the so-called winter of discontent which brought Mrs Thatcher to power. Successive bouts of deflation, Common Market membership, the intervention of the IMF and the cuts in public expenditure upon which the world bankers insisted, led to rising unemployment worsened by the wider world slump.

Thus the explicitly socialist ingredients of the post-war consensus which had created welfare capitalism could not be afforded and were progressively whittled away.

In the last few years this process has accelerated under the policies of the present Government which has launched a three-pronged attack upon the unions, and which the Cabinet has correctly identified as the main obstacles that stand between their objective of restoring Victorian capitalism and its realisation.

The attack upon the unions is much more political than economic in its motivation. Whatever the attractions there may seem to be in describing it as monetarist, it is in practice a carefully orchestrated political campaign to weaken labour, strengthen capital and undermine the unions and the ballot box as instruments for achieving greater social justice.

Unemployment which is designed to weaken the bargaining power of workers has been deliberately created and there is clear evidence that it has had precisely the effect that was intended. Anti-union legislation has been drafted to render industrial action ineffective, and if enforced it would certainly succeed in doing so.

But perhaps the most powerful anti-union campaigns of all have come from the mass media, including Fleet Street, the BBC and ITN. The unions have been presented as undemocratic, subversive and greedy and their role as the protectors of working people over the whole range of their lives from health and safety to compensation have been completely ignored.

At this moment, in early 1983, there is evidence to suggest that the Government strategy is succeeding so far and the political implications of this situation are beginning to surface.

This passage from *Mein Kampf* reads like many leading articles in our daily newspapers, or might even appear in a Cabinet minister's weekend speech without sounding out of place:

> In the course of a few decades under the expert hand of social democracy, the Trade Union movement grew from being the means for protecting the social rights of man into an instrument for laying national economics in ruins. The interests of the workers were not going to count at all with the promoters of this object. For in politics the use of economic pressure always permits extortion when one side is sufficiently unscrupulous and the other has sufficient stupid sheepish patience.
>
> By the beginning of this century the Trade Union movement had long ceased to serve its earlier purpose. With each succeeding year it fell more and more under the influence of social democratic politics and ended by being used merely as the battering ram for the class war.

There are those – and I am one of them – who believe that if the attack on the unions were to be pressed home as completely as the Conservative Party would like, our political liberties would be gravely undermined.

It would not however be fair to attribute everything that has happened to the power of capital or its political and parliamentary and media representatives. The Labour movement itself must bear some of the responsibility for what has happened. The trades unions and the Labour Party are now paying the price for neglecting to defend their own role and for failing to maintain a sustained programme of political and socialist education. The challenge stemming from the growing internationalisation of capital, from the impact of new technology, and from the obvious failure to re-equip our old industries and move quicker into new ones, was often under-estimated or left too tamely to market forces to sort out. There was also a failure to reform state capitalism within the nationalised industries, some of which proved bureaucratic and insensitive to the demands for reform by their employees and their customers.

The Labour movement, as a whole, was slow off the mark in recognising the urgent demands by women for real equality of treatment, and not always sensitive to the problems of discrimination experienced by black workers.

Some within the trade union and parliamentary leadership looked with suspicion upon the re-emergence of socialism within their own ranks and with outright hostility to the clamour for greater democratic accountability.

The Need for a New Industrial and Political Strategy

The time has now come when the Labour movement, as a whole, must begin to develop a combined political and industrial strategy to protect what has been achieved, to reverse the trend to the right, and to begin to rebuild a more democratic and egalitarian society.

This means that we shall have to recreate an effective progressive alliance, bringing the industrial and political wings of the movement closer together. The basis of that alliance must be a campaign to reconstruct our industrial strength by recruiting actively for membership of the trade unions themselves, and by doing so around clear and legitimate demands that are simple and relevant to those that work; the best form of political education has always been the experience of struggle itself.

It is at the very moment when the wage claim goes in to the employer and is rejected that workers learn where power lies under capitalism and the pressing of that claim, whether it involves a withdrawal of labour or not, breeds unity, collective leadership and confidence which Labour must have if it is to survive.

When people band themselves together and demand jobs, or homes, or schools, or hospitals, or better pensions, or peace, then the movement grows in strength.

The people's march for jobs in 1981, and again this year, the campaigns against education cuts or for the National Health Service, the pensioners' charter or the Greenham Common women, have all shown us how to mobilise in pursuit of our aspirations.

But to be really effective, these struggles need to be linked together and to be mutually supportive. That is what solidarity is all about. It is no good seeing each campaign as separate and then picking which ones you will support and which ones you won't. We are all fighting our battles and if any are lost we each lose. That is what class consciousness is all about.

I believe that the erosion of the strength of working people and their organisations over the last generation can be largely attributed to the decline of class consciousness and the neglect of the role of struggle in the achievement of even most modest demands.

But Britain has the cleverest ruling class in the world and its survival, more or less unscathed, in a world full of successful revolutions, proves that. While the French and the Russian working-class leaderships stormed the barricades and brought their aristocrats down, some British working-class leaders leaped over the barricades and became aristocrats themselves.

The need for unity in the face of the growing monopoly of capital explains the trend towards trade union amalgamations which will help to move us nearer to the old syndicalist objective of industrial unionism. The next development which is already well advanced is the establishment of joint shopstewards' committees, bringing together representatives of all the unions working in a factory and through combine committees bringing together all the workplaces in a firm or industry.

The Lucas Aerospace initiative, developed at the top level of the unions, shows what energies and talent such a development can release. It is here, at the smallest unit of industrial organisation, that political activity needs to develop. Workplace branches of the Labour Party, which have long been discussed, need to be established as quickly as possible to provide a forum for political discussion that can feed the experience of those at work directly into the party and its policy making.

This concept of partnership between the unions and the party has been developing at national level since the TUC–Labour Party Liaison Committee was set up in 1972. It took two years of hard work after the 1970 defeat for this committee to be brought into being, but it has been meeting regularly now for eleven years. Our partnership in the future will be based not on the extension of government control over the economy but on the extension of control by workers through their trade unions.

This is the point of difference between Tory and Labour approaches to economic policy and planning.

The Tories are determined to govern without the unions. The price is mass unemployment and a deliberate strategy to undermine union power.

By contrast, the Labour approach is not to restrict the power of workers in relation to employers, but to promote the maximum possible development of this power to allow new forms of economic control. Labour will establish new statutory rights for workers and their representatives in joint union committees, and a strong National Planning Council with sectoral committees to channel and develop workers' own plans and priorities beyond the individual enterprise into the economy as a whole.

As workers extend collective bargaining over investment decisions at company level, they will play an increasing part in the allocation of resources between investment and consumption. This means that they will assume a new responsibility for planning incomes as an aspect of the production process.

Past incomes policies have restrained wages in favour of profits, which have not been directed into investment. Our new approach will enable workers themselves to control the use of resources for investment.

The partnership we propose between the Labour Government and trade unions will give rise to a 'new politics' in the Labour movement. It will no longer be a question of whether 'our team' can manage the economy better than 'their team'. Political activity will be linked for the first time to the everyday economic activity of working people. The success of our drive for full employment, industrial revival and social justice will be dependent upon the initiatives and creativity of workers themselves. We see a radical extension of collective bargaining as the indispensable basis of economic planning and socialism.

At the other end of the scale the unions would be involved in collective bargaining over all the main areas of policy making, through the legislative programme, the budget, cash limits and industrial strategy. This concept marks a sharp shift away from the idea of imposing pay norms which were rigid, unfair and unworkable.

Thus, as the Election [1983] approaches, the real nature of

that partnership will be seen to have a very different feel to it than it has had in the past.

It has to be recognised that a withdrawal of labour as the ultimate weapon in the armoury of the trade union movement can easily be misrepresented as being directed more against the public than against the employers with whom the unions are in dispute. For example, the ASLEF drivers and the Health Service workers were widely criticised for endangering the transport and health services of the nation, when in fact they were engaged in trying to defend those very services. And with the leaked Think Tank report which forecast the end of the NHS as we know it, and the Serpell Report which would destroy our rail system, it has dawned upon the public that it is the Government and not the unions which are threatening these services.

The strike weapon is essential as an instrument of last resort, but there may well be a case for developing new forms of industrial action which would make this clear.

For example, the provision of emergency cover as decided by the unions in the Health Service dispute marked a significant move towards workers' control and it would only be one small step beyond that for the Health Service employees to take over full responsibility for the administration of the service from the chief executives of the health authorities in a future dispute, maintaining all those services, but under *their* supervision.

If, in their campaign against privatisation, workers in British Telecom concentrated their stoppage on the City of London rather than on the general body of telephone customers, the effect would be far greater.

This is the technique used by capital to get *its* way in that wage cuts, redundancies and closures occur at individual plants and thus attack the employees in them, without alienating the community. And similarly, when the bankers demand cuts in public expenditure, they do so by insisting upon supervising the economic policy of the Government which is nothing less than 'Bankers Control'.

The Importance of International Labour Links

To be effective against the internationalisation of capital and to contribute to the development of policies for detente, disarmament and peace, the trade union movement will need to strengthen still further its international work.

The first priority is to bring together trade unions, representing members in all the plants owned by international
companies, to plan joint strategies that can be pressed in the
interests of all the employees worldwide. This would not only
protect workers from the loss of jobs through the export of
capital to low wage areas, but would help to build trade union
strength in the developing countries to which the multinationals
may move their work.

The second priority should be to heal the breach caused by
the breakaway of the ICFTU from the World Federation of Trade
Unions in the post-war years. It is gravely damaging to the
cause of Labour for the world trade union movement to be
divided on Cold War lines. If ministers from East and West can
meet at the UN, and if multinationals can sign technical and
trade agreements with the communist countries, unions should
be able to confer together on a regular basis.

The Unions and Political Action

Effective political action is going to be crucial if the unions are
to realise the historic aspirations of their founders. The Labour
party was created by the unions and they must have a significant part to play in the revitalisation of the party in terms of its
organisation and its socialism.

But this cannot, and should not, stem from the top but from
a greater diffusion of trade union influence at every level in the
party.

Locally the trade unions are already the largest and most
effective community groups and they can and should work with
other such groups and with the women's movement, the ethnic
and other community groups, including those campaigning for
peace and the environment – all of which should be able to rely
upon support from the unions and the party. And the deeper
the trade unions become involved in local Labour parties, the
easier it will be to tackle the thorny problem of the balance
between the union and constituency votes at Annual
Conference.

Despite the immense pressures under which trade unions are
working, and the apparent setback to socialism which we have
experienced in recent years, I want to conclude by reaffirming
my commitment to and faith in the future of both.

For as the public learn by bitter experience the price that has
to be paid, in unemployment, poverty and inequality, for the

policies that seek to exorcise socialism and cripple trade unionism, they will turn again to the working-class movement to lead us out of the crisis and towards a fairer society and a safer world.

Full Employment:
the Priority

Mass unemployment has undermined the living standards of millions of working people and their families, has eroded many essential services and has been used to justify a major assault on hard-won trade union and democratic rights.

For these reasons the restoration of full employment must necessarily be, and be seen to be, the first objective of a new Labour Government.

That task cannot be achieved unless we are ready to make substantial changes in the way we work, and in the way we think.

There are many people who now believe that unemployment is inevitable because of the recession in the western world or the advent of the microchip revolution, and hence they have come to live with it.

Others, while not actually accepting unemployment, simply do not see how it can be ended, and are deeply sceptical of anyone who claims to have the answer.

There are still others who would welcome a new deal for jobs but suspect that if an attempt were made to implement it the international bankers or industrialists would soon step in to prevent it from being put into effect.

Perhaps the biggest group is to be found amongst those who attribute almost all the blame to the members of the present cabinet personally, and believe that a different government, without any real change in the economic system, would do the trick.

We do not believe that unemployment is inevitable or insoluble; nor that policies to resolve it, if pursued resolutely, could be frustrated; but neither do we, for one moment, believe that it could be overcome by a bit of fine-tuning that left market forces in charge.

There are many decisions that would have to be taken by any

government that was serious about ending the dole queues, and what the benefits would be if we were to do so.

The measures required are radical but they can all be seen to emerge from the situation that would confront a Labour Government, and, for that very reason, they are both compelling and credible.

What stands out most clearly is the need for policies that counteract the economic and political power of capital, and are implemented with a determination.

The British economy, seriously weakened by years of decline, is now being rapidly de-industrialised and only the massive oil revenues, so criminally wasted, have obscured what has really happened.

We cannot correct these deep weaknesses by bringing a little pressure to bear here, and offering a few financial incentives there, within a basically unchanged market economy.

If we are serious about restoring full employment we shall have to be ready to make some significant changes in the structure of the economy and shift the balance of power towards working people and their families for whom useful work and good services are essential.

We must give hope to millions of people who are now in despair, and those in the Labour movement will recognise them as the authentic and legitimate inheritance of our democratic and socialist traditions.

The surest way to win the majority support which we must have if we are to end the present nightmare and re-establish our society on a basis that is fair to those who create the nation's wealth, is to give full employment the priority it needs if it is to be achieved.

Standing on the plinth below Nelson's column, in Trafalgar Square, last Sunday, and listening to the speeches of the Jarrow marchers at the great rally held to greet them, I realised that there is no one, and no organisation, in this country, which has been given the responsibility for seeing that every man and woman has a job, and that all the basic needs of the community are actually met.

Head postmasters are responsible for seeing that the mail is delivered, chief constables for the maintenance of law and order, the health service for the care of the sick, generals for the defence of the country, and local authorities for the education of the pupils in our schools.

But no one is responsible for seeing that everyone's basic

needs are met, and that those who want work are able to get it, since all that is left to chance.

The Chancellor of the Exchequer accepts overall responsibility for the state of the economy, imposes taxes, and supervises the task of deciding where the nation's money will go.

Public authorities have certain tasks imposed on them, and local authorities are allowed, within certain strict limits, to raise a rate to help pay for their services, but they are not required, for example, to see that every disabled person is able to live a full and useful life, or that everyone in their area has work offered to them.

For, in our list of social priorities, which we all unconsciously accept, the right to work and the right to be able to lead a full and useful life do not actually feature at all.

In the last few days I have had a visit from someone who works for the disabled, and is trying to alert the community to the many problems that disabled people have to face, and to win public support for better facilities for them; and it is an uphill task.

Others have been to see me about the new and brutal scheme for the cross-examination of those who are unemployed, about their 'availability for work', all designed to cut as many as possible off the register, to make the dole queues look shorter by the time the election comes, and to pay for more nuclear weapons and tax cuts for the rich.

But, instead of accepting all this, why should we not decide, as a community, to insist, as a matter of national policy, that most basic needs must be met and that all those who are unemployed must be offered work, at trade union rates, to meet those needs?

There is no reason why we should continue to allow urgent needs to be neglected and so many talents to run to waste, when those who want to be employed could be used to meet those needs, and everyone would be better off as a result.

If we were to decide, for example, to widen the scope of responsibilities for local authorities to include the provision of all the services necessary for a civilised life for all and to see that there was work for all it would mean developing and extending the functions that local government has developed over the years.

From the early years of Victorian England, many local councils have taken over responsibilities for housing, planning, sewers, hospitals, water supply, education, transport, libraries. To add a legal requirement to meet a comprehensive range of local needs, and to offer work to all those who were unemployed, would be a giant step forward, and it would certainly mean making the necessary funds available, partly by cutting down sharply on wasteful defence expenditure on, for example, nuclear weapons and the Falklands.

The whole public sector would have to broaden their objectives from the pursuit of profit to the provision of work, and we should have to extend common ownership in private industry and the banking world. The cost should not be prohibitive since every man and woman who is on the dole costs the nation no less than six thousand pounds a year in benefit and the loss of tax and national insurance, and the cost of leaving people without the services they need, already causes human hardship that cannot be measured in purely financial terms.

This sort of imaginative approach to popular planning will have to be seriously considered if we are ever to end the despair and hopelessness that has demoralised so many people and brought the Jarrow marchers back to London fifty years after their first historic march.

The Common Ownership of Land

Nine hundred years ago this month, William the First, who was spending the winter near Gloucester, resolved to have a survey made of land ownership in the Kingdom of England, which he had conquered twenty years earlier after defeating Harold at the battle of Hastings. Survey teams were despatched everywhere, and recorded the names of all those who had owned the land before 1066.

King William understood the value of owning the land as a source of power and wealth, and so the Domesday Book records the names of his Norman friends to whom that land had been given, together with the number of slaves, serfs and workers there were on each farm, as well as the number of implements and animals.

That is how the Domesday Book came to be compiled and it was a formidable achievement, the whole project being completed within a year.

Yet today, 900 years later, there is no proper land register, and we know that vast areas of the country are still owned by relatively few great landowners, including the Dukes, and increasingly by major corporations, who are living well as a result of the escalating price of land.

Meanwhile spiralling land values are raising rents and costs in the big cities and helping to cause, or worsen, the inner city poverty crisis; while, in the rural areas, the same increase in land prices is driving small farmers and smallholders off the land, causing depopulation and increasing the drift to the overcrowded towns.

Yet the money needed to develop both town and countryside is being withheld by rate-capping and the reduction of the rate support grant. Indeed the Government is now talking of replacing the rating system altogether with a flat rate poll tax of £160 a year which would increase the burden on the poor while the richest people would continue to live, literally, off the fat of the land they own.

These are some of the reasons why the demand for the common ownership of the land is now being reopened – a demand that goes back over many centuries, and was taken up by the Liberals who happily sang Lloyd George's famous land song which said it all: 'The land, the land, the land on which we stand; why should we be paupers with the ballot in our hand? God gave the land to the people.'

In Scotland the memory of the highland clearances, which expelled so many crofters from their homesteads, is still alive. The abuse of power by Scottish landowners is still resented.

There is another factor too, which has given a fresh sense of urgency to this whole movement for common ownership, and that is the emergence of the environment as a major political issue. The Green movement especially has campaigned to prevent the despoliation of our countryside in the interests of profits, as is bound to happen under private ownership. Moreover, the huge giveaway of public assets, in the name of privatisation, has reminded people that a similar policy was used to steal our common lands in the Middle Ages, by passing thousands of Enclosure Acts which handed our land to big land-owners, some of whom are still in possession.

It is for these reasons that, in a few weeks time, a number of Members of Parliament are going to introduce a Bill to bring the land of Britain back into common ownership – exempting every single piece of owner-occupied land worth less than a quarter of a million pounds.

It has been estimated that if we did own our own land again, the gross revenue payable to the community could amount to £70 billion a year.

Even allowing for some modest compensation, according to need, for those big landowners who had been required to give back our land, the new income might even replace the rating system altogether.

A few years ago, when oil and gas were first discovered off our coast, it was considered normal and natural to demand that the British people be allowed to own it, so that the revenues would come to us all. Some such action will have to be taken soon to find new sources of revenue to pay for community services, if we are not to end up with some poll tax plus further savage cuts in local community services.

We must now put the question of land ownership back at the top of the political agenda and the proposed new Common

Ownership of Land Bill will start us talking about it. And when better to begin than on the 900th anniversary of the Domesday Book of 1086.

The Case Against Nuclear Power

Mr Tony Benn (Bristol, South-East): I am sure that the House will give the Bill a Second Reading. It deals with the safety of nuclear materials, about which there is much public concern. I should like briefly to tell the House why, in the eight years for which I was ministerially responsible for civil nuclear power, I was converted, first from support of it to scepticism and anxiety and then to the feeling that it was undesirable for Britain to use it.

When I was Secretary of State for Energy, as some hon. Members may remember, I introduced legislation to allow the arming of Atomic Energy Authority constables to be sure that there was no theft of plutonium or of other nuclear materials from Atomic Energy Authority establishments. The House accepted that legislation because it felt that it contained necessary safeguards.

I believe that the time has come for a wider discussion about the risks associated with nuclear materials in both their civil and military context.

First there are now grounds for believing that in the mining of uranium the workers who are involved can be subjected to health hazards that were not hitherto publicly understood and discussed. We have a small amount of natural uranium in Britain but we have never mined it. We have bought our uranium from abroad. Were there the same health and safety standards in the mines from which Britain draws its uranium that we insist on at home, the cost of uranium would be very much increased. We have never included the true social costs of uranium mining protection in the costs of nuclear power.

My second point relates directly to the convention that has been drawn up by the International Atomic Energy Agency. On many occasions in the House, as Minister of Technology and as Secretary of State for Energy, I have referred to what are loosely called international safeguards in respect of nuclear operations. I must tell the House that there are no safeguards. In the handling of nuclear material there is no guarantee that there is no leakage from civil to military purposes. I say that with a particular case in mind that will be familiar to those who followed it.

Pakistan developed its own nuclear weapons programme – or was thought to be developing its own nuclear weapons programme. When it came to the attention of the then British Government and the Cabinet, of which I was a member, that Pakistan was engaged in developing the bomb, the only way we could bring any pressure to bear on Pakistan was politically, economically and through trade. We refused to supply Pakistan with certain materials. That was the way in which the so-called safeguards were to be maintained. But after the invasion of Afghanistan when the Americans wanted Pakistan to be drawn back as part of the American response to what was happening in Afghanistan, all those pressures on Pakistan were immediately lifted. There are no safeguards. There is a crude monitoring system but if the monitoring system throws up an anxiety about the misuse of civil nuclear technology to produce the bomb, one is back in the political arena and the matter can only be dealt with there.

In signing the convention the Community has registered some reservations about arbitration. Under EURATOM there is a requirement that all new nuclear materials that come to any country should be available for transfer to any other country in the Community. Since the French are not signatories to the non-proliferation treaty, materials that are brought under safe-guard once they get into the area of EURATOM can be transferred throughout the whole of the Community. That is another leakage in the international safeguard system.

My third anxiety relates to the need for higher safety standards in nuclear processes. Two factors relating to this are important. First, when nuclear technology was first developed, people knew very little about it and had to learn as they went along. I do not intend, in any way, to criticise those who learnt as they went along. As they faced new hazards, they tried to stiffen their safeguards. Indeed, many of the safeguards are what one might call gold-plated compared with safeguards in other industries. But that does not alter my point. We are dealing here with extremely dangerous material.

In December 1978 the Atomic Energy Authority at Windscale, in carrying out a normal examination of its site, discovered that there had been a major leakage of what it calls liquor – which is the highly toxic waste, the most dangerous stuff of all – out of a sump and into the ground. It was analysed three months later in March 1979, and was one of the last things brought to my attention as Secretary of State. When I investigated the matter and discussed it with Sir John Hill he told me that to recover that highly toxic waste that had sunk under the earth would involve building a new plant at Windscale, so dangerous was the material that had leaked into the ground.

Another important question is the movement of plutonium nitrates by sea from Dounreay to Windscale which is probably now taking place. In the United States the movement of plutonium nitrates is not allowed; nor is the movement of uranium and plutonium by air with the possibility that an aircraft containing this material may crash or be involved in an ordinary accident.

We know much less about the military control of these processes than we do about civil control. Anyone who has had anything to do with civil nuclear power will know that there is the most meticulous monitoring of milk and grass growing around the nuclear power stations. They are examined to see whether there is any adverse effect on the environment. Does that happen around military establishments? I do not know because they are handled under a totally different regime. It is all very well to say that we protect military materials with greater care than any other materials – I do not doubt that – but are the people around the establishment where nuclear materials for military purposes are processed, or developed, treated with the same care?

Another hazard is the final disposal of nuclear waste. For a long time the Atomic Energy Authority at Harwell argued that the so-called 'Harvist system', or glassification system, would provide a final solution for the disposal of highly toxic waste – the so-called liquor which is the nice word they use about it. It is now apparent that this system is not proving satisfactory, that the borings that were to have been made with a view to finding long-term solutions to the problem by putting the waste in glass blocks underground have not proved satisfactory. It appears now that these wastes may continue to be stored in the zinc-lined tanks on the surface, from one of which came the leak from Windscale in 1978.

I move on now, to complete the picture – because I will not argue a wider case by referring to the nuclear weapons side – to the risk of nuclear accident. The risk in a military use is very apparent. Another issue is the effects of tests of nuclear weapons. I know that there is a test ban treaty but it does not cover underground tests. This brings me to my next point, which is arousing considerable public interest. Are we satisfied that the compensation, for those who for one reason or another – I do not allocate any blame – have been subjected to a health hazard through an involvement in nuclear work, is adequate?

It has recently been reported that the Government are to carry out a rough and ready health check on those who were present at the Pacific tests after the war. We know that soldiers who were exposed in America to the first Nevada tests have revealed a high incidence of cancer. If we really take seriously the long-term hazards to health arising from what at the time seemed a quite safe use of nuclear power or, indeed, the testing of nuclear weapons, we may find that a large compensation bill faces us. As in all compensation cases, the authorities are anxious not to move for fear of creating a precedent.

The next point hinges on all that I have said so far. One consequence of nuclear power is the great secrecy surrounding all nuclear matters. I fully understand that. If one is to have the bomb, one does not tell people where it is or how to make it. Indeed, the post-war Labour Government did not even tell Parliament that they were making the bomb. But behind that framework of legitimate secrecy, very powerful international lobbies are operating. The House would be foolish if it believed that secrecy concealed only matters involving the national interest. It also covers things that it would be greatly in the national interest for the public to know.

No one could argue that nuclear material should be pushed around like an ordinary industrial material. But, as with the legislation that I introduced on the arming of the Atomic Energy Authority constabulary, I must tell the House that all the safeguards take their toll in civil liberties. It would be extremely foolish to suppose that we could preserve such a curtain of secrecy and security around such a growing operation without impinging on the rights of the public in various respects. Potentially, indeed, nuclear power is a threat to the rights of Parliament.

Sir Russell Fairgrieve (Aberdeenshire, West): Is the right hon Gentleman arguing that this country's industry should be denied cheap energy when our European competitors obtain far cheaper energy for their industry by using nuclear power?

Mr Benn: I had intended to come to that at the end of my

speech, but it is so important that I shall deal with it now. If the full costings to which I have referred – health protection for uranium mining, full protection for nuclear processes, compensation for those who become ill and all the necessary safeguards throughout the processes – were added to the bill, I do not believe that nuclear power would be cheaper. If the proper safeguards existed – they would be very costly – and if the costs were properly allocated, this would add enormously to the cost of nuclear power. If proper compensation were paid for those who may have suffered as a result, I do not believe that the House would approve the building of any more nuclear power stations. That is the conclusion that I have reached. I also believe that we should adopt a non-nuclear defence strategy.

Nuclear
Accidents

Mr Tony Benn (Chesterfield): I should like to express sympathy for the terrible tragedy that the Soviet people have suffered in terms not only of the immediate loss of life but of the loss of life that may come later and of the contamination of their crops. I am aware that it is not the responsibility of the Secretary of State for Energy, but if it were possible to make a gift of food, which is at present held by the Common Market, that would assist the Soviet Union at this time, I believe that would be much appreciated and would contribute to better relations between East and West, which may result in lessening the risks of nuclear war.

I have risen to put on record the reasons why I take the view, to which I have come slowly over the years, that we should have an energy policy that does not incorporate a nuclear component. I say that, having been responsible for the Atomic Energy Authority as Minister of Technology from 1966 to 1970 and again as Secretary of State for Energy from 1975 to 1979.

Nuclear power began as a military operation. In the countries which have adopted it, it remains primarily necessary for military purposes. In India, Pakistan, Iran and in Britain, it was wanted for military purposes. The first British reactor was built when Mr Attlee decided that Britain needed the bomb. That desire was not confided to his Cabinet or to Parliament. That was the origin of the development of British nuclear power.

It is an expensive technology, concealed by the fact that the research and development has been paid for by the Ministry of Defence. Recently the French stated that it would cost 40 per cent of the cost of construction of a new power station to decommission a nuclear power station. It would cost about £600 million to decommission each nuclear power station.

We have no answer to the waste problem. I accept that whether we proceed or – as I believe we should – stop and phase out nuclear energy, there will be a residual waste problem. Is nuclear energy safe? It was only by an act of God or of chance that the accident occurred in Chernobyl, not here.

In 1969, I was Minister of Technology when the corrosion occurred at the Magnox stations. I was told in great detail how a meltdown might occur if it was impossible to close the reactor down and if the heat exchanger ruptured. At Windscale there was a serious fire, and serious leaks also occurred.

There was a near-disaster at Three Mile Island. But people may not be aware of what happened at Brown's Ferry in America. A fuse blew at that site. A scientist was sent to look for the fuse box with a candle, and he set fire to the safety circuit.

There was serious corrosion at Winfrith. It was discovered that a dissatisfied employee had urinated into the equipment, and Scotland Yard had to be called in to discover how the corrosion had occurred.

At Hunterston a valve was turned the wrong way and sea water was brought into the station. As a result, the power station was out of action for a year.

One cannot exclude human error. There have been many cover-ups. When there was a big explosion in Khysthym in the USSR, American intelligence picked it up and told the International Atomic Energy Agency in 1958, but American intelligence also told it not to tell British ministers. When 200 tonnes of uranium was stolen from EURATOM in 1968 I was Minister, but I was not told on the ground that Britain was not a member of the Common Market.

The biggest cover-up of all, for which I shall never forgive those responsible, was that throughout the period when I was Minister, plutonium from our atoms-for-peace reactors was going to America to make bombs and warheads that would return to American bases here. That view has been confirmed by ministers in this Government. I was cross-examined about it at the Sizewell inquiry, and only recently has it been admitted that the atoms-for-peace power stations are in reality bomb factories for the United States.

The environmental hazards of nuclear power both now and later are too great for us to take. The cumulative effect of radioactivity is very different from the reassuring statements that we receive about little doses that may come from time to time. The military implications of what happened at Chernobyl are phenomenal. People must now know that if we bomb Russia, the bombs that we drop will release radioactivity that will ultimately destroy us, and if conventional weapons are dropped on our nuclear power stations radioactivity comparable to that from a nuclear attack will be released.

The civil liberties of which we are so proud are bound to go by the board when dealing with such a dangerous technology that has military implications. I have been to the plutonium store in Dounreay. It is like a bank vault. One can understand why the Atomic Energy Authority constabulary is armed with orders to shoot to kill in the event of an attempt to steal plutonium. We must phase out nuclear power. We must cancel the PWR, abandon the Dounreay project, close Sellafield and decommission nuclear stations, beginning with the older stations. Anyone who thinks that the industry's skills will not be required should bear in mind that it will take the skill of every nuclear engineer for ten years to clean up what has, alas, been created.

The miners were right to say that coal should be the basis of our future energy needs. In the 1960s the pits were closed on the ground that oil would always be cheaper. In the 1980s they were closed on the ground that nuclear energy was better. We should go for a coal programme. My Department admitted that, even with the fiddled figures for nuclear energy, coal was as cheap as nuclear power. We should also go for conservation and for alternative sources of energy.

I fear that Chernobyl will not be the last accident. I listened to the debate and wondered how different it would have been if that accident had occurred in Bradwell, Hunterston, Oldbury or Torness. I share the view expressed today. This is a technology that humanity cannot handle, and, not for the first time, the public are ahead of Parliament in perceiving that.

The Nuclear Lobby

Mr Tony Benn (Chesterfield): I spent four years as Minister of Technology and Minister of Power and four years as Secretary of State for Energy. I entered into that task, just after the Dungeness B power station was ordered by my predecessor, Frank Cousins, with all the energy and enthusiasm at my command, believing, like many of my generation, that civil nuclear power was a classic example of 'swords into ploughshares' and that, after Hiroshima and Nagasaki, to be able to use that hideous power for constructive purposes was advantageous. I must confess that my experience over that period persuaded me, in my opinion all too slowly, that none of the arguments were true, and before I left office I wrote to the then chairman of the Atomic Energy Authority, Sir John Hill, just after the Three Mile Island accident, telling him to stop work on the pressurised water reactor. I also raised with him the latest and most serious leak at Windscale.

We are facing in the nuclear business the most powerful lobby in Britain. I have been in Parliament for many years, including eleven as Minister, and I have never come across a lobby with such power as the nuclear lobby. That lobby has known for years what it wanted. I have mentioned Frank Cousins' decision to go for Dungeness B, which was an advanced gas-cooled reactor [AGR]. At that time, the Ministry of Technology wanted the boiling water reactor, which was in the pressurised water reactor family [PWR].

In 1974, the brief given to incoming Labour ministers was that they should get the PWR. The lobby waited and waited until it could get a Government who would agree to that plan. Lord Marshall, my adviser, told me that he had seen the Shah of Iran, who had offered to buy half the British nuclear industry if we would adopt the pressurised water reactor. In other words, if we ordered it, the Shah would also, and so on. With

Westinghouse, the Ministry of Defence – because of its military interests – and the lobby here, the Government and Parliament are facing a lobby in which American interests are very strong. The Star Wars contracts allow the Americans to vet our technology if it is exported.

What will be the limitations on any possible export of technology deriving from a British purchase of the American reactor now?

I advise the House to reject the pressurised water reactor. I believe that, as the nation is self-sufficient in oil and gas, and will be for a long time, and as our coal will last for 300 years – although the Romans thought that it would run out in about 200 AD – with conservation not fully developed as a possibility, and with the alternative sources of energy including the Severn barrage, in which I have had a long interest, we should recognise that nuclear power has realised none of the claims that were made for it. The public, not for the first time, are well ahead of the Government in recognising that fact for themselves. I hope to God that the next nuclear accident – and there will be one – does not happen in Britain. If it does, a heavy responsibility will rest upon all those who advocated it, as I did, and even more upon those who decide to prolong it, if the PWR at Sizewell B goes forward to construction and completion.

Evidence Against
Sizewell B

The CEGB has always pressed for American style reactors in the long run, i.e. beyond the immediate ordering needs, and has been opposed to the building of more British reactors. I think this question as to why that should be the case merits examination.

It was the same story with the High Temperature Reactor, the Dragon Reactor, which was under development in the UK at Winfrith, which the CEGB declined to support, even though High Temperature Reactors have the advantage of offering the combined heat and power facility, which potentially has great long term value in terms of higher thermal efficiency. Similarly, it was the CEGB that forced the cancellation of the Steam Generating Heavy Water Reactor, which had been ordered in 1974, also under development at Winfrith, and which had offered the possibility of being constructed on a modular basis, i.e. without having to up the scale, and which had some similarity to the Canadian CANDU reactor, which had proved itself.

I believe the Inquiry should go into these matters with great care and, if it does, it may well conclude that the motivation of the CEGB is best explained by a desire to drop all British systems in favour of an American system, rather than by the establishment of any real need in terms of domestic energy demand in the United Kingdom.

A study of past energy forecasts will also reveal that the input from the Treasury in terms of expected economic growth has also proved to be consistently wrong, in that the British economy and the energy demand that would flow from that assumed growth has never justified the forecasts, either in terms of the growth itself or in terms of the energy demands within that growth. This has left the industry with an excess capacity that has actually increased electricity prices to consumers, who have been called on to pay not only for the electricity that they use but for the unused capacity in the system and, because of that extra cost, this has contributed to reduce the demand still further and push up the levels of excess capacity again. I think this is an important point to stress because the early claims that nuclear electricity would be cheaper have not been justified in the event.

Indeed, if the Inquiry asks to see the figures over the years it will be shown that the excess capacity, over and above the planning margin, and the very size of the planning margin, exceeds all the electricity produced by nuclear power, and thus makes it questionable, at any rate, whether the nuclear power stations that have been ordered and built over the years have, in terms of contemporary energy demand, ever been necessary at all.

If the matter is examined still more closely it will be seen that the very high planning margins adopted by the CEGB have in part been dictated by the fact that delays, breakdowns, plant failures and outages – and I cite Dungeness B, Hunterston, corrosion in Magnox and the derating that followed from it – for nuclear power have been greater than for coal-powered stations, although there have been some failures of big generating sets, and thus the decision to use nuclear power had, of itself, driven the CEGB to push up the planning margins.

I would put it to the Inquiry that one of the dominant factors which explains the policy of the CEGB and the Atomic Energy Authority, which is itself a Defence Agency, in pressing for an American PWR is that there are strong military reasons, with which Government is concerned, for doing so, and that to some extent the economic and energy arguments are a cover. I come back to that point later.

The British Navy uses PWRs in its nuclear submarines, and this has led to a close link with American reactor systems that they hoped would lead to the ordering of PWRs for electricity generation, especially as there has been a virtual standstill of PWR ordering in the United States itself. It is interesting that this is an American system that has not been ordered, as far as I know, in the United States since 1977 or 1978. In addition it has only recently become publicly known that for a number of years some of the plutonium which is produced in British power stations has been made available to the United States for weapons purposes, and since the USA has a weapons programme that requires more plutonium than can be produced in the much curtailed US civil power stations they need to get it from Britain, which could continue to supply the plutonium if this country expanded its civil nuclear power programme. I must say, in expanding that point, that I personally feel betrayed in that I was never told of this arrangement for the trading of the plutonium from our power stations into the American weapons programme.

To put it more plainly, every British nuclear power station has, or could, become a nuclear factory for the United States, which puts a very different light upon the much publicised argument that civil nuclear power is all about 'Atoms for Peace' and the finest example of beating 'Swords into Ploughshares', which are arguments that in good faith I used and can be found in speeches of my own as Secretary of State in the House of Commons.

In this context it should be pointed out – this is an economic point – that nowhere in the world has nuclear power ever been developed in response to market forces, as compared to government evidence that the coal industry must find its own level in terms of the market. This test has never been applied to nuclear power, nor has any nuclear power been completely paid for by private capital: indeed, it has depended for its origins and its development upon massive State funding, usually motivated by the defence interests of the nation which adopted it, which is true of the United States, of the Soviet Union, of the United Kingdom, of France, of China, of Pakistan. These raise wider questions, but the point I want to make is that it is the one exception, even to the philosophy of this Government, which believes in profitability above everything, that nuclear power should be protected from those stern tests.

The next series of questions which the Inquiry should examine relates to the true costs of the alternatives open to us.

I submit that the true costs of nuclear power have never been made explicit, partly because so many of them have been carried in the Defence Budget, which has never been candidly disclosed in respect of nuclear expenditure, and partly because there has never been a proper allocation of these costs to the civil programme. It has always been open to change the economics of civil nuclear power simply by allocating less of the costs for R & D, which are then carried on the Defence Budget.

The Research and Development of nuclear power was, and remains, immense, and yet the royalties which fell to be paid by the CEGB never took full account of them, for if they had, the cost of generating electricity by nuclear power would, or perhaps I should say could, have been shown to have been far greater than by conventional methods. Indeed, the strict comparison would be the historic costs of the mining industry, which are carried by the industry in terms of capital costs, and the R & D costs of nuclear power which have been wished away in the Defence Budget.

In addition, the costs associated with the hazards of nuclear power have never been properly allocated, partly because some of these health hazards have been experienced by those who work in the uranium mines which are privately owned, as with RTZ, in Namibia, where the rigid standards which we maintain under the Health and Safety at Work legislation do not apply. I think it worth noting here that the decision to shift from acquiring uranium from Canada, where we thought it would come from in the late 1960s, to Namibia not only gave the Authority the right to get unsafeguarded uranium, but also, of course, uranium from mines where the wages were much lower.

It should also be stated that the RTZ contracts are in breach of the UN resolutions on Namibia and thus future supplies under those contracts may not be secure.

Nor is allowance made – a new point – for the payment of compensation to those who live near nuclear processing plants, as at Windscale or Sellafield, were it to be discovered that there is a real hazard.

What matters now is that the public investment should be shifted towards coal and conservation and alternative energy sources to cut the delays that would occur if these investments were held back so that nuclear power could go ahead.

In this context I would draw your attention, Inspector, to three points. One is the enormous subsidies to coal in the Common Market compared to the very meagre or non-existent ones in Britain; secondly, the existence of the enormous reserves of coal in the North Sea which, with technologies not difficult to contemplate and develop, you would be able to scour and pipe the coal ashore as slurry. Therefore, it is probably true to say we have one thousand years of coal and not three hundred years, and this coal for oil-conversion, for gas, for feedstock is of great value. A Government report said that after a nuclear war Britain would depend on coal and therefore special shelters should be built for mining engineers so that they would survive a nuclear war, which indicates that even the Government, wearing one hat, thinks coal has a future.

In conclusion, I submit to the Inquiry that the case for the PWR cannot be sustained on energy or economy grounds, and that the PWR is the wrong system for Britain, even if a limited nuclear power programme is to be sustained.

I also recommend that the right course for the Inquiry to recommend would be to step up the investment in coal, conservation and alternative sources of energy, and to urge that the necessary investments be put into them. Thank you very much indeed.

SOURCES

THE UNEMPLOYMENT TRAGEDY
Extracts taken from the House of Commons Official Report (*Hansard*) of proceedings on 12 November 1985

TRADE UNIONISM IN THE EIGHTIES
George Woodcock Memorial Lecture, March 1983

FULL EMPLOYMENT: THE PRIORITY
Extracts taken from the Foreword to *A Million Jobs a Year* by Andrew Glyn, September 1985, and the *Chesterfield Star*, 5 November 1986

THE COMMON OWNERSHIP OF LAND
First published in *Chesterfield Star*, 8 January 1986

THE NUCLEAR ENERGY DEBATE
Extracts taken from the House of Commons Official Report (*Hansard*) of proceedings on 8 February and 13 May 1983, and 23 February 1987

EVIDENCE AGAINST SIZEWELL B
Extracts from Tony Benn's evidence for the NUM to the Layfield Commission of Inquiry, 1984

6
THE ARROGANCE OF POWER

The Case of
Sir Anthony Blunt

Mr Tony Benn (Bristol, South-East): This debate is essential because it provides the House with one of its rare opportunities to discuss our political liberties and how they should be maintained and protected from enemies at home and abroad, and whether Parliament has any role whatever in upholding those rights and liberties.

The first question that the House must ask is: Is anybody requesting details of the operational work of the security services? To my knowledge, nobody is asking for those details. What we are concerned about is the policy upon which those services operate. Certainly the defection of Anthony Blunt revealed a weakness in those defences. The secrecy which the right hon Member for Sidcup (Mr Heath) properly said is necessary to cover the operations of the security services also covered a serious failure by them in allowing Blunt to remain for so long.

The second aspect of our civil liberties depends upon much more than national defence. It depends upon our being satisfied that we are governed by ministers who are elected by the people and accountable, through Parliament, for all the major policy decisions that they take, including those on defence and security matters. What the Prime Minister and my right hon Friend the Member for Leeds, South (Mr Rees) and the right hon Member for Sidcup are all agreed about is that there can be no true accountability in this sensitive area of security. We are talking not about operations – nobody in the House is interested in that – but about the policy on which the security services rest. We are entitled to be sure that the defence and security services, and the civil servants who work in them, report directly, immediately, fully and truthfully to the ministers responsible.

What has been really interesting to me, observing this debate, is that minister after minister has either said 'I was not told' or 'I was told.' Nobody has said 'I demanded to know what was going on in the security services.' Ministers are not passive people to be told or not told. If a minister is in charge of the security services, his first duty is to satisfy himself that they are efficient. Where, in any of the speeches that we have heard, has there been an explanation that the duty of an elected minister is not to wait for the Director-General to come and see him, but to call the Director-General and say 'What is the position?'

That is the sort of problem that arises because a minister is not accountable to Parliament. After all, if one can ask a parliamentary question about health, housing or education, an angry minister, hounded in the House, goes back and raises hell with his permanent secretary. A minister involved with security, who cannot be hounded in the House, gets into a cosy relationship with the security services. I am not making a personal attack on anyone. I am making a constitutional point. The reason that democratic self-government works in Britain is that Parliament presses ministers, and ministers in turn must press officials. Take the pressure of Parliament off a minister, and before he knows what is happening he becomes part of the Establishment that he was elected to control.

The right of Parliament and of the people to know the policy under which the military and security services operate – not the operational details – is basic. If we did not know the budget of the defence services, or the policy under which they operate, that would be held as a denial of the long-established rights of Parliament.

Mr Wellbeloved: Can my right hon Friend explain whether he considers the decision taken about Mr Blunt to be an operational or policy decision? Can he define exactly what he means by 'operational and policy matters'?

Mr Benn: I am drawing the same distinction as that which is drawn when we discuss defence matters. Defence is much more publicly discussed than security. We have a White Paper every year on defence policy. Even the Birkett figures on the number of telephone interceptions recorded in 1957 has never been updated. We do not know today how many telephone calls are intercepted or how many letters are opened. Is that a matter of operational secrecy, or a matter of policy that the House should know? How many people are on police dossiers? How many people are on Special Branch files? We do not know. The degree of supervision of the security services cannot be a matter of operational secrecy.

The third point is the right of the citizen, alone or with others, and of the media, to probe the conduct of the Government, to report on it and to criticise. It is a coincidence that the Protection of Information Bill, which would have clamped down on studies such as the one Andrew Boyle published, should have come at the time of Blunt. Those people who exercise the very responsibility of running the security services are also those who are most keen on tightening up on security. By that I mean they are most keen on the 'Protection of Information Bill' which has the advantage of covering their own conduct, as well as covering the legitimate secrecy of the security services.

The other issue is the legal aspect of our liberties. Democracy depends not only upon national security and self-government but upon the maintenance of certain legal rights, including the right to know that the law will be applied impartially. When hon Members say that if their constituents had been guilty of these offences they would not have been treated in the same way, they are making not a class point but a legal one. There must be one law for everybody, and not a different law for those who have friends in high places. That is a matter of legal rights, upon which our liberties depend. Also, the courts must be kept free from political or administrative pressure. There is nothing that can so influence the courts as to deny their right to prosecute or judge a man because he has been covered by a pre-empted immunity.

The right hon Member for Sidcup went back to the McCarthy period. Perhaps we have to be of a different age group to recall it. That was a terrifying period when people were guilty as of opinion and not for what they had done or not done. Another freedom is the right to express opinions freely and without harassment by the authorities and the right of conscience to be respected.

The fact that Blunt has tried to justify his treason and his spying by reference to conscience must not lead us to say what the *Daily Express* said today about 'damn your conscience'. Ultimately conscience is the basic safeguard of our liberties. It is hard to say this in a debate today when a man who is a spy and traitor has pleaded conscience as justification, but it must be said. The laws are man-made and men must have, and have had historically, the right to refer to matters of right and wrong. It was as serious a matter to be an atheist 100 years ago as it is to be a Marxist today. There are the rights of the conscientious objectors who, in the war, were allowed to pursue their faith. We hanged the Germans after the Nuremburg trials because we said that conscience must come above an order from the duly authorised officer.

If there is to be a public outcry against dissidents, against men and women who claim conscience, against homosexuals and Marxists, we shall endanger the very liberties that this House is today trying to maintain. If a nation were to be hounded by public hue and cry or, worse still, to contribute to it, it would find that it had lost what it had sought to uphold.

The central question for the House of Commons today is how to secure the democratic control of our security services. Why is that? First, to be sure of their efficiency. The Blunt case suggests that they are not. Secondly, to be sure that they are accountable to ministers. The Blunt case throws serious doubt on that. Consider the contorted convoluted descriptions about who should talk to whom. Should an official speak to the Attorney-General, should the Attorney-General have told the Home Secretary? Our former Attorney-General said that he had discovered that his predecessor had not been told ten years ago. He went to the Cabinet Office to ask if he could tell that man who was then Lord Chancellor.

The right hon Member for Sidcup dismissed what Mr George Young said on the radio on Sunday. I heard it, and I obtained the transcript five minutes ago. He said: 'There's a curious convention in Whitehall: you can inform the Prime Minister without telling him'. Mr Young was asked about Lord Home and he said: 'This may have happened or it may be that Sir Alec was rather dim, I can't remember.' That is a statement from the deputy head of MI6.

He was asked about my right hon Friend the Member for Huyton (Sir H. Wilson). The deputy head of MI6 said: 'I would be rather hesitant to have informed Harold Wilson.'

Then came the key passage:

> The higher reaches of the Civil Service undoubtedly make most of the decisions for ministers. They put them in front of them and say, Ministers, do you agree? The ethos of the higher reaches of the Civil Service is not one of stirring up hornets' nests, particularly if some of your best friends are hornets, but in my experience of dealing with ministers – and I've met a fair amount off and on over some twelve years – they don't hear what you say; you tell them something, it goes in one ear and it's out of the other and they are busy thinking up the next parliamentary answer to the next parliamentary question.

I am not confirming Young. I have never met him, but it is one thing to hear the former Prime Minister saying that he was in charge and another thing to hear the voice of the man who was under the control of the former Prime Minister giving his view about what happened. The reality is that the House is entitled to know.

We need a Freedom of Information Act which will exclude operational secrecy. We want to know the budget and the staffing. We are entitled to know the names of those who are in charge of MI5 and MI6. We need to know the policy, the number of dossiers and the names of countries with which we have intelligence links. Did we have intelligence links with Savak when we had a relationship with the Shah? Did we have relations with BOSS in South Africa? I do not know. All I know is that intelligence links are part of foreign policy, and the House of Commons is entitled to know with which foreign intelligence agencies our intelligence officers exchange information.

We are entitled to a Select Committee which would look at these policy matters. What is important here is the issue of accountability. We cannot entrust our liberties to a State within a State, with its own policies, its own prejudices, its own friends, and its own enemies; with unlimited powers of surveillance, of scrutiny, of blacklisting or of granting immunity. The freedoms that we are trying to defend are too important to be trusted to the security chiefs or the secretaries to the Cabinet, however high principled they may be.

Sir Norman Brook, Sir Burke Trend, Sir Robert Armstrong and Sir Maurice Oldfield are all distinguished public servants, but they were not elected to run the system that safeguards our liberties. They cannot be removed for what they do, because everything that they do is behind the tightest secrecy that covers their failures, their successes, their friendships and their prejudices.

This debate requires us to reassess the freedoms that we are seeking to uphold. It also requires us to reassess, as a House, the control that we believe we should exercise, on behalf of the people, of the means that we use to protect them.

The *Belgrano*–Ponting Debate

Mr Tony Benn (Chesterfield): I doubt whether this is a good occasion on which to refight the naval strategy of the Falklands War, first because the ministers now responsible were not there at the time.

I doubt whether it is a good idea, either, to try to reopen the Ponting case, because the jury has acquitted him. I doubt whether we are doing justice to the importance of the issues that face us if we think that the responsibility can be placed simply on the shoulders of what are quite minor figures in the story.

I shall, therefore, draw attention to what I believe to be the real importance of the debate, for which it will be studied in future years, long after the names of the participants and maybe even the Falklands War are forgotten. That is what we are discussing today a central question, which must be decided, as to the proper relationship between the Cabinet, the Commons and the courts. That is what the debate is about— *[Interruption.]* – and if the House will listen, I will establish the point.

It arose, in the first instance, because the Cabinet, who are there by virtue of having won the election, and exercise the prerogatives of the Crown, believe, and have argued, that civil servants, once appointed, are bound in duty simply to work for the ministers of the day, and that point was put powerfully by the Secretary of State in his speech.

I wonder whether hon Members think that what happened in the Ponting case happened for the first time. I remind the House of a report in the *Daily Telegraph* on 13 November 1976 under the heading: 'Whitehall spies fed Churchill secrets in the 1930s':

Sir Winston Churchill received hundreds of secret documents surreptitiously removed from official files sent to him in breach of the

Official Secrets Act when he was fighting appeasement as a back bench MP. Mr Martin Gilbert, Sir Winston's biographer, reported that these documents had been found in the Churchill Archives at Chartwell and said 'there was total, consistent and persistent breach of the Official Secrets Act'.

I do not know, looking at it now, whether Conservative Members think that it was wrong for senior civil servants to keep Mr Churchill informed when he was a back bencher. I remember, as a boy, in 1937, seeing Mr Churchill sitting where the former Prime Minister, the right hon Member for Bexley and Old Sidcup (Mr Heath) now sits. Were the civil servants wrong to inform Mr Churchill? They thought they were doing a public duty. Mr Churchill was getting information which allowed him to destroy the appeasement policy of Neville Chamberlain, in much the same way as my hon Friend the Member for Linlithgow (Mr Dalyell) has undermined the credibility of the Government in regard to the Falklands War. But whatever view we take, we must not think that that question has always been resolved in one way.

I happen to think that civil servants, ministers, Members of the House of Commons and political parties should never put their consciences in hock to anybody else. If we think that a course of action is wrong, we have a duty to say so. Our religious liberties in Britain would not have been won if people had not broken the law in order to worship as they wished. It was that which laid the foundation for our political liberties.

Was it right of the Attorney-General to prosecute Mr Ponting when Mr Ponting was informing a Member of Parliament? There is a precedent for that. I cited it the other day, Mr Speaker, in a rather unhappy exchange with you about privilege. In 1938, Mr Duncan Sandys, a Member of the House and a territorial officer, received information from a fellow territorial officer as a result of which he tabled questions in the House of Commons. Following that, Mr Duncan Sandys, although an MP, was told to appear before a court martial. He sought the support of the House. The House, in a famous Select Committee report on the Official Secrets Act, published in 1939 – my father was a member of that Committee, so I was brought up on the doctrine within it – made it clear that Parliament would not allow people to be prosecuted when their only offence was to tell Members of Parliament things that they should know in order to perform their parliamentary duties. Indeed, the House laid down clearly in that decision in 1939 that to prosecute in regard to information falling under the Official Secrets Act, when it is given to a Member of Parliament, is in itself a breach of privilege. Indeed, I believe that the Attorney-General, in bringing that prosecution, was guilty of a contempt of the House.

The Prime Minister is head of the Civil Service and head of the Armed Forces – indeed, with the nuclear button, she is especially responsible, without any holidays as part of the package. The Prime Minister is also head of the security services and, of course, she is the head of the Government. Therefore, it is inconceivable with the Whitehall network that exists, that any contemplated prosecution, under Section 2 of the Act, of a most senior civil servant, known to the Prime Minister personally, would not have been reported to No 10 along the network. The prosecution would not have taken place if the Prime Minister had not given assent. Perhaps, like Henry II, all she said was 'Who will rid me of this turbulent priest?' and left it to others to do what was necessary. No one will persuade me that the Prime Minister was not involved. But in any event she should have been involved.

There are other aspects, all of which bear on the relationship between the Cabinet, the courts and Parliament. In his judgement in the GCHQ case, Lord Fraser said

> The decision on whether the requirements of national security outweighed the duty of fairness is for the government and not for the courts; the Government alone has access to the necessary information, and in any event the judicial process is unsuitable for reaching decisions on national security.

If a minister, using the prerogative that he has temporarily acquired by election, says, 'This is a matter of national security', the courts now will not even attempt to be fair. Indeed, in the Ponting case, Mr Justice McCowan said that 'the interests of the state' were the same as 'the policy of the Government of the day.' That is a doctrine that every dictator in history would have liked to enshrine in capital letters above his presidential palace. It would be a deadly danger for any party, Conservative, Labour or other, to allow such judgements of the courts to go unchallenged. If we were to accept, in the Commons, that doctrine about national security, the Commons would be capitulating to a Government who had decided to rule by prerogative instead of by accountability to the House of Commons. That is what the debate is about, and it is much more important than whether we can catch each other out with little quotations.

The Secretary of State for Defence has made great play – I

am not being personal – about the need to protect the troops. What he is clearly saying is that the Government received all their information about the movements of the *General Belgrano* from United States intelligence. Everybody who knows anything about such matters knows that we do not have satellite intelligence in the South Atlantic; the Americans do. The Americans intercepted the Argentine messages and sent them to GCHQ. We are not talking about protecting a soldier from being shot tomorrow by a sniper. That is what is usually meant by protecting the boys in uniform in the middle of a war. At the insistence of the Americans, the Government are protecting the fact that it was American intelligence that won the Falklands War by giving us the necessary information. I believe that as a quid pro quo the trade unions at GCHQ – which is a part of that international intelligence system – had to be abandoned.

These are central questions that reopen matters that I was brought up to believe were settled in the 17th century – that the prerogative could not be used so that ministers could take matters to the courts and get the judgements that they wished; that the prerogative could not be used in Parliament to buy the silence of the Commons in order to accept whatever a Government said; that the prerogative could not be used to put at risk a man of conscience who chose that course rather than his career. Unless this House comes back to those questions and resolves them, we shall find that the so-called *Belgrano*–Ponting case will turn the clock back not to Victorian days but to a much earlier, less glorious and less democratic period in our history.

Westland Helicopters

Mr Tony Benn (Chesterfield): I have found it hard to believe the Prime Minister since my hon Friend the Member for Linlithgow (Mr Dalyell) raised the *General Belgrano* question, so today is not the first time that doubts about her trustworthiness have crossed my mind. But the debate will be wasted if we do not understand the lessons that may be drawn from it. First, why did the Government lose two senior Cabinet Ministers over this matter? We are at least entitled to know that. The answer is that when Westland got into difficulty, in pursuit of their policy of non-intervention, the Government said, 'We do not care what happens to Westland.' They said the same about the steel, mining and manufacturing industries, so there was no surprise about it.

However – this is why the matter became a central political question – the vultures from Washington and Brussels moved in. As Minister with responsibility for aviation, I used to deal with Westland and I know of its long link with Sikorsky.

Sikorsky wanted to use Westland to expand its arms sales in Europe. The Prime Minister could not ignore that view because she was close to President Reagan and she wanted contracts for Star Wars. However – this is why it is a big issue, not a little issue – there is a growing feeling among Western European industrialists that American domination must end. Therefore, the Prime Minister tried to withdraw from a major international industrial matter by pretending that the decision should be left to the shareholders. Of course, her idea of democracy is to hold ballots to elect trade union executives, but if employees want to ensure their future employment, they must buy their votes and become shareholders. We saw the disgusting slave market of the Albert Hall, with people such as Mr Bristow and Lord Hanson buying shares to trade the future of Westland workers. So much for the workers at Westland having any rights.

The matter became more complicated because one minister supported the American bid and another supported the European bid. The Prime Minister deliberately used the mechanisms open only to a Prime Minister, first, to encourage legal advice and, secondly, to release that advice to destroy the Secretary of State for Defence, who left the Government. Thereafter, she had to sacrifice her Secretary of State for Trade and Industry by saying that he, alone among ministers, had authorised the leak. That is what happened. That is what people outside know to have happened. It was not simply a matter of who telephoned whom on what occasion. This was, and still is, a major industrial conflict between Europe and the United States, with ministers taking different sides and the Prime Minister using her powers, first, to undermine one minister and, secondly, to get another minister – very close to her – to take the blame so that he felt he had to resign.

It was good to see those two ministers go. The former Secretary of State for Defence led the Army against the Quakers at Molesworth, so I am pleased that he has gone. The former Secretary of State for Trade and Industry, when he was responsible for the Home Department, told the police to batter the miners at Orgreave and now he has gone. The loss of those two ministers is a plus, and it must have delighted the National Union of Mineworkers and the Campaign for Nuclear Disarmament.

However, the House must discuss other matters. The first is the Official Secrets Act. Some months ago, Sarah Tisdall, from a sense of principle, released to the *Guardian*, which did not protect her – it might be remembered that Bernard Ingham came from the *Guardian* – details of something that had happened, and she was put in prison for six months. No doubt the Prime Minister, who believes in law and order, endorsed that sentence. Clive Ponting of the Ministry of Defence was charged under the Official Secrets Act. Yet the Prime Minister retrospectively authorised – today she takes responsibility for what she pretends she did not know – a leak to undermine a colleague.

The incident also throws light on the lobby system and all those people sitting there in the Press Gallery— *[Interruption.]* If I am not allowed to refer to them, Mr Speaker, that is another absurdity added to many. There are people in this Palace who go twice a day to No 10 and get from Bernard Ingham an account of what the Prime Minister wants them to know about Government business. Then people appear on television saying,

'Our political correspondent understands', but they never tell us from where the information comes. They do not understand it. That is because they got it ten minutes before from Bernard Ingham on the instructions of the Prime Minister.

When the briefing gets a bit touchy they appear on television or write in the papers about a grave constitutional crisis. The lobby correspondents are involved in secret arrangements with ministers of all parties. I hope I will not be accused of being a leaker when I say publicly what has to be said. I do not leak through the Lobby. That is a vicious system, because it creates a sort of cosy conspiracy between ministers, shadow ministers, civil servants and the lobby correspondents.

The third thing that the Prime Minister did was to blow up the questions of procedure that she sent to her own ministers in 1979. The Prime Minister broke her own rules. [Interruption.] The main reason we are debating this is, first, because it is a major constitutional question. Because of the Official Secrets Act and the way in which the right hon Lady treated her Cabinet and because the Government misled Parliament and the public we have had to have this debate. We are told that parliamentary democracy is what we uphold but we cannot have parliamentary democracy if ministers do not tell the House of Commons what is happening and have to be hauled up under Standing Order No 10.

This is an important debate. It goes well beyond whether the Prime Minister talked to Bernard Ingham, which I am sure she did. I know that other people who know Bernard Ingham will agree that he would not have so acted if he had not had the clearest instructions so to do. The debate is important because of Westland and all the other matters. The Prime Minister must be wondering why what she sees as such a small issue should have been exploded to the point where it appears to the minds of some correspondents to threaten the premiership.

The reason is that 'Thatcherism', which the right hon Lady created and believes in, was a myth. People are asking whether that myth is capable of leading the Conservative party to victory at the next election. The Conservative party is looking for a new leader. Members on the Government side will go into the Lobby tonight and the resigned Secretaries of State will be rubbing shoulders with the Prime Minister. The reality of the matter is that they are looking for a new – [Interruption.] – leader.

Surcharge and Disqualification of Councillors

Mr Tony Benn (Chesterfield): The speech of the hon Member for Streatham (Mr Shelton) and the hon Member for Nuneaton (Mr Stevens) together represent two of the clearest statements that I have heard of the Conservatives' attitude towards democracy. Their view of society is that if the Tories are in power, by definition they are behaving responsibly, even if they sell off our most priceless assets, run down the welfare state and destroy the prospects of employment. That is responsible and non-political. If, however, a group of people win the support of the electorate for a contrary policy and the Conservative Party finds itself not in a majority, it no longer believes in the democratic principle. The district auditor is called in to decide what action is to be taken in a local authority.

The question of acting responsibly is a central question, but reasonable to whom? The district auditor is responsible to nobody. He is not responsible to the House, he cannot be defeated in the House and he cannot be dealt with by the electorate. The core of the argument is that the Conservative Party says that if one is anything other than a Conservative, one is, by definition, political and irresponsible. Therefore, if by chance such a person wins, the Conservative Party says that it will have other ways of dealing with him.

I am proud to be a supporter of the Bill. I think that my hon Friend the Member for Liverpool, Garston (Mr Loyden) has done a great service. He has brought into focus the real issue, which is that in Britain we have an unjust law, and the prime victims of that unjust law are not the councillors but the people they represent. It is their interests which are adversely affected.

I shall draw a contrast between the conduct of private capital and local democracy. If any two Conservative Members set up a company, make some money and the company goes bankrupt, they are not bankrupted or surcharged. They are protected by the Companies Act 1980 and could set up another business the following day. In some cases, I have heard it said that companies go bankrupt and the old owners then buy the assets of that company from the receiver at a knockdown price. If one is a private business person, one can leave a trail of bankruptcies among sub-contractors, buy the company back, sack the people employed and still be free the following day. However, if one is a locally elected councillor, there is no such protection.

I shall take a classic case of two famous men who reduced fares – Freddie Laker, and Ken Livingstone. Freddie Laker reduced fares and went bankrupt. He left many people out of work and others could not manage to pay their bills because they had been sub-contractors. Freddie Laker is a hero of the Government and has been knighted for his pains. Ken Livingstone, only a symbol of the local authority, introduced cheap fares and was taken to court by Lord Denning. Somebody later explained to judges what a bus was, and in the end they reached a compromise. The reality is that if local government tries to meet transport needs by lowering fares, councillors, if they do not pay their fines, are at risk of imprisonment, bankruptcy and surcharge, but private business men can make profits by leaving a trail of ruin behind them. That is what the Bill is about.

In a clinical sense, we are seeking to change class legislation. Since Victorian times class has not been allowed to be mentioned. In Victorian times the upper classes looked down on the lower classes. When Karl Marx told the lower classes there were more of them and that if they banded together they could change society, class ceased to be a respectable word to use. If we are returning to Victorian times, let us resuscitate Victorian language and discuss the fact that there are more poor people than rich ones. Democracy in local government allows poorer people to buy collectively, by the ballot box, what they cannot afford individually.

That is what democracy is about. I do not know how many hon Members are dependent upon public provision or require council accommodation in which to live, but if one cannot afford the services that one needs – home, nursery school, education or pension – democracy is about buying it collectively by using the ballot box.

That is what the Chartists and the suffragettes were about. They were not interested in obtaining seats in this place. They saw democracy as a route to social justice. The same is true of trade unions. We are not discussing them, but if people band together they can get back in wages from their employer a share of the profit that they make. If not – that is why Murdoch has stopped trade unionism – one has to put up barbed wire and publish the Wapping lies which come out in the *Sun, The Times* and the *Sunday Times*.

This Bill brings out the point that the Tory Party hates democracy because it gives the people the power to get a fair share of the wealth that they create. Democracy limits market forces and it must be hammered on the head wherever it appears. That is why the GLC has been abolished. That is why rate capping has been introduced. That is why the latest Local Government Bill has been introduced. It prevents people from even speaking to one another if they have elected their local authority. That is why the Government use the courts against councillors, to make them seem to be criminals. That is why the Government are now talking about development corporations. If there is a local authority they do not like to which they do not want to give money, the Government set up a corporation. It is not democratic. It is put in the heart of the inner city. The Government then give money to their business friends to make a profit out of the poverty of the inner city without that corporation being responsible to the electors in the towns.

The Tory Party is the enemy of democracy. That point comes out through all the legislation. I heard the speech by the hon Member for Nuneaton. He talked about how marvellous it was in the old days when councillors behaved responsibly.

The roots of municipal socialism began in Victorian England. If the Conservative Party tries to take us back to that period, it will find that it is not just attacking socialism; it is attacking the tradition of public responsibility in government.

The Bill removes disqualification and in doing so would restore two controls on local councillors. If a councillor is corrupt, he or she should be prosecuted by the police. If he or she behaves in a way that the electorate does not like, he or she should be defeated at the polls. There should be nothing between the police court and the polling station to prevent councillors from serving the interests of their people.

The Bill merely restores the position to what it should be. The police court or the polling station are the only hazards that councillors should face. Councillors should be free to provide any services which are in the interests of the people – to acquire by purchase or to hold any land or buildings; to establish any company, as any Government can; to assist by way of grant, loan or subsidy; to make grants to voluntary bodies; to provide services of news and information; and to undertake any activity not explicitly prohibited by Act of Parliament.

The greatest and most sensitive agent of public expenditure is local government, because councillors know what needs to be done. They can meet the needs of people for twenty-four-hour-a-day care for old people, day-care provision for mothers with children, proper libraries and sports facilities. In that way we can restore full employment and demobilise the riot police, because there will be no need for them.

That is the issue that we are discussing. By introducing the Bill, my hon Friend (Mr Loyden) has performed a great service, because without the normal hype of a debate about controversial Government legislation, the House has an opportunity, through his wisdom, to focus attention on the real question – whether profit is to take precedence over need, and whether we are to have democracy or market forces running the country.

The Ordination of Women

Mr Tony Benn (Chesterfield): This is an important debate because it raises far wider issues than the one raised by the hon Member for Wokingham (Sir W. van Straubenzee) in presenting the Measure. We are, as Parliament, first responsible – apart from our relationship to the Church of England, to which I shall refer – for the rights of women in Britain. We are also bound to consider, because the Measure deals with it, the attitude of the Anglican Church towards women. But also, necessarily, because of the nature of the Measure, we are bound to consider the legislative relationship of the Church to Parliament and, inevitably, the issue of the establishment of the Church. I want to touch briefly on some of those questions.

The campaign for the full ordination of women in the Church of England is not a new one but a very old one indeed. It was 70 years ago that Maude Royden sought permission to be ordained. It was refused and she became an assistant at the City Temple in London, where she continued to preach until her death.

In the same year, 1916, Constance Coltman was the first woman to be ordained as a Congregational minister and she practised as a minister. The ordination of women since then has spread over a wide number of denominations.

I must admit to the House a long family interest in and connection with the ordination of women. In 1920 my mother, now in her ninetieth year, joined the League of Church Militant, the name of the organisation then seeking the full ordination of women. She was summoned to Lambeth Palace in 1926 by Archbishop Randall Davidson and told that it was impossible that women could ever be ordained into the priesthood. Following that came the Anglican Group for the Ordination of Women, which continued to argue the case, then the Society for the Ministry of Women in the Church, of which Bishop

Montefiori was the Anglican chairman and my mother was once the Free Church president. Now we have the Movement for the Ordination of Women, which has been arguing the case in the Synod.

I would go further. During the war the Reverend Lee Tim Oi, a Chinese woman, was ordained by Bishop Hall of Hong Kong because in wartime circumstances nobody else could administer the sacrament in his diocese. It is to the eternal disgrace of the Church of England that after the war it threatened to withdraw its financial support from the Church in China unless the Reverend Lee Tim Oi resigned, which she did. She visited Britain a little while ago.

Meanwhile, other denominations accepted women as ministers. If I may be allowed one other family reference, forty years ago this year my father, as Secretary of State for Air, appointed the first woman chaplain to the Forces, a Congregationalist, the Reverend Elsie Chamberlain, much against the opposition of the then Archbishop of Canterbury. When the Air Force list was printed my father found, to his rage, that his officials had listed her as a welfare officer. He had the Air Force list pulped and reissued showing her as a full chaplain in order to establish that the rights of women could not be dismissed in that way.

Since then, Anglicans have accepted the ordination of women in other countries. There are women priests in the United States of America and the Episcopalian Church in Australia. They have been considering the appointment of a woman bishop in the United States and it is not impossible that at the next Lambeth conference the Anglican community will have to receive a woman bishop as a full member of that conference and the Archbishop of Canterbury will have to receive her in that capacity.

The only churches that do not accept the ordination of women in England are the Catholic Church, the Greek Orthodox Church, and the Church of England *in England*.

It is not for me, for a reason that I shall come to in a moment, to go in detail into the argument within the Church of England, beyond saying that the Bishop of London has played a wretched role and was recently censured in the Church for his intervention in a parish in the United States. He has stirred up prejudice against women in an established church which, I might add, is presided over by a monarch who is a woman, where the bishops are appointed by a Prime Minister who is a woman. Yet the hon Member for Wokingham begs the House to believe that under no circumstances under the Measure, and he is correct, could a woman become a priest. That is the background against which we have to discuss the matter.

There has always been prejudice and obscurantism in relation to women's matters, but there is much sympathy. Everybody is always sympathetic to the principle – but not now. That was the way in which the House discussed the women's vote and now we are invited today to vote for a Measure that explicitly makes it unlawful for a woman to be a priest, and that has to be taken into account.

One of the factors – I can only say this from observing the scene – that leads the Church to object to the ordination of women is a fear of prejudicing reunion with Rome, although there is an Alliance for St Joan in the Catholic Church and, judging from the speed with which the Catholic Church has moved on many matters, it is not inconceivable that it will ordain women before the Church of England gets round to it. But that is a matter for speculation.

The opposition to the Measure highlights the central question – the absurdity, drawn out by my hon Friend the Member for Liverpool, Walton (Mr Heffer) – that Parliament, the Members of which do not have to be Anglicans or even Christians has the final word in deciding whether women should be deacons, priests or bishops in the Church of England. It is absurd for the hon Member for Leicester, East (Mr Bruinvels), who is a member of the Synod, having lost in the Synod, where at least he is surrounded by members of his own denomination, to appeal to Parliament, where anybody could be Catholic, Jewish, Sikh, Muslim or humanist, to defeat that Measure. That is what makes the establishment of the Church of England unacceptable.

The political control of the Church is a total anachronism. Over the years there has been quite properly a distancing between the Synod and Parliament and a greater formalisation of our relationship. But it is the Prime Minister who appoints the bishops. Anyone who has read the recent scandalous stories about the Archbishop of Canterbury must know that it was hoped that he would resign because of those stories, to pave the way for a more acceptable Archbishop appointed by the Prime Minister— [HON MEMBERS: 'Nonsense.'] I give that as my opinion.

If any hon Member were to suggest that establishment is so successful that we should nationalise the Catholic Church, the Baptist Church, the Methodist Church and the Jews, people would say that it was a gross abuse of spiritual freedom and they would be right.

We are a nation of many religions and of none. This House is a Parliament of many religions and of none and the time has come to complete the steady progress of separation between the Church of England and Parliament.

The Zircon
Affair

On Thursday 22 January 1987 Speaker Weatherill ruled that the BBC Television film Secret Society *should not be shown within the House of Commons to MPs. This ruling followed a High Court injunction against the film on the grounds that the subject – the Zircon satellite project – was a matter of national security. On Tuesday 27 January the House debated the Speaker's decision. The Government's motion proposed to continue the ban while the injunction remained in force. Tony Benn submitted a late manuscript amendment and was responsible for persuading the House to refer the matter of the film to the Committee of Privileges.*

Mr Tony Benn (Chesterfield): I am grateful to you, Mr Speaker, for allowing me to put before the House the manuscript amendment standing in my name that would transfer the matter to the Committee of Privileges. The amendment is, in line 1, leave out from 'That' to end and add 'Mr Speaker's ruling of 22 January, relating to the showing of a film, be referred to the Committee of Privileges.'

Mr Speaker: Order. The right hon Gentleman may move the amendment at the end of the debate, but he may speak to it now.

Mr Benn: I think it is obvious to the House that the issues we are discussing go far beyond the immediate matters of controversy between the Government and the Opposition, the related question of the Campbell article in the *New Statesman* on the film or the project. I do not wish to go back over the issues of last week when you took a decision, Mr Speaker, at very short notice, because it is today that we face the big decision.

   Those of us who have anxieties about the implication of the decision that you took last week, Mr Speaker, wish to make it clear that those anxieties are in no sense personally related to you. Nevertheless, those anxieties are clear and specific and can be set out in the following way. If the Government are asking that we should 'confirm' your ruling, or if, as the amendment put down by my right hon Friend the Member for Islwyn (Mr Kinnock) states, we should 'accept' that decision, the difficulties go far beyond the Opposition and extend to the Chairmen and members of the Select Committees. That is why I am moving that the matter should go to the Committee of Privileges, which was set up by the House many years ago to examine matters that require complex examination. We should not reach a decision until the Committee of Privileges has reported.

The issue that we are discussing is a fundamental constitutional one on the relationship of the Commons, Members of Parliament and the electors on the one hand; and the Executive and the judiciary on the other. Although you quite properly said, Mr Speaker, that you did not wish your ruling of last Thursday to be treated as a precedent, if we confirm or accept it tonight it will appear in *Erskine May* and will be quoted in future Parliaments and have a profound effect upon Parliament.

I do not believe that there is any precedent for the ruling that you gave, Mr Speaker. I have searched carefully through *Erskine May* and I can find no precedent, nor can I imagine that when the Committee on Accommodation was set up it was ever intended that the organisation of Committee Rooms of the House should be used to prevent the showing of a film on the provision of information that might assist hon Members in the course of their work.

It is right that we should look at your role, Mr Speaker, in this connection, because it is the highest office that we can bestow and you speak for us and defend us from the Executive. I have cited before, and will cite again, the words of Mr Speaker Lenthall. On 4 January 1642 the King came to the Commons to seize the five Members. Mr Speaker Lenthall, described as 'a man of timorous nature', knelt and said: 'May it please your Majesty, I have neither eyes to see nor tongue to speak in this place but as the House is pleased to direct me, whose servant I am here.'

That was the precedent. It could be argued that if it was not in relation to five hon Members and the King that precedent would not apply. However, we have taken it, ever since, as a statement of your role. Now when a new Speaker is elected he goes to the other place to claim the ancient privileges of the House.

I am sorry to go back to the texts, but people may not always appreciate their importance. In 1668 the ninth article of the Bill of Rights stated: 'That the freedom of speech, and debates or proceedings in Parliament, ought not to be impeached or questioned in any Court or place out of Parliament.'

Hon Members may ask whether a film shown somewhere else in the Chamber can be described as a proceeding in Parliament. Fortunately, we have a precedent for that as well. In 1938 Duncan Sandys, a Member of the House and also a member of the Territorial Army, received from a colleague in the Territorial Army information that there were defects in the air defence of London. He tabled a question and the person from whom he got the information was charged under the Official Secrets Act 1911. Duncan Sandys came to the House to appeal to the House to protect him by way of privilege and the person who gave the information.

I remember most vividly the debate in the House. The House upheld the view – I shall refer to it because it refers directly to the question as to what is a proceeding in Parliament – and did so in a case involving the Official Secrets Act. I shall quote from *Erskine May*, page 93, commenting on the Committee that examined the Sandys case:

> Cases may easily be imagined of communications between one Member and another or between a Member and a Minister, so closely related to some matter pending in, or expected to be brought before the House, that, although they do not take place in the Chamber or a committee room, they form part of the business of the House.

That was one of the most important judgements reached by the House, especially when one considers, to its credit, that it was in the middle of war. As far as I recall, the matter was discussed in the House in May 1940, when it may well have had other matters to consider. Nevertheless, it entrenched the right of its Members to receive information from someone who is not a Member of the House even when that information is in respect of the security of the country.

I give that historical and legal background only to underline the enormity of the decision that it is proposed we should take without any further examination of the issues at stake. My amendment does not prejudge any of those issues, but invites the House to put the matter to the Committee that is best qualified to judge.

It is an issue that is not just of historical and legal importance, but one which will have immediate, practical importance to the future workings of parliamentary democracy. I ask the House to ask itself these important questions before hon Members go into the Lobby to vote on any of the amendments, other than the one referring to the Committee of Privileges.

First, is it right for the Government to engage in major military projects without telling Parliament? This question, as my hon Friends will know, points a finger of criticism at both Labour and Tory Governments. I think I am one of the few surviving Members who sat in this House when Mr Attlee was Prime Minister and Mr Attlee developed the atom bomb without telling Parliament. At the time that may have been considered acceptable, but I do not believe that any hon Member would accept that it would be right to do that today.

The House does not want technical details about the defence of secrets when the question of security arises. I have not read the article in the *New Statesman* and I do not particularly want to read what Duncan Campbell may say about a particular satellite. However, Parliament must know the general nature of major defence projects, their purpose and their cost. If Parliament does not know that it is abdicating its responsibilities.

The second question is whether it is right that ministers should be able to go to any court and use the magic words 'national security' as the basis for a court injunction. In a democracy it is for the House and electors to decide what is in the national interest. And when there is a General Election, it is the people's judgement as to what is in the national interest that counts. It is not for civil servants, generals, scientists or ministers to determine what is national security. The judges of the Cheltenham case have said that if the magic words national security are used they will not allow the matter to be raised.

The third question that I would like the House to consider is whether it is right that any Speaker – so as not to personalise it – hearing news of an injunction that has been issued should be able, without the explicit and specific authority of the House, to prevent hon Members from seeking available information that would assist Parliament in its work of holding Governments to account. As the court in question declined to grant an injunction against some hon Members, it is clear that it recognised the limits of its powers. Page 204 of *Erskine May* states: 'the courts admit: That the control of each House over its internal proceedings is absolute and cannot be interfered with by the courts.'

I do not know, and it is not my concern, to what extent that aspect was in your mind, Mr Speaker, when you took what you feel to have been interim action, but that is the question that we have to ask today, because we are reaching permanent decisions.

The next question is whether we should accept and confirm a limit on our freedom as Members of Parliament that would assist the concealment of any matter by any Government of any Parliament – this is not just in relation to this matter – by the use of national security and injunctions. I worry greatly over the other implications of your ruling, Mr Speaker. What if the police had gone to a magistrate and asked for a warrant to search the papers of my hon Friend the Member for Livingston (Mr Cook) at the time they were going to the home of Duncan Campbell? What would have been the position? Is it the case that the House could ever allow the courts or a magistrate to send policemen into the Palace, where already a film may not be shown, to discover the sources of information of a Member who might be contemplating a parliamentary question?

If we accept the motion or the amendment, we would be placing the House of Commons and Members of Parliament for ever under the effective control of the Government, in that ministers could bring an injunction, the court could accede to the injunction and – nobody would wish this less than you, Mr Speaker – Mr Speaker would become an agent of the minister and his injunction and the court that upheld it, to enforce upon Members the denial of the right for which we were elected. I cannot believe, knowing you, Mr Speaker, that it would be your wish to be remembered as a 'Counter-Lenthall' whose protection did not extend to hon Members in this position.

I should like to make a final comment as an old Member of the House. We all take children and visitors round the House. I do and have done for many years. We tell them that we keep Black Rod out. We tell them about the Outlawries Bill, we tell them that the House decides on its own business before it gives attention to the Gracious Speech. We tell them about the Army Annual Act and the order to prevent a Standing Army being maintained and we tell them about the five Members. Those are not meaningless rituals. They are reminders of monumental struggles to build democracy against tyranny. It is important that we should not treat them simply as tourist attractions.

In thirty-six years in the House I cannot recall a debate as important as this and I am grateful to you, Mr Speaker, for allowing my manuscript amendment to be put on the Order Paper tonight along with the motion and the other amendments before us.

Spycatcher

It was here in Hyde Park that free speech was established over a hundred years ago, and we are meeting today in an attempt to prevent ministers and the judges from destroying our inherent, inalienable and ancient democratic rights.

Mr Peter Wright has alleged in his book *Spycatcher* that certain public servants, working for the security services, have broken the law many times, and have even attempted to subvert an elected government, in which I, along with others, served as a Cabinet minister. But instead of investigating these allegations the Attorney-General has applied for, and won from the judges, injunctions to prevent these reports of alleged illegalities from being published at all, and even the House of Commons has been inhibited from debating the issues on the grounds that they were sub judice.

Let me quote now from the book itself. On page 31 Mr Wright alleges: 'We did have fun. For five years we bugged and burgled our way across London at the State's behest, while pompous bowler-hatted civil servants in Whitehall pretended to look the other way.'

On page 160 Mr Wright alleges: 'At the beginning of the Suez crisis, MI6 developed a plan, through the London Station, to assassinate Nasser using nerve gas. Eden initially gave his approval to this operation . . .'

On page 274 Mr Wright alleges that James Angleton of the American Central Intelligence Agency told him: 'We're going to have a beefed-up CIA London Station, and half those officers are going to work directly inside MI5. We'll have access to everything.' Wright comments on this, on page 275, as follows: 'Angleton's ambitions were obvious: he wanted to swallow MI5 up whole, and use it as an Agency outstation.'

On page 360 Mr Wright alleges: 'We had always been able to get material from the National Insurance records if we really wanted it. We had a couple of undercover officers posted up there who could be contacted for our files. But establishing a direct computer link was something completely different.'

On page 364 Mr Wright reports: 'After Harold Wilson became Prime Minister in 1964, Angleton made a special trip to England to see FJ, who was then director of counter-espionage. Angleton came to offer us some very secret information from a source he would not name. This source alleged, according to Angleton, that Wilson was a Soviet agent.'

And on page 366, he alleges that 'once the Conservative Government came to power they began to take a great interest in the material as well. Victor (Lord Rothschild) often used to complain about the quality of the intelligence reports No 10 received from F Branch. "They pull their punches all the time" he would say, "can't you give us something better?" '

Writing of the end of the Heath Government Mr Wright alleges:

> As events moved to their political climax in early 1974, with the election of the minority Labour Government, MI5 was sitting on information, which, if leaked, would undoubtedly have caused a political scandal of incalculable consequences. The news that the Prime Minister himself was being investigated would at the least have led to his resignation. The point was not lost on some MI5 officers.

And on page 369 Mr Wright, dealing with the period after Labour was elected in 1974, spelled out his allegations in these words:

> The plan was simple. In the run-up to the election which, given the level of instability in Parliament, must be due within a matter of months, MI5 would arrange for selective details of the intelligence about leading Labour Party figures, but especially Wilson, to be leaked to sympathetic pressmen. Using our contacts in the press and among union officials, word of the material contained in MI5 files, and the fact that Wilson was considered a security risk would be passed around. Soundings had already been taken, and up to thirty officers had given their approval to the scheme. Facsimile copies of some files were to be made and distributed to overseas newspapers, and the matter was to be raised in Parliament for maximum effect. It was a carbon copy of the Zinoviev letter, which had done so much to destroy the first Ramsay MacDonald Government in 1928. [sic] 'We'll have him out' said one of them, 'this time we'll have him out.' Shortly afterwards Wilson resigned. As we always used to say in he office 'Politicians may come and go, but the security service goes on forever.

Those then are just a few of the quotations from Mr Wright's book, in which he makes a large number of very serious allegations.

If any of them are true MI5 officers were incited to break the law, have broken the law, did attempt, with CIA help, to destroy an elected government, and any responsible Prime Minister should have instructed the police to investigate, with a view to prosecution, and the Courts should have convicted and sentenced those found guilty. The charge which the Prime Minister, the Lord Chancellor, the Law Officers, the Police, have to face is that they have all betrayed their public trust, and the judges who have upheld them are in clear breach of Article One of the Bill of Rights of 1689. For if ministers can arbitrarily suspend the law, and claim that issues of confidentiality, or national security, justify a ban on publication; and if the judges issue an injunction, there could be no limit to the suppression of any information which might embarrass any government.

I have come here today, first as a citizen, but also as an elected Member of Parliament, a Privy Councillor and a member of the Committee of Privileges of the House of Commons to warn that we cannot, and should not, accept this restriction on our liberty.

Protection of Official Information

Mr Tony Benn (Chesterfield): We have had an interesting debate
and the hon Member for Hampstead and Highgate (Sir G.
Finsberg) made a powerful case for the cancellation of *Hansard*,
because if people were to read what was said here hon Members
might be nervous of speaking. Then when the right hon
Member for Plymouth, Devonport (Dr Owen) offered to go on
the Committee I thought that that would be another little group
that he could split into five parts.

We have had a marvellous debate, but the House should be
candid with the public, who will be reading *Hansard*, probably
with some interest.

Why are we having the debate? It is because certain public
servants, for one reason or another and in many cases honour-
ably, have spoken the truth on matters about which the Government did not want the truth to be known. Sarah Tisdall was
betrayed by the *Guardian*, which is supposed to be a liberal
newspaper, and served a sixth-month sentence. In my opinion,
that woman was moved by conscience. Clive Ponting came out
with information that was embarrassing to the then Secretary
of State for Defence. Cathy Massiter said that people who were
active in the peace movement were having their telephones
tapped. We have also had the case of Peter Wright, and I shall
return to him later.

An interesting factor in the debate is the way in which
alliances have run. As the right hon Member for Devonport
said, this is not a party matter. We have seen an alliance of
former Home Secretaries – who have been involved to some
extent and who do not want the degree of freedom of information that, on the whole, the public want. The public are not
fools. They have watched Colonel Oliver North being grilled
before the American Senate under what I would call the thirty-
minute rule, whereby the news comes out as soon as the event

has occurred. Here it is concealed. People want to know more about what Government do. Of course they do. Why else was there such a struggle to elect people to Parliament in the first place?

I must say one thing for the Government: I understand why they have a three-line Whip. I understand why they sent Sir Robert Armstrong to Australia and ruined the end of his Civil Service life. I understand why they brought injunctions against the newspapers. The Government do not want what the security services are doing in Britain to come out. There is no point in saying that the Government have been silly and absurd and made people look ridiculous. In a limited way I can confirm, from my knowledge as a minister in a Government which Peter Wright tried to destabilise, that what he said happened. Who benefited? The Conservative Party. That is why the Prime Minister defends MI5. It helped to get rid of the right hon Member for Old Bexley and Sidcup (Mr Heath). I have evidence of that as well. The right hon Gentleman must know – this appears to have come out of the Cavendish Christmas card, which I have not read because I am not on his mailing list – that efforts were made to discredit him as leader of the Conservative Party. I have evidence of some of the reasons.

Of course the Prime Minister does not want to bring to light the process by which Wilson was removed and the right hon Member for Old Bexley and Sidcup discredited. MI5 is still doing it. Does anyone think that it ended when Peter Wright resigned? MI5 is still discrediting people whom it regards as acting contrary to the national interest, as MI5 defines that national interest. Does anyone think that the fabrication of false information and its publication in the foreign press ended when the Labour Government left office? Of course it did not. It still continues. That is what the three-line Whip and the threats in the press are about. Any Conservative Member who wonders how such a nice Government could do such a horrid thing had better think about the reality behind the argument.

Then we come to this marvellous principle about confidentiality – whatever one's position in the public service, until one dies everything learnt while there must remain secret. The whole idea is absurd. The hallelujah chorus does not rely on press releases; it relies on Bernard Ingham, who is paid to issue confidential information daily to benefit the Prime Minister. Whatever damage Clive Ponting did to the right hon Member for Henley (Mr Heseltine) was nothing compared with the damage done to the right hon Gentleman by Bernard Ingham on the Prime Minister's instructions. A Prime Minister who talks about keeping everything secret but who, using a civil servant, pumps out secret papers to get rid of a Cabinet colleague is an absolute disgrace.

There has always been a highly selective leaking of confidential information. I must confess that I have rather less sympathy than perhaps I should with all the pompous editorials about the freedom of the press. The warnings about what the security services have been doing in Britain have been given time and time again over the years by my hon Friends. But when we said it, those editors said it was the paranoid Left talking about those wicked 'conspiracies'.

But when there is interference with the papers' right to publish what they want on a Sunday they are on their high horses and talking about the need for a free press. They know what we ought to tell the public through *Hansard* today: government is lubricated by the selective leaking and briefing that go on all the time. Therefore, it is in the interests of the press to support the wider question.

It is for Parliament to decide the categories of secrecy. For my part, I do not want to know any of the secrets that the security services know, if those secrets would impinge upon national security.

The underlying question is, 'What is the real issue?' As has emerged from the debate, it is the relationship between Parliament and the Executive. What are the powers that Prime Ministers use – be they this Prime Minister or the other Prime Ministers to whom I shall come in a moment? The powers of the Royal Prerogative are abused by Prime Ministers to preserve the security services from public scrutiny. Ministers are appointed by the prerogative, as are the heads of the security services. The security services have the power to bug and burgle under the prerogative, just as the Postmaster General had the power to open letters under the prerogative. With that power, the Prime Minister decides on classification, defines security – through her ministers – prosecutes, or orders injunctions, appoints the judges and then appoints the chairman of the BBC to ensure that there is no public discussion of matters that she does not want to be discussed.

The BBC is supposed to be an independent agent. When its programme on the security services was banned, it should have broadcast forty-five minutes of silence, punctuated by the statement that the Government had banned the programme. Through the powers of patronage, the Prime Minister has reduced the BBC to a crawling, creeping servant of Government policy. She has followed that today with a three-line Whip designed to do to Tory Members what she has done to the BBC.

To be fair, I should say that all Prime Ministers have been the same. In case hon Members cannot wait for it to appear in my diaries, I should tell the House that James Callaghan was passionately opposed to a Freedom of Information Act. He loathed the idea of anyone knowing anything. There was a hint of memories of the armalite coming from the recesses of the mind during the speech of my right hon Friend the Member for Morley and Leeds, South. No Executive wants Parliament, the public or the press to criticise it effectively.

The most important matter is the relationship between Prime Ministers and the security services. We do not know whether Prime Ministers know too much about the security services, or whether the security services know too much about Prime Ministers, but neither position is satisfactory.

I understand why the Government believe that, but I do not understand why Parliament accepts it. Today, we have the power, if we choose, to carry this Bill into Committee – no more than that. Not even the hon Member for Aldridge-Brownhills (Mr Shepherd), who introduced the Bill with a lucid speech, honestly believes that he will get it through with the entrenched power of the Premier against him. After all, the final reserves of prerogative power of any Prime Minister is the witholding of honours from Tory Members who do not vote according to a three-line Whip. Peerages do not come so easily to those who have been difficult. I warn Conservative Members who might be influenced by the arguments that I understand they may not be invited to the royal garden parties if they are a bit rebellious.

But the House has the power to enforce its will today. By enforcing its will, it will not be endorsing the Act that would emerge from this Bill, but enforcing the right to debate the central questions at greater length. I have been in this place for far too long for my good, although that has been compensated for by the benefit which the House has received from my sacrifice. I did not think that I would live to be a Member of Parliament where clerks are vetted, research assistants are vetted, members of the press are vetted, Members are vetted and Mr Speaker receives a briefing on behaviour from the Serjeant-at-Arms. I did not think that I would live to serve in a Parliament vetted by Government. We were elected by the people to check and control the Government. Until we get that right, we cannot complain if we continue to have the problems from which we have suffered in recent years.

SOURCES

THE ARROGANCE OF POWER
Extracts taken from the House of Commons Official Report (*Hansard*) of proceedings on 21 November 1979, 18 February 1985, 27 January 1986, 14 February 1986, 28 October 1986, 27 January 1987 and 16 January 1988
SPYCATCHER
Extracts from a public reading of *Spycatcher* in Hyde Park, 2 August 1987

7
DISESTABLISHING THE ESTABLISHMENT

Power, Parliament and the People

The Labour movement is primarily concerned with the immediate problems confronting the people: unemployment, a run down of essential services, gross inequalities of wealth and income, the threat of war abroad and a 'law and order' tyranny at home.

Experience has shown that substituting Labour ministers for Tory ministers cannot achieve our objectives if we limit ourselves to the more humane and efficient management of capitalism, which depends on maintaining unacceptable inequality.

The Labour movement's commitment to parliamentary democracy, from the days of the Chartists, stems from the belief that the industrial organisation of labour, plus the use of the ballot box, can become the agents that will alter the structure of society. This will be done peacefully by electing a government with a majority in the House of Commons, which can then use the statute book and the machinery of the state to bring about that transformation by consent.

But the assumption that Parliament and the machinery of government, once they are at the disposal of an elected Labour majority, can be used freely to achieve the objectives of that administration raises a number of questions for socialists.

Traditionally, many on the Left have believed that the state machine in capitalist society existed primarily to uphold and re-enforce that system, whichever party is nominally in office. They sensed that it operated through its natural links with the Establishment, links that remain in existence whoever forms a government.

In recent years the continuity of the policy objectives of the mandarins in the Civil Service, and the power which they exercise, has come under close examination, and tends to confirm the Left's analysis. The role of top officials in the Treasury, the

Foreign Office, the Home Office and the Ministry of Defence in particular have been seen as having central significance in controlling economic policy, defence, the police, the intelligence services and Britain's relations with the rest of the world, whoever is in power.

Labour can win a majority. What then are the prospects for a Labour Cabinet, appointed personally by a Labour Prime Minister to form part of 'Her Majesty's Government', to take charge in a meaningful sense after they have received a popular mandate?

This question has come to the centre of discussion in the Labour Party for intensely practical reasons. It arises in part out of the necessary and proper post-mortem which followed the devastating election defeat in May 1979.

There were important achievements during those years in power, but none of those governments secured the central objective of bringing about 'a fundamental and irreversible shift in the balance of wealth and power in favour of working people and their families'. And none of them was even able to protect the hard-won gains that are now being dismantled.

It is natural, in searching for an explanation for this failure and in regrouping to secure a better future, that the role of the state should have been studied. It is equally natural that this study should have led to a charge of hostility to parliamentary democracy, for any deep analysis of the true nature of our system of government has led many people to question just how democratic it really is.

Let us consider the situation that would be created by the election of a Labour Government, with a working majority, at the end of this Parliament. Beneath the euphoria, all socialists will know that the real task of taking power will only just have begun.

True, a monetarist and militarist group of Tory ministers will have been swept into opposition. True, the new House of Commons will contain Labour MPs in sufficient numbers to repeal old legislation and enact new laws and budgets. True, there will be genuine good will among a majority of electors, or else we would not be there.

But in another sense nothing will have changed. Those who control the centres of financial, economic, military and administrative power, and those who own or run its mass media, will be meeting to discuss urgently the best way of preventing the new Government from carrying out policies to which they are bitterly opposed.

The House of Lords, determined to prevent its own abolition, will still have a huge Tory majority and will be planning how to use it to protect its own position and frustrate the wishes of the electors, perhaps with the help of the judges.

The senior ranks of the Civil Service, who have played a large part in shaping the policies of the out-going Government, will be in conclave to defend those policies and to deflect ministers from reversing them too far.

The defence chiefs, fearing the removal of their nuclear weapons and a cut-back of their budget to bring it in line with European levels of expenditure, will be discussing, probably with their NATO colleagues, how to obstruct the new Cabinet.

The Governor of the Bank of England will be considering how the City can be mobilised effectively to safeguard the profits it has been making from its global transactions.

And big business, together with the bankers and financial houses, will be arranging discreet gatherings to discuss how to insulate themselves from the effects of the new policies they fear will be introduced.

The security services, whose files will contain full entries on all the new MPs, will be hoping to influence the allocation of portfolios to exclude certain people from key jobs and to prevent those whom they dislike but who do get appointed from having access to information that MI5, MI6 and Special Branch regard as especially sensitive.

The newspaper proprietors will permit a short honeymoon for the Government in their editorials, partly because the public support for Labour, as expressed through the ballot box, will include some of their readers and cannot be ignored at the outset; partly to build up a wholly false reputation for their newspapers of having given the new Government 'a fair chance'; and partly because they may cherish a secret hope that a highly selective diet of skilful praise and criticism could be used to woo some Cabinet members away from their commitments.

In the Common Market Commission in Brussels and the NATO headquarters nearby, in the IMF and at the head offices of the multinationals, position papers will have been prepared of two kinds. The first will be for use in direct negotiations with the new Labour Government, to show how far these organisations are prepared to go to accommodate the Government's aspirations and how it would be impossibly dangerous to seek to go all the way with it.

The second set of strictly confidential papers would consist of contingency plans to frustrate those policies in case it became clear that Labour really meant business and could not be shifted by persuasion.

Across the Atlantic in the White House, the Pentagon, the State Department and the Treasury, they would be studying more detailed plans, based on long-term appreciations, updated regularly and given added urgency as soon as the polls in Britain had begun to hint at the possibility that a Labour Government might be elected. The options set before the President and the National Security Council would include every possibility, from an offer of extending special economic and defence aid to buy off unwelcome policies, to highly classified plans to discredit individuals in the Labour Government or destabilise it completely.

The listing of this formidable array of opposition which the next Labour Government will face is not intended to create a sense of despondency or to divert us from the tasks we have set ourselves.

Quite the reverse is the case. It is to encourage us to think through the consequences of what we have decided is necessary if we are to tackle the basic problems that beset society by methods that are both democratic and socialist.

The cruellest hoax we could play on the electorate would be to pretend that we could transform their prospects or realise their hopes without major reforms of the institutions that wield power in Britain, whoever sits in No. 10 or occupies the ministerial offices in Whitehall.

Those who say it will not be easy when Labour is returned to office are right, but not always for the reasons they believe. We must not deceive ourselves into believing that our opponents will accept fundamental change provided it is carried through democratically. They will not. Their interest lies in preserving the power and wealth that they have against all attempts to change it. It is we who are the advocates of democracy and they who only pay lip service to it.

When a Labour Government with socialist policies, and the will to implement them, is elected we shall soon learn that they will fight it all the way and seek to undermine it. That is why democracy, even more than socialist rhetoric, is so much feared and hated by those whose power derives not from a parliamentary majority but from the ownership and control of land and money, and the occupancy of key power bases in the administration, the military or the media.

It is for all these reasons that the next Labour Government's success or failure will depend critically on its readiness to adopt a major programme of institutional reform designed to widen and deepen the democratic influences in our society, at the same time as it implements economic and social reform.

The Crown prerogatives, most of which are exercised by ministers, confer immense powers which can, if abused, frustrate the wishes of the electorate and undermine democracy. The House of Lords still retains a crippling power of delay. The Prime Minister enjoys immense and unacceptable powers of personal patronage, working with a Civil Service elite in a highly secretive manner. They are outside the effective control of the House of Commons which has, in key respects, abandoned its responsibility to hold the Government to account, to itself and to the electors.

The Labour Party and the trade union movement are still held at arm's length from the Government, even when the party is in office and they suffer from serious defects in their own democracy, despite some improvements in recent years. Thus that direct connection between the people who are governed and those who govern, which should characterise a democratic system, is far from being effective, leaving much real power where it has always rested, free from the reach of public accountability.

Labour ministers may gain office from time to time, but Labour will never be in power and socialism will never be achieved however many electors vote for it.

It is against this background that the reforms we need can best be understood. They all involve practical action early in the lifetime of the Government, for which explicit endorsement should be sought in the manifesto.

The Right of the Electors to Know How the Government Works

The 1974 commitment to introduce a Freedom of Information Act to replace the oppressive Official Secrets Act was never honoured by the Labour Government and indeed was strongly resisted by it. This was not for the lack of a Commons majority, which was always available, given the consistent support of the Liberals and some Conservatives for such legislation.

Secrecy protects strong civil servants and weak ministers from parliamentary and public criticism and undermines Cabinet as well as Commons control, without the knowledge of the electorate.

The Right of an Elected House of Commons to Legislate for the People

This demand – on the face of it so simple and uncontroversial – would involve radical changes in our present constitution and our relations with the EEC and NATO.

It requires the abolition of the House of Lords, which consists of members who have inherited their seats in Parliament or have been appointed to it as peers, law lords or bishops. These men and women enjoy great legislative power – a complete veto in the case of delegated legislation and a damaging power of delay over all other Bills, save those certified as Money Bills. The Lords have a huge, permanent anti-Labour majority and even those who are Labour peers are usually converted to the merits of their House.

All the laws passed under the authority of the Treaty of Rome, none of which requires parliamentary approval or are subject to repeal by Parliament, have to be brought back under the control of our electors.

Full Commons Control of Crown Prerogatives

Parliamentary democracy, as it has developed in Britain, has two main characteristics. One is the right of every man and woman over eighteen to have a vote and use it to elect the House of Commons, a majority of whom are needed to sustain a Government.

The other is that the leader of the majority party is invited to form an administration ('Her Majesty's Government'), which then acquires the right to use the Crown prerogatives to control the Civil Service and Armed Forces and to proffer advice to the Crown, which by an established convention is regarded as mandatory.

Prerogative powers provide a virtual armoury of extra-parliamentary powers, from the declaration of a State of Emergency, through to the right to make orders in council, make war and sign treaties, grant reprieves and confer honours, all without explicit Commons approval or ratification.

It is high time that we looked at these powers too. For

example, all treaty-making powers should be made subject to parliamentary ratification. This practice, long established in the US Senate for example, would force Foreign Secretaries and their officials to be accountable to MPs exactly as other ministers are for their legislation.

Two prerogative powers only remain within the personal control of the Crown – the power to dissolve Parliament before the expiry of its full term, and the power to invite a person to form a Government.

The use of either prerogative power in a controversial manner in Britain would draw the monarchy into the heart of the political debate.

The best way to avoid this would be to follow the practice of other commonwealth countries where these powers are sub-contracted to the Governor-General and transfer the power of dissolution and the power to ask a person to form a Government – both of which are matters of high constitutional importance – to the Speaker of the House of Commons, subject to its confirmation by that body. The Speaker knows the Commons intimately and is therefore specially qualified to reach a judgement about the appropriate moment for granting a dissolution and who is most likely to command a majority. He stands apart from the political parties and is directly answerable to the Commons for the conduct of the chair.

The End of Patronage

The powers now concentrated in the hands of a modern British Prime Minister are enormous, have been growing over the years and now exceed those of an American President relative to Congress. This issue had been the subject of comment that goes way beyond the Labour Party.

The election of the Cabinet when Labour is in office is the next logical step in the process of accountability. It is inexplicable that Labour MPs should only be permitted to choose their own front bench when in opposition. If the PLP is to have real influence it must have the power by election to appoint and remove Cabinet ministers even if the Prime Minister is to allocate port-folios, subject to general PLP approval.

A similar power to appoint permanent secretaries to all departments, which makes the Prime Minister overwhelmingly powerful in comparison with his or her Cabinet colleagues, should also be modified by permitting ministers to approve their own Civil Service heads or have the power to secure their transfer. This would do more to establish democratic control of the Civil Service than any other reform.

The Labour Party should put an end to this absurd Hollywood version of medieval England, which reinforces the class system and replenishes the ranks of the establishment with working-class leaders who earn their promotion by means which may damage the interests of those they were originally elected to represent.

A Bigger Role for Labour MPs, the Labour Party and the Trade Unions when Labour is in Power

The Parliamentary Labour Party must be allowed to play a larger part in the implementation of Labour policy.

First, Labour MPs, in addition to electing the Cabinet each session, should be entitled to be consulted before portfolios are allocated, before major policy initiatives are decided, and before ministers are dismissed. Second, the subject groups of Labour MPs for each department should be invited to choose perhaps ten of their number to constitute the 'cabinet' for each elected minister to work with in each department.

In this way Labour MPs, who have a fund of experience that is never used, would be able to play a far more constructive role than has ever been permitted in earlier periods of Labour government.

In this context the party has a special responsibility for seeing that the interests of the affiliated trade unions are not ignored. When the Conservatives are in power they maintain close links with the financial and economic interests which they represent. These links do not have to be formalised because the Cabinet, senior civil servants, the City, big business, and the media owners and managers share the same economic interests, the same values and many of them came from the same social class.

Labour cannot and does not work that way at all. The unions and the party, which are voluntary organisations, can only function through their own democratic machinery by which collective decisions are slowly argued out and settled.

If a Labour government is to connect closely with the unions at all levels new mechanisms need to be developed. Openness of government proceedings could play a significant part in building such links. The process of government decision-making, which is often quite slow, could then go in parallel with trade union discussions, which would offer the best prospects of mutual influence.

More specifically, the trade unions should be invited to second staff to act as liaison officers in the private offices of all ministers, just as industrialists have been seconded to assist previous Conservative (and Labour) ministers in the past. The success of the next Labour Government is going to hinge on the development of a proper system of committees that brings the unions, the party and the Government closer together.

Socialists need to give at least as much attention to the institutions of the State as to the power structure of the economy, since both are riddled with privilege and they combine to deny the people of Britain their rightful inheritance.

Our efforts must go into defending our interests now and preparing for the day when we can secure them more fully by the election of a reforming socialist Government.

The Civil Service

Questions put by the Treasury and Civil Service Sub-Committee

Memorandum of Evidence

Q: Has the Civil Service as a whole or in departments any constitutional responsibility to come to a collective view of what the long-term interests of the country are?

If so, how is this view evolved and expressed, particularly to ministers?

What evidence is there of the means by which conflicts between such a collective official view and Government policy have been resolved?

A: The Civil Service as a whole, or departments within it, do not have any machinery for coming to a collective view and the power within them is concentrated in the hands of the permanent secretary who may consult anyone he or she chooses.

The regular meetings that take place within Whitehall which are attended by permanent secretaries, represent the highest centre of official power with direct access to the Prime Minister and to all other ministers.

The permanent secretaries enjoy all the power associated with a permanent bureaucracy, have many opportunities to set the Cabinet agenda and, because of their power in their own departments, to shape the agenda in departments as well.

Moreover when they have reached a view they have the capacity to see that that view is known to all the senior officials in all departments, and that simultaneous pressure can be brought to bear on all ministers to secure their acceptance of that view.

They also have the power to frustrate policies that are produced by individual ministers by mobilising the support of other departments and other ministers against it, and the power, through the Cabinet Secretary, to undermine the position and reputation of a minister whose views are unacceptable to them.

The main instrument for following up the policies which the permanent secretaries support is the advice they give to departmental ministers, and in the sub-structure of official committees which prepare the papers for the ministerial committees, and for Cabinet.

The Think Tank set up under Lord Rothschild carried this process of official policy making a stage further in that his group was free to initiate policy, and Sir Kenneth Berrill who succeeded him was invited to attend ministerial meetings on the same basis as ministers, and to put in papers which ran counter to those submitted by ministers, which provided a direct method of countering the policies that the Civil Service did not like.

On one occasion I have known a permanent secretary who actually refused to help to prepare a Cabinet paper which his minister wished to submit to his colleagues.

There is another aspect of the role of the Civil Service which should be noted, namely its position as part of an international official committee, as for example in the European Communities. Under the Treaty of Rome, ministers of member countries are only allowed to accept, or reject, proposals that come to them from the Commission, and are not allowed to submit papers of their own. This system, common on the continent but unknown under British practice, reserves the power of policy initiation to civil servants, and at COREPER, (Committee of Permanent Representatives) at ambassadorial level, civil servants will negotiate arrangements with the Commission, which are then presented to ministers as a packaged fait accompli.

This has then to be accepted or rejected en bloc, which involves a major reversal of the normal relationship between officials and ministers.

Similar official negotiations may go on under other treaty arrangements, as with GATT, the IMF or NATO, where the officials will do the preliminary work, and it will be presented to ministers for approval, but the difference between these proceedings and the EEC is that, in respect of the latter, there is an outcome which may not need to come to Parliament at all and is directly enforceable under Community law.

Indeed so simple and extra-parliamentary is the procedure for community law-making, that civil servants who want to get certain legislation enacted without all the fuss and bother that

is needed to find a place in the Queen's Speech, and the conse-
quential booking of precious legislative time, may find it
attractive to steer their proposals through the Community
procedures, where the civil servants are in charge and the
House of Commons is not involved.

I cite these examples because we are all tempted to ignore
the immense impact that Community membership has had
upon our domestic legislation, upon the relationship between
ministers and officials, and upon the relationship between
ministers and Parliament under the written constitution which
we adopted upon entry to the EEC in 1973.

Q: Does the convention limiting ministerial access to papers of
previous administrations indicate a wider responsibility than
that to current ministers?
Are there any such other indications?

A: The restriction over the papers that new governments are
permitted to see is not, of course, absolute since records relating
to international negotiations, undertaken by previous governments, which carry a continuing obligation, or may not be
concluded, are disclosed to incoming administrations, though
at the discretion of officials.

Obviously officials who serve successive governments know
more than any of the differing groups of ministers whom they
serve, and are able, by discriminating between those pieces
of information which they do pass on, and those which they
withhold, to influence policy making.

This may apply in other ways in that, when there is a reshuffle, an incoming minister from the same party may never
be told what were the decisions reached by his predecessor,
and as he is in ignorance of that, a reversal of his predecessor's
policy can be carried through.

Alternatively civil servants may adhere to a decision of his
predecessor, without putting the same point to his successor,
and prevent a change of policy from being accomplished.

This once occurred, in a case of which I have knowledge,
when a minister decided that he did not want to be troubled
with a particular matter so meant that his successor was never
given any papers by officials on that subject thereafter.

There is another aspect of the role and power of officials
which merits consideration, and it relates to sensitive matters
of military, intelligence or nuclear importance, when a minister
may be excluded from knowledge either on the direct instruc-

tions of the Prime Minister, or arising out of international arrangements as with the supervision of our security services by the United States, or in respect of the subordination of our nuclear policy to the US atomic authorities.

In theory, the Prime Minister is in a position to vary all these arrangements but it cannot be safely assumed that either he or she will always be told what is going on. Britain is in practice governed by the Prime Minister of the day, together with the permanent secretaries, the heads of the armed forces and the security services, and is free to bring into his, or her, confidence such ministerial colleagues as he or she wishes to consult.

And the instruments for government are increasingly the prerogative powers, loaned by the Crown to each administration, of which by far the most significant are the treaty-making powers, which are not subject to any form of parliamentary approval, and where, by definition, the role of the Civil Service is correspondingly the greatest.

Q: What should permanent secretaries and the Head of the Civil Service do if they believe that the policies of the Government of the day are damaging the Civil Service?

A: The Civil Service is, in theory, there to serve the Government of the day, and its capacity to do that depends on its independence from improper pressure. But to state that proposition baldly is to oversimplify the situation, and hence to confuse the issues that the sub-committee is considering. To begin with a distinction must be made between the policy function, and the more straightforward executive function, which can be undertaken in a practical way.

In constitutional theory there should only be two routes to the corridors of power – the one through popular election and the other through a, rigidly enforced, selection of people based upon their capacity to maintain high professional standards of administration. But, in practice, it is not like that at all, and ministers want to have permanent secretaries and senior officials who are actually sympathetic to what they want to do, while officials very often want to bend ministers to their own will.

If a Government stays in office long enough, the opportunity for promotion of politically sympathetic officials will come automatically as retirement vacancies occur, and any Prime Minister who failed to use those opportunities for placing the people he or she liked into the top jobs would be failing in elementary common sense.

But where does that leave those people when there is a change of administration and a new minister, from a new Government, is saddled with a permanent secretary who was probably the real architect of the very policy the new minister was elected to reverse? There is no easy answer to this problem but the options open to those concerned are obvious. For the civil servant there is retirement, or more likely the chance of an appointment elsewhere, in the public services, or in business. The number of senior civil servants who have moved from Whitehall into firms with which they have had dealings, as officials, needs to be examined for other reasons, but at least it takes them away from a task that would be impossible for them, and for their new minister. A new Prime Minister may then be able to fill those vacancies with officials thought to be more sympathetic to the policies of the new Government, but that is a hit and miss affair, and it politicises the Civil Service in a very haphazard way.

Another solution, which has become more commonly adopted, is for ministers to bring in advisers, who work closely with him or her and, though denied executive powers, have immense influence, as they are intended to have. It is of enormous help for a minister, in a department, to have access to sources of expert advice from politically sympathetic people, and, under our present arrangements, it is really not possible to function without them.

But the danger of adopting the American 'spoils system' has to be guarded against, since it brings dangers of its own. Probably the best defence against that danger would be for the names of all advisers to be listed and put to the House of Commons for approval, since this would provide some safeguard against abuse. But the real answer may lie in the re-examination of the proposals made by Fred Jowett MP before the First World War, when he suggested the appointment of ministerial 'cabinets' of Members of Parliament who would go into a department, with each minister, and assist him or her in the running of that department. At least such a proposal would retain the principle of power by election, but the consequences for the role of select committees would need to be considered if a large number of government backbenchers were to be co-opted into government in that way.

It must however be said that there would be some advantages for the integrity of the democratic system if it were to be buttressed by allowing MPs to be used to provide a stronger elective element in policy making.

Q: Should restrictions on political activity be revised or are they adequate and acceptable?

A: The political rights now available to civil servants ought to be extended, under new arrangements, that would fit in with the provisions of a Freedom of Information Act.

As things stand the discreet nods and winks of the permanent secretaries in the right places, which everyone knows go on, are accepted as normal, whereas far less serious breaches of the rules governing political activities by more junior officials would lay them open to severe disciplinary measures.

Q: What is the duty of a civil servant if a minister rejects policy advice and proceeds in a way which he believes may be impracticable or positively harmful?

A: If a minister, having considered the options available, decides on one which the Civil Service think impracticable or harmful, it is still its duty to help the minister to carry through the decision that he or she has made.

Ministers are under no legal obligation to consult their own civil servants, or to take their advice, though it would be foolish not to do so, or not to listen carefully to what they say.

But political decisions are essentially political, and there can be no objectively right and wrong way to tackle any problem. In practice, there are many methods open to civil servants to obstruct their ministers, or to place information before them that points in the direction that the Civil Service want the minister to follow.

The Official Secrets Act, which protects the process of decision-making from any public scrutiny, greatly helps the Civil Service in their objective, since, if it is not known that a decision is to be taken beforehand, the only stream of advice that is available is the official advice, thus keeping the minister in ignorance of other solutions. Since some ministers are nervous of being subjected to outside criticism, there is a temptation to shield behind the official advice, and rely upon the formidable Civil Service machine to protect them and, since many civil servants know that their own power and influence depends upon secrecy, it is true to say that the Official Secrets Act is sustained by a common interest between weak ministers and strong civil servants – both of whom believe it to be to their advantage to sustain it.

Where a minister rejects official advice, the power of the Civil Service to frustrate him or her derives from the network of official contacts within Whitehall, which carries the news to other departments. These will then brief their own ministers to write letters of objection to the 'recalcitrant' minister, to ask that the matter be taken to a committee, or to Cabinet itself, and there to kill off his proposal, or to suggest that the matter be looked at by an official committee, which will then recommend against.

The Think Tank can also be used for this purpose, or, if necessary, British posts abroad, as in Brussels or Washington, for example, may be induced to send telegrams to express their anxiety that the course proposed may be harmful to British interests. It has also been known for senior civil servants to leak the disagreement to the mass media, and then bring external pressure to bear to shift policy back again.

Q: Are there circumstances when a minister could require a civil servant to release information in a manner contrary to obligations under the OSA and the memorandum?

Have there been examples of such official leaking?

A: This is the most common form of leaking, and it goes on all the time, in the name of briefing, ordered, or assented to, by ministers who are the biggest leakers of all, topped by the Prime Minister, who leaks through his or her press office all that No 10 Downing Street wants to get across, on a daily basis.

It would be quite wrong to suppose that the OSA provides any sort of real protection for official secrets, since the leaking and briefing network – undertaken under the Lobby system – that involves ministers, MPs and civil servants, constitutes the mechanism by which all forms of news management takes place.

One of the reasons why a Freedom of Information Act has not been passed, is that it would replace that system, which works to the advantage of all those who take part in it, and it would provide an accurate flow of news that would undermine the present cosy relationships that official secrecy encourages.

Examination of Witness

Q: Does the Civil Service have legitimate interests of its own in your opinion?

A: Oh, yes and the Civil Service has clear policies of its own. There is a document – I do not know how I am covered on this – there is a document called 'Brief for Incoming Ministers' – I have the copy given to me in 1974 after the second election. That document is a document prepared by the Civil Service during the election campaign, because, as the Committee will appreciate, when Parliament is dissolved, civil servants stop even formally working for the Government of the day. They go away and read both manifestos and prepare a brief for each possible Government that might be elected. In that document, which is a very important document, handed to an incoming minister when he is very busy, so he probably does not read it, you will discover what the departmental policy of that department is, presented to make it attractive to the incoming minister. I have only, of course, ever seen briefs to incoming Labour ministers. But, for example, in the illustration Mr Sedgemore gave a moment ago, the brief for Eric Varley in 1974 to the Department of Energy made it clear that the department wished to have American reactors. I declined to accept it and it did not happen. It came back again for the present Government. I think if you followed those briefs over a period of years, you would find Civil Service policy is very often – if not always – implemented after a passage of time. What the civil servants will offer a minister is this arrangement: 'If you support the policy we believe in, we will put out to the press what a very able minister you are, and help you to pretend that the policy you are following is the policy you said you would follow in the election!' That is the nature of the deal and unless people understand that deal they do not understand the power of the Civil Service and their infinite skill in using it until they get their way.

Q: Can I question you on loyalty of civil servants to ministers?

A: Well, I think they are very free with it. If I take the Department of Energy where I followed Mr Jenkin, on the question of the pressure water reactor, my department wanted it very much and I considered the argument and I said: 'I want an advanced gas cooled reactor'. Then the permanent secretary marched into my office, with all his officials, including the deputy secretaries, the chief scientist and he said: 'We want the pressure water reactor' and I said: 'Well, I have taken a contrary view, I want you to draw a paper on the advanced gas cooled reactor', and he declined to do so. I had to go to my political advisers to do it and the permanent secretary then briefed the CPRS and other departments in the Cabinet against me. This is one example, I could give you others but that is probably the most important.

Q: Mr Benn you say in your paper that any Prime Minister who failed to take the chance to appoint to senior vacancies civil servants who were 'politically supportive' of the Government would be failing in 'elementary common sense'? In your experience did that actually happen?

A: I had a number of permanent secretaries, one Sir Richard Clarke – now dead – who was outstanding. I used to have great arguments with him but in the end when the decision was made he loyally supported. I also had two very unhappy experiences with permanent secretaries but the experience that burned most clearly in my mind was when Barbara Castle wished to get rid of her permanent secretary Sir Thomas Padmore at the Ministry of Transport. When she tried to get rid of him it was leaked to the press – a classic case – and the Prime Minister was confronted with such an angry group of mandarins that Padmore remained at the Ministry. So, I never tried to get rid of my permanent secretary because I knew it would not work. I had to find other ways of getting advice that was helpful. I think you have to face the fact that the one thing civil servants will stick together about is if a minister tries to replace a permanent secretary by somebody more favourable. If there is a vacancy, then that is a different position but I was never faced with the position of having a vacancy in a department in all the eleven years that I was there. I always had to live with the person I inherited. Had there been a vacancy I would have insisted on having somebody broadly sympathetic to the policies that we were pursuing and I think any Prime Minister would be bound to do the same.

Q: When Mrs Thatcher has been criticised for making senior appointments amongst people who are broadly in support of her ideology, you would support her in saying she was only acting according to precedent as had been done under the previous administration?

A: I think every Prime Minister behaves the same way and I think one of the problems of the headlines of the past few weeks is to give the impression that the conduct and motivation and power and so on, of one Prime Minister is in any way different from any others.

Q: You also said, Mr Benn, that senior civil servants inherited by a new administration can be retired or found posts elsewhere. Do you actually advocate this?

A: Well, I think you have this problem. I do not know what the future holds for anybody but I must confess I would not be prepared to work with somebody in a department who had been there before and was, candidly, a major architect of the policy that an incoming Labour Government had – as it were – been elected to replace. I do recall the case of Sir Richard Clarke, to whom I paid tribute (I did not appoint him) – he was very quickly retired after the defeat of the Labour Government in 1970. He was given an honorific post to write the 'History of the Ministry of Technology' and then left the public service. I think that must surely have been because Mr Heath did not want such a committed interventionist to run a Government under Geoffrey Rippon and then later John Davies and, therefore, he was quickly shunted into the background. I imagine that that would be a proper and sensible thing to do.

Q: Supposing that the present exaltation of Prime Minister's power was to diminish and we were to get back to something approaching Cabinet Government on the classic lines, in order to make sure that policies of the Cabinet of the day were being implemented throughout Government, would it not still be necessary for each permanent secretary to consider whether his Secretary of State was, in fact, carrying out the policies of the Cabinet rather than different policies of his or her own?

A: Well, I think you have to have rules and I have never argued against that. What I think is outrageous about the rules [Questions of Procedure for Ministers] I have submitted to you – and am making available to other Members of the House – is that those rules never have been collectively discussed. They never went to Cabinet, they were never disclosed to Parliament. Thus so far as this House is concerned there are two classes of Members: those who had those rules given to them and are expected to obey them for life and those who have not. The House has been so craven in its submission to the Executive, it has never asked for them and that is one problem. The other problem is the problem of what is meant by real collectivity. Now, real collectivity would mean that matters were brought to Cabinet but if Prime Ministers want to avoid opposition in the Cabinet, they set up what are called 'Misc' or 'Gen' committees (miscellaneous and general). They do not tell other ministers that they have been set up. They then meet in secret, reach conclusions and then you get minutes – as I had from Mr Wilson – saying that even though they are only Cabinet committees they carry the full weight of collective Cabinet responsibility. You see, it is a bit difficult if you are asked to carry responsibility for something you do not know about, particularly as Mr Callaghan said in the House of Commons in answer to a question from Mrs Thatcher: 'collective Cabinet responsibility only applies when I say it does.' It is not a constitutional principle, it is an instrument of power by Prime Ministers of the day. Now, in different circumstances, where there was genuine collectivity, permanent secretaries would realise you could not bypass one minister and go to a Prime Minister and get that particular minister isolated enough to be dismissed.

The Crown, the Church and Democratic Politics

The Church of England, which is an established Church, is in a unique position to warn the Crown not to intervene on the question of sanctions against South Africa, or indeed on any other political issue. It may be tempting for those, including many Churchmen, who think that the British Government should impose sanctions, or who regard its domestic policies as uncaring, to welcome an intervention by the Crown. But the Crown has no constitutional right to interfere in political matters, which must be decided by Parliament, even where the future of the Commonwealth is involved, important as that is. If the Crown was allowed to act against one Government it would then feel free to act against a future Labour Government, on any policy, to which it was opposed. We saw that actually happen in Australia when the Governor-General used his prerogative to dissolve Parliament to remove an elected Labour Government under Prime Minister Gough Whitlam.

Those of us who want to get rid of apartheid, and campaign for social justice, should remember that, throughout our history all progressive change has been secured by moral teaching, and by popular pressure brought to bear on Parliament; and more recently through the ballot box and in the House of Commons, and not through the agency of the Crown.

Unless we understand that, and re-affirm this constitutional principle now, we could find that in the pretence of helping to establish democracy in South Africa, we were actually undermining it in Britain. It was, in part, to guard against the risk of any Crown intervention in their domestic politics that many Commonwealth countries decided to become Republics. If the Crown in Britain were ever to act, politically, to by-pass, undermine, challenge or threaten the authority of the House of Commons, or the sovereign rights of citizens who elect it, a much more fundamental re-appraisal of its constitutional role would become inevitable.

The idea of having an established Church is itself an anomaly, and all Churches should be free of all state control. Here, then, is an issue where the Church should be speaking up, both against apartheid and social injustice, and against any interference by the Crown in democratic politics.

A Moral Crisis

Most of my life at Westminster has been spent during a period when Parliament and politics were contained within the consensus, and most of the argument was about which party or persons could best manage a progress that seemed to be inevitable.

But however we look at it now everyone is aware of a sea—change in our circumstances. The industrial decline has gone on unchecked and whole areas of the country have been destroyed. There has been a lack of investment – a world slump – and narrowing options for those who have tried to manage that system. Mass unemployment has returned, with the hopelessness that goes with it, welfare has been eroded and the arms race gobbles up money as if there were no other demands for our resources. We are witnessing the serious contemplation of nuclear war as an instrument of policy, an idea that had been entirely banished from the minds of my generation – who returned from the war believing that that must be the end of war, using atomic weapons.

But above all we have witnessed a failure to satisfy the basic and simple needs of our people, which are moderate and not extreme: for jobs, and homes, and schools and hospitals, dignity in retirement and peace. Welfare capitalism has failed.

From the politics of progress we are now into the politics of regress. Of course, new technologies are still developing – television, computers, robots and nuclear power – but those technologies are now imperceptibly shifting and they are being seen not as agents of expansion but in some cases as instruments of repression.

I can visualise a police state brought about by nothing more complicated than the fact that half the population might be working in such highly technical industries that they all have to be watched in case they do anything that dislocates our vulnerable and interdependent system and the other half might be permanently unemployed having to be watched in case they cause trouble because they will not accept a permanent life on the dole queue.

I believe that what we are witnessing is not just – nor even primarily – an economic crisis. It is a political, a social, a constitutional and a moral crisis. And we are seeing a widening gap between Parliament and people deriving from the fact that those who see no answer to their problems drift into hopelessness, apathy, protest or violence, combined with a lack of credibility that attaches to politicians and their pronouncements.

To understand all this we have to go back to our history. It is currently argued by the Establishment that what is happening in our society is due to the appearance of left-wing extremism. By contrast, I think we are witnessing the reappearance of right-wing extremism.

If you look back at the 1930s, only Roosevelt's America, which was the greatest capitalist country in the world, opted for Keynesianism and the 'New Deal'. Most of the countries of Europe faced with the economic problems that now face us – Italy, Germany, Spain, Portugal, Greece and today Turkey – opted for a very different solution to the crisis of their economies. And the characteristic of that reaction can be seen quite clearly by identifying its main features – nationalism, chauvinism, xenophobia, militarism, contempt for true democracy, the hatred of trade unionism, the emergence of the corporate state and the harassment of dissent.

Those same right-wing ideas are now at work again in our society. Most of them lie at the heart of that huddling together of the Establishment. But outside Parliament the reaction that is emerging to the crisis reveals a great vitality of popular movements.

We all know that the trade unions, weakened by unemployment, harassed by legislation, fearing the re-introduction of the Combination Acts and suffering from media attacks on such a scale as to make it almost inconceivable that they can survive, are not at the moment in such a strong position as they were some time ago.

But the unions are no less determined to defend themselves and to find new ways of expressing the interests of their members.

The peace movement has grown rapidly with a very strong moral appeal both to the young and to the old who have been through the experience of war. The Church of England has come out with its important document on the Church and the Bomb, and the women of Greenham Common have been prepared to pay a price for their beliefs by going to prison.

The ecological movement is reacting strongly against the rape of our environment. Like the Green movement in Germany, it argues that the stewardship of the land is an essential interest of every generation, going back to what was said about the earth being 'a common treasury of mankind' – an old Leveller and Digger plea – and to common ownership espoused by many generations from John Ball to Lloyd George.

The black community, suffering most strongly from unemployment, and feeling itself harassed and experiencing racism, is determined to establish its right to be treated like other citizens.

The devolution movement, now strong again in Scotland, is only waiting to express itself in a new form through Labour's old demand for Home Rule. Elsewhere unemployment is bringing about the return of municipal socialism: Ken Livingstone's vitality in London; David Blunkett's in Sheffield; and in the West Midlands. And if devolution applies to Ireland how could any of us really believe that a combination of the Royal Ulster Constabulary and the SAS will hold us in Ireland for another 300 years. It is a ludicrous supposition.

The women's movement is perhaps the most important of all these popular movements because women are a majority in our society and the victory of the suffragettes did not bring to them all the gains they expected when they sought the ballot box as a route to equality.

The Disestablishment of the Church of England

I would like to take this opportunity to argue the case for the liberation of the Anglican Church from the British State by the disestablishment of the Church of England.

Though I was confirmed as an Anglican I have, over the years, become more and more interested in the relevance of the social message of Jesus the carpenter of Nazareth about peace, justice and the brotherhood and sisterhood of all humanity, from which so much of the socialist faith derives, and less and less concerned with matters of doctrine, mystery and mythology, though I deeply respect those whose beliefs centre on the creeds.

I was brought up to believe in 'the priesthood of all believers' and retain considerable scepticism about those bishops and clergy who might claim a prescriptive right to interpose their own interpretation of the gospels, or the faith, between the people and the Creator – still more if those same bishops have been appointed by political patronage.

In short, I regard myself as a serious student of the teachings of Jesus – no more and no less.

My argument is a simple one and can be briefly summarised. It is that the teachings of Jesus, about brotherhood and sisterhood and peace, and the need to preach them freely, have acquired a new urgency and importance in the crisis which now threatens to overwhelm the world, and must necessarily lead many Christians to challenge the role of the State as the instrument of Government, and the status quo which it sustains, and hence should not be subject to State power.

The debate about the establishment of the Church of England goes far back into our history, and has, in the past, aroused great passions. As recently as 1970 the Chadwick Commission on 'Church and State' dealt with this very issue.

Britain has a tradition of Christianity dating back many

centuries and the Synod of Whitby in 664 recognised the Pope as the head of the Church in England, with powers over its organisation and theology. He also had discretion in the appointment of archbishops and bishops, and supervision over the work and discipline of the Church – with considerable powers over taxation. Indeed, in 1376 a petition to the House of Commons protested that the taxes paid to the Pope 'amounts to five times the tax from all the King's annual benefits from the whole kingdom'.

Canon Law was made in Rome and modified to meet local customs. Moreover, the King depended upon the Church to provide financial, diplomatic and administrative talent. In that sense, the Church was established even during those centuries before the Reformation and the break with Rome; because it was the religion of the Crown, and successive monarchs upheld the authority of the Church and, in turn, had their authority upheld by the Church.

The Crown accepted papal supremacy because it embodied the doctrine that the King derived his legitimacy and authority by 'divine right', which the Church then defended against republicans, democrats, pretenders to the throne and other troublemakers. The survival of the Coronation as a quasi-sacrament is a reminder of that principle. It was equally convenient for the Pope, who required the submission of the King in matters of faith and relied upon the King to protect the Church against heresy, schism, apostasy and other troubles. Thus was Henry VIII recognised as a Defender of the Faith for his denunciation of Martin Luther in 1521, a title retained by successive monarchs to this day, centuries after the break with Rome, of which we are reminded with the abbreviated words FID DEF (or just F D) on our coins.

Nor should it be thought that this medieval version of the position of the Crown has vanished from the teachings of some clergy. A few weeks ago I visited Canewdon parish church in Essex and the vicar, the Rev. Norman Kelly, gave me his parish letter dated November 1982, in which he had written: 'The Monarch, the Queen, is the Law, and no one else . . . Why cannot the Queen do wrong and be prosecuted like us? Because the Monarch is the source of law, just as God cannot sin, because God is the source of goodness.'

The conflict which developed between the Pope and Henry VIII culminated in a complete break and the Acts of Supremacy of 1534, and those that followed it, required all subjects to recognise the Crown as head of the new Church of England,

and to accept that Church as the only legitimate Church. This was a political and not a theological breach. It protected the State from criticism by the Church, thus creating the very problem which now strengthens the State and weakens the Church.

The real issue hinged on who should exercise ecclesiastical power in England, and the controversy over the King's marriage to Anne Boleyn in 1533, which the Pope would not allow, was the occasion rather than the cause of the dispute. But what emerged was a nationalised Church, suppressing others, first subject to the King's personal authority; then, as the powers of the Crown came, over the centuries, to be shared with Parliament and people, the control of the Church passed with it.

Theological arguments ebbed and flowed within the Church, and Parliament insisted upon conformity with its decisions. The Blasphemy Act of 1697, which made it a criminal offence for Christians to 'deny any one of the persons in the Holy Trinity to be God', was only repealed in 1967. The Bible, long kept out of the hands of the laity for fear that it might undermine the authority of the priests, and encourage those who were campaigning for social justice, could only be printed by the authority of the King, as it had first been by Henry VIII. The Book of Common Prayer was a schedule to the 1662 Act of Uniformity and the original text, in the Houses of Parliament, still carries the jagged ribbons by which it was attached to that Act. These successive acts of uniformity were strictly enforced against all dissenters and independents.

The Royal prerogative, by which archbishops, bishops, deans and others were appointed, was transferred to the de facto control of successive prime ministers who still today are free to exercise their discretion between candidates recommended by the Church's Crown Appointments Commission, as Mrs Thatcher did in appointing Bishop Leonard to the diocese of London in 1981, though it is believed he was not the first choice of the Church.

The two archbishops and the bishops of London, Durham and Winchester automatically sit in the House of Lords along with others who enter, in rotation by seniority, all exercising, as Lords Spiritual, their rights to speak and vote as legislators. At the same time Anglican priests are held to be disqualified from election to the House of Commons on the grounds that they are represented by their bishops in the House of Lords – a disqualification criticised by the Bishop of Bath and Wells in his 1982 Christmas message. The argument for this disqualification is not sustainable since the appointment of bishops precludes a democratic election from that clerical 'representation'.

In addition, the Church has its own Assembly for handling its own internal affairs, which was made possible by the Enabling Act.

In practice, the Church of England has become a residual and comprehensive spiritual home for all who wish to use its services in the parishes in which they live, providing official support for the role of religion under the Crown as part of the social fabric of our society, now tolerant of all religions. Opposition to disestablishment would come from those who accept this system and fear that if its continuity was disturbed it might destabilise and secularise our whole way of life and diminish the influence of religion in all its manifestations.

We have grown so accustomed to these arrangements that their manifest absurdities and dangers are hardly noticed and rarely discussed in public.

How, for example, can we justify a situation where the Monarch combines the functions of being, at one and the same time, supreme governor of the Church of England when in England, but who changes her denomination to preside over the Church of Scotland when in Scotland – even though in that capacity she enjoys no power of patronage nor can Parliament intervene in Scottish Church affairs.

Is it not strange that the Church of England, which still will not allow the ordination of women to the priesthood, should accept a woman as its supreme governor, albeit with powers that do not extend into spiritual matters?

How can a Church preserve its spiritual integrity when its Prayer Book may still, in theory, be amended, or a new one rejected, as in 1928, by a Parliament composed of members who are not required to be Anglicans or even Christians? How can the Church accept a situation in which its archbishops and bishops are appointed by a Prime Minister who could be a Catholic, a Jew, a Congregationalist, a Humanist, a Muslim or a Hindu?

Suppose for a moment that the Church of England was not now established and imagine the public outcry there would be if a Member of Parliament were to demand the nationalisation of that Church to subject its leaders to political patronage and control of the order of its services. Or suppose it was argued that State control should now be extended to cover the Catholic,

Nonconformist, Jewish, Buddhist, Hindu or Muslim communities.

These are all powerful arguments for disestablishment, but the case is stronger still if we examine the actual effects of having an established Church in the current situation.

Take first the attitude of Christians to the issue of nuclear war. Many Christians who are not pacifists have now concluded that the old doctrine of a just war cannot apply to the production, ownership or use of nuclear weapons which would escalate armed conflict to the levels of genocide.

The Bishop of Salisbury, who chaired the Committee which wrote the report 'The Church and the Bomb', has raised this very issue and has won wide public support for its conclusions even though it was rejected by the Synod. In 1982 the Assembly of the Church of Scotland voted by 255 votes to 143 in favour of unilateral nuclear disarmament.

But could the established Church of England take up a position on nuclear weapons that brought it into direct conflict with the Government, while the Crown remained the titular head of both Church and State? Mr Peter Blaker, the Minister of State for Defence, made this point on ITN on 6 August 1982, when he said: 'Obviously we would not be happy if the Church of England was to adopt a policy different from that of the Government.'

Even the mild and reasonable arguments for the spirit of reconciliation, which the Archbishop of Canterbury introduced into his sermon at the Service of Thanksgiving at St Paul's Cathedral after the Falklands War, apparently incurred the displeasure of the Prime Minister, who seems to have wanted a more militaristic celebration of the victory. And why not, since she appoints both archbishops and bishops?

Given that power of patronage, what bishop or cleric, with hopes of moving into Lambeth Palace or Bishopthorpe, would now dare to mount a sustained campaign against the militarism and jingoism which are officially blessed from No 10 Downing Street?

But even if all these problems could be resolved, a national-ised Church could never take its proper place in the world ecumenical movement. Yet the teachings of Jesus have spread across the world and know no national boundaries. Like the ideas of socialism, they are international in outlook and perspec-tive. That is another powerful reason for liberating the Church from the control of any nation state with its national, rather than its international, outlook. Religious conviction is also a very personal act and cannot be regimented by legislation or enforced by the State. So, both the international nature of Christianity and its reflection in personal faith point away from the idea of having a State religion.

I believe that the time has come to begin a national campaign for disestablishment. How it is to be done can be safely left for future discussion. It would certainly end all ministerial and parliamentary control over appointments, doctrine and worship, and end the automatic right of bishops to sit in the House of Lords. It would necessarily free the Monarch of the day to worship in any way that he or she might wish, or not at all, as a member of any Church or none.

The financial arrangements would need to be looked at separately, and if Parliament thought it right that any public money should be paid to the Church of England, for example for the upkeep of cathedrals or church buildings, the financial claims of other denominations would need to be considered on the basis of absolute equality.

All this could be settled once the principle of disestablishment had been agreed. There are of course clear precedents to guide us. The Church in Wales was disestablished in 1920 after the passage of the 1914 Welsh Church Act. Since then the Crown has not had the power to appoint bishops in Wales and such bishops do not sit in the House of Lords, and no significant body of opinion has been expressed in favour of re-establishing it as a State Church.

There is certainly support within the Church of England for disestablishment and many in the Anglican community worldwide might welcome and approve the liberation of the Church of England to release it to work more effectively. Disestablishment might also appeal to the large Catholic community, to the Free Churches and even to the Church of Scotland, which is in a special position, established but not under direct State control. In addition, there are over a million Jews, Buddhists, Hindus, Muslims and Sikhs and, according to the gallup polls, over a quarter of the whole population who would classify themselves as Humanists, following no particular faith, who might favour a change that gave them equality of status.

The case for disestablishment thus rests on various grounds: historical and theological; practical and moral; constitutional and democratic; international and equitable. But the strongest case of all, as it would need to be argued within the Anglican community, would necessarily hinge on the argument for liberation. As the crisis of our society deepens, the moral basis that must underpin all political judgements is becoming clearer and clearer, and the Church must be liberated from its subservience to the State.

Britain needs a liberation theology which has the courage to preach against the corruption of power by speaking for those who are its victims. Nowhere is that more necessary than in the inner cities where the poverty and deprivation are most acute, and where hard-pressed Anglican clergy feel themselves under the greatest pressure compared to their colleagues with more prosperous suburban or rural parishes. The Church needs freedom, to challenge the decisions of government, Parliament and the whole Establishment, and the materialist values which have elevated the worship of money above all else – and the people need to know that these rotten values are not endorsed by a State religion.

If democracy is to reflect through its decisions the deeper needs of humanity, and its aspirations for international peace and justice, and for brotherhood and sisterhood in our relations with each other, we must now break the link between Church and State.

Television in a Democracy

I would like to judge the role of the media, and particularly television, against the enormity of the perceived experiences and problems of the people in this country today. There are three, or probably, in truth, four million people out of work; our public services are being run down; we have an enormous arms race in progress, and indeed, almost every problem that has been discussed and has caused disturbing repercussions of thought throughout the whole of our history is now back on the agenda.

It is a very remarkable period politically, and, in this situation, there are a lot of interests involved. People inevitably perceive life through their own eyes. If you are one of the 8 million people living below the poverty level, or if you are one of the many hundreds of thousands of people waiting for a home, or if you are a woman who was in work but has now been thrown out of work and driven back into the home, if you are a member of the black community where unemployment – particularly among young blacks – is far, far higher than among others, if you are a trade unionist engaged in some attempt to protect your own living standards and the living standards of your members: that experience is the beginning of your perception of society.

If you take the view of the monetarists, now represented very strongly in the Cabinet, the problem is that we have a lazy workforce and incompetent managers and trouble-makers in the trade unions; and if only we could concentrate on high productivity and greater discipline against these lawless elements in society, then everything would be all right, and Phoenix-like out of the ashes of an old economy would grow a new one. That is a very rough, but I hope not unfair, account of the monetarist position, as we hear it on TV every day.

If you take the view of what are now called the 'mould-breakers', who actually represent the old consensus from the post-war years, the problem is not best dealt with by mass unemployment, but is dealt with by a statutory incomes policy and stronger trade union legislation. In this way, they argue, we can get all reasonable top men and women together and they will solve the problems of society and everybody else will fall into line. That is the view widely reported on television of the Conservative wets, the Liberal Party and the SDP, and some people in the Labour Party.

But there is a socialist tradition as well which deserves a full coverage, and does not get it.

The first comment I would like to make about the television coverage of current affairs is that almost everything we see and hear is presented from a central Establishment viewpoint. I don't know exactly where to place it: perhaps somewhere between the *Guardian* and the *Daily Telegraph* but it does present all problems as if normality lay somewhere slightly to the Left of Mrs Thatcher and very much to the Right of mainstream Labour thinking. This Establishment viewpoint is justified by the media on the grounds that if the Labour Party doesn't like it and the Cabinet doesn't like it, it must be fair. This is the basic principle upon which almost all the television producers justify what they do. That was broadly the position of the Medieval Church which presented on a daily basis the view of the then Establishment.

I will give you a few examples I've picked to illustrate this argument. Take the treatment of trade unionism and industrial disputes which has been brilliantly documented by the Glasgow University Media Group. They have established that by the use of language, all industrial disputes are presented in a particular way. Unions always 'demand' and 'threaten', management always 'offer' and 'plead'. Pause for a moment to consider the impact of that language. Or put it the other way round. Take any dispute. You could say that the trade unions are 'offering' to work for an 8 per cent rise when inflation is 10 per cent and are 'pleading' with their management not to cut their real wages, and management are 'demanding' they work for 5 per cent and 'threatening' to sack them if they don't. Now, it does make quite a difference how you use the language. But we take it as natural that all disruption is caused by trade unions. I haven't seen any programmes discussing whether it is right for the Government to cut the real wages of Health Service workers, or to cut the real wages of railwaymen. It just isn't put on the agenda by the media.

If you compare this with the coverage of other interests, for example, the endless programmes that are in the interests of investors: the *Money Programme*, *The Financial World Tonight* and so on, you will find tremendous coverage of the problems of those who are deciding where to invest their money. I doubt frankly whether lower-paid workers, along with the pensioners, watch or listen and sell their Yen and buy their Deutschmarks in response to the best advice that the BBC may offer. Even a radio programme I listened to early on Saturday morning, *Farming Today*, treats farming quite differently. Farmers are allowed to criticise the Government. The programme ends with somebody on his farm in Northamptonshire having a comfortable breakfast on a Saturday morning at 6 o'clock. There is no programme called *Trade Unionism Today*. There is not even *The Scargills: An Everyday Story of Union Folk*. But you *could* and should properly reflect class interests in a balanced way.

Gerald Priestland did the most marvellous series, *Priestland's Progress*, about religious denominations. I saw a TV programme recently on the Evangelicals, who are Fundamentalists, and, although I don't share their view, they were treated with great respect. Liberation theology has been treated with enormous interest. But when it comes to the socialist tradition, which is equally interesting and which has been argued about all over the world, it is presented with the utmost crudity of language, and socialists as the 'hard Left', almost beyond the pale.

This bias applies also to the coverage of world affairs. How many people in this country realise that Turkey, which is a member of NATO and one of our allies, has been under martial law for longer than Poland? The coverage of Poland has been enormously full and the coverage of Turkey miniscule. People are simply not aware that there are problems of civil liberty to be found both in the socialist world and the capitalist world. We were only told that the Argentine had a military junta *after* they had invaded the Falklands.

The third example, the most immediate and interesting, comes from the handling of the peace movement and the Falklands War. CND is probably the fastest growing political organisation in the country. There are about 60,000 members of the SDP and nearly 400,000 members of CND. Yet compare the coverage of the SDP during the period of its birth with the coverage of the CND: probably 100:1. Even at the height of the Falklands War, when 83 Members of Parliament, of whom I was one, signed a resolution calling for a ceasefire and the transfer of responsibilities to the United Nations, a total of MPs four times as great as the SDP parliamentary strength – what sort of interest did it get? Coverage of the peace movement was minimalised. I was deeply shocked by the TV coverage of the CND march in London, which began with a lot of people with painted faces and gave a very brief report of one or two speeches. On the occasion of the Falklands demonstration when there were two priests speaking (Bruce Kent and Donald Reeves) all the TV showed was a long dwelt-on photograph of the Communist Party banner and a short interview with me. On another Falklands demonstration when a Roman Catholic bishop was speaking in Trafalgar Square, there was no mention of him whatever: but the TV dwelt upon the Revolutionary Communist Party banner.

In parallel with the domestic debate about war you have questions of censorship. Let me give you one important example. Were there any nuclear weapons on the Task Force fleet? I raised this in the House. Mr Paul Rogers from the Bradford Peace Institute raised it. I wrote to Mrs Thatcher who replied: 'We never confirm or deny the presence or absence of nuclear weapons in any part of the world.' But it is widely suspected that, for example, on *HMS Sheffield* there were nuclear depth charges that went down with the ship. Some war correspondents were very concerned about this. Where have you seen that issue discussed on television? During that war the BBC and ITV became virtual agents for Government policy.

Other techniques of language are used. If you introduce one man as 'a former President of the Commission of the EEC with a long experience as Home Secretary and Chancellor' and another man as 'one of the most controversial hard Left figures who has ever appeared on the British scene', you are in effect issuing a Government Health Warning: DON'T LISTEN TO WHAT HE SAYS.

The problem in essence is that there are no programmes, or very few, that ever reflect the point of view that a lot of people, including myself, hold. The Glasgow University Media Group evidence has hardly ever been discussed, though it is probably the most serious academic study of its kind.

The effect of all this on our society seems to me to be as follows. First of all, the possibility that there is a valid alternative is blacked out. There are wide 'extreme' alternatives but not *valid* ones. And if you ignore the hopelessness of people's positions, but give it mass coverage when they protest, television actually encourages violence. I believe that television *is* a major factor in encouraging violence. Who was interested, for example, in Toxteth until the riots? Indeed, Michael Heseltine took a busload of businessmen around Toxteth and they were amazed by what they had seen. Why? Anyone who had ever been to Toxteth or had lived in Toxteth could have told them. We have a TV system which will bring you every football match from Spain and endless coverage of Wimbledon, but no coverage of Brixton or Bristol or Toxteth until the rioting occurs. Then all the cameras arrive en masse and cover it. TV actually offers desperate people a short-cut. If you want to have your problems discussed, you get a quicker discussion, it might appear, if you throw a brick through a window than if you actually organise, discuss, try to argue for an alternative solution. Television plays a very large part in ignoring real issues and in encouraging violence, but above all it simply lowers the quality of debate.

The Establishment is almost totally ignorant of what goes on. On *Question Time* a couple of weeks ago David Steel attacked Militant for their support of import controls, when anyone who knows anything about Militant knows they are absolutely opposed to them. Michael Heseltine said to a woman in the audience who put the Militant view 'Well, if it was always put as charmingly as that, it would be different.' We have a British Establishment who are largely ignorant about what is happening and what people are saying, unless it conforms to the Establishment view.

I would like to conclude with a few points to put on the agenda. First, that television should be required to reflect all viewpoints, all standpoints and all interests fairly. The test of fairness is very simple: when you hear *your own* view on the television, does it seem fair to *you*? That's the test of fairness. It is the distortion of a view attributed to people that is the test of unfairness and it goes on all the time. Second: there must be much greater accountability nationally and locally, and that may best be done by introducing into the upper echelons of broadcasting a stronger representation of women, of the ethnic community – which is a sizeable community – and of the interests of labour which need to be better represented. This could, in part, be achieved by decentralisation. Third, much wider access to the media; at the moment, there is only one way of getting on the television: if a producer asks you on. The right to be heard is as important as the right to free speech. We may have the right to free speech at Hyde Park Corner, but we don't have the right to be heard from Hyde Park Corner. This must inevitably involve a break-up of the monolithic structures to disperse programme units where programmes can be produced and published. A new financial structure must be developed in which advertising and grants are mixed together to fund a genuinely public service system.

This is not a marginal issue, it is a central one. There is more hostility to the BBC and ITN in the Labour Party than there is even to Mrs Thatcher. That might sound strange, but it is true; it is one thing to be governed by somebody whom you don't agree with, but it's another to have your view ignored, distorted, suppressed, or misrepresented on a regular basis. If anyone thinks that this *is* a marginal issue – the preoccupation of a few people with a grievance – they should recognise that what we are really talking about is something as important as the religious conflicts of the seventeenth century, which led to the great and bitter religious wars between the established Church and the dissenting denominations, the independents, and so on. We are up against the same argument again. The people who control and run television are as hostile to any change in their own structure – that is why they won't let it be discussed on their own programmes – as would have been the Church towards the Fifth Monarchists, the Shakers, or the Quakers in the seventeenth century. And it is against that background that I would like to see the matter discussed: quietly and calmly, but recognising that we're talking about something very important indeed, upon which I believe the survival of our democracy might ultimately depend.

Televising of the House

Mr Tony Benn (Chesterfield): I hope that this debate will not be diverted into minor matters. As some hon Members may know, there is a periscope in the Gallery and anyone can watch the House at any time. In the thirty years that I have been here I have often taken children to see it. I do not know whether a camera could be attached to that, but the technical obstacles to televising the House do not exist. Nor does the argument about violence. A tragic death at a Conservative Party conference has not stopped broadcasting taking place.

What is wrong with the House is that it has given up fighting for its rights. This debate is not about television at all; it is about the role of Parliament in a modern society. The right hon Member for Brighton, Pavilion Mr Amery and the right hon and learned Member for Richmond, Yorks Mr Brittan put their fingers on the real question.

Walter Bagehot, in his famous book on the English constitution, gave us a completely new perception of the British constitution – which at that time people thought was run by the King or Queen – by dividing the constitution into the dignified and the efficient. The Crown he defined as the dignified; the Executive as the efficient. The House of Commons is now part of the dignified part of the constitution. It is not at the heart of anything. That is in part – I hope to show – because it has capitulated and abandoned the right to its privileges. It has failed to raise matters that it should have done.

When I go past the Tower of London I often wonder for how many centuries the Beefeaters thought that they were part of the armed services before they realised that they were a tourist attraction. Let me consider what happened in this House in my lifetime alone. I leave aside the end of empire, because when I was born in 1925 one quarter of the earth's surface was governed from this Chamber and I am glad to see the empire go. That is where I would disagree with the right hon Member for Pavilion. I was not glad to see American forces based here in breach of the 1688 rule against standing armies. I was not in favour of the transfer of legislative power to Brussels. I was not in favour of the International Monetary Fund dictating the economic policies of successive Governments. I am not in favour, and never have been, of the new technology of television replacing the House, as it manifestly has done, as the central forum for national debate.

We are discussing whether the House is content – this has come out in some of the serious speeches, and I leave aside the others that have been made – to be the Beefeater guard of parliamentary democracy? Are we really so poorly placed in our own estimation that we queue up at the Admission Order Office to try to get tickets for the Gallery, and then say, as my hon Friend the Member for Bassetlaw (Mr Ashton) said in a deeply cynical speech – if I believed one tenth of what he said I would repeal the Representation of the People Act – that he has no confidence in the public, in the media or in the people's judgement. My hon Friend thinks that all one has to do is to write a popular article in a Sunday newspaper and that people need not be influenced by us.

We have no merits other than that we have been elected here. This is the only job in Britain for which no other qualification is required. That is why it is an interesting Parliament. There is no diagnostic testing – to use the Labour Party's phrase on the national curriculum.

Let us compare us with the media. I began life as a BBC producer. Producers have their own agenda. They ring up only those hon Members who they think will boost their ratings. They are not producers in the way that Mr Speaker is a producer of an order of speakers. They are casting directors. They look round at the Tory Party for two wets, two dries, a minister who was sacked and another who resigned. They look at the Labour Party for the hard Left, the soft Left, the moderates, the old Left, the Trade Union Group. The producers sit there and plan their programme. If there is trouble in the Labour Party, they say, 'What about Mr Benn?' I have refused about a dozen invitations over the past week, because I know what they are up to.

When we speak here, we speak with the authority of our electorate, chosen to speak by a Speaker, whom we have chosen. Mr Speaker does not label us according to the BBC's political classification. He says, 'The Member for Chesterfield', or 'Mr Benn' or 'Mr Amery'. In this House we have a duty to articulate the anxieties of the people, and we have a duty to see that when we articulate them they are entitled to hear what we say.

Of course, we should not hand the job over to the BBC or ITN. The *Official Report* should take over the handling of television here. It should keep the archives so that some of the great speeches that may never be shown will still be there, just as the sound records are there. It is a tragedy that none of the speeches made here by Winston Churchill, who left the House long after the technology of broadcasting was established, were recorded. We should start a video archive now under the control of Mr Speaker, under the direction of the Editor of *Hansard*, and then let the BBC broadcast the proceedings on the basis of proper balance.

The House should not have ceded its central role as an elected forum to an unelected forum created by producers and media people. It should not have done it. But it is not too late to recover it. I have not been here as long as some hon. Members, but I have been here nearly as long, and some great debates and turning points in history have come out of this place. The one difference between this place and *Question Time* or *This Week, Next Week* or *Last Week*, or whatever they call the various programmes, is that decisions flow from this place.

We had the Marconi debate, the famous debate, which my mother now aged ninety-one heard, when Rosslyn Mitchell defeated the New Prayer book in 1928. When I first visited here fifty-one years ago Churchill was sitting where the right hon Member for Pavilion is sitting. He was a back bencher, with his spectacles on the end of his nose, and he spoke on the Naval Estimates. I was eleven years old and I have never forgotten that.

Then there was the Norway debate. I heard Bevan's resignation speech, the debates on Suez and the Falklands; and, although not popular politically with the Conservative Party, the articulation of the anger and anxieties of miners, printers and nurses must be spoken of here. We have had some conflicts with Mr Speaker, and rightly so, about whether the Moonies should take preference over the nation's medical services. If Parliament is to be a centre, it must allow people to bring their anger here. If there is an angry scene, people speak as though Parliament has failed. It is the day when they do not bother coming here, but take the bus to Brussels or picket Broadcasting House, that I will be frightened.

The reputation of the House of Commons depends on what we do, whether we are faithful to the electors, whether we present our arguments with honour and integrity and whether we stick to our views, even when they are unpopular.

Unpopularity is a strange phenomenon. Two years after I saw Churchill sitting on the Conservative back benches in 1937 he was First Lord of the Admiralty and a year after that he was Prime Minister. We must stick to our guns and say what we believe here, even though the media may marginalise a point of view at a certain time.

Given the drift of argument that we have heard, I assume that the House will reject the motion. It will do so for the strangest reason – a jealousy of the media. But it is in our power to make the microphones – a powerful media means not only people or producers, but microphones and transmitters – and the instruments of modern technology available to the elected representatives of the British people. That is the question, and if we dodge it, let it go and wake up in the morning and say, 'We wish that television had never been invented', the people who will suffer initially will be ourselves. That will not matter as much as the deepening discontent of those who put us here that we should have abandoned a responsibility to be the forum to articulate their feelings, to reach decisions and to insist that what we say is at least available to those who sent us here so that they can make up their minds about whether to renew their mandate when the next election comes.

SOURCES

POWER, PARLIAMENT AND THE PEOPLE
First published in *New Socialist*, September 1982
THE CIVIL SERVICE
Extracts from the Minutes of Evidence taken before the Treasury and Civil Service Sub-Committee, 22 January 1986
THE CROWN, THE CHURCH AND DEMOCRATIC POLITICS
Extracts from address to the Modern Churchmen's Conference, 25 July 1986
A MORAL CRISIS
First published in the *Guardian*, 31 January 1983

THE DISESTABLISHMENT OF THE CHURCH OF ENGLAND
First published in *The Church and State*, ed Donald Reeves, Hodder and
Stoughton, 1984
TELEVISION IN A DEMOCRACY
Taken from the *Guardian* Lunchtime Lecture, 29 June 1982
TELEVISING OF THE HOUSE
Extracts taken from the House of Commons Official Report (*Hansard*)
of proceedings on 9 February 1988

8
LIGHT AT THE END OF THE TUNNEL

The Radical Tradition: Past, Present and Future

We are all taught to accept, almost without question, that our freedom and welfare depend on centralised power structures, and that we have a duty to obey the orders that are passed down to us from on high. A few individuals make it to the top in every generation, but once they have got there they are expected to defend the status quo which has made it possible for them to advance personally. Meanwhile the source of much authority remains with the old elites and with some new ones. The Crown, the Lords, the land, the Church, and the professions retain considerable political power. These have now been joined by the new financial, multinational, military and media establishments which have skilfully integrated themselves into the hierarchies of the older order. Parliament itself has lost many of the powers that it won so painfully over the centuries, and the electors have witnessed their own rights shrinking too. This oppressive political culture has now spread over the whole of our society, affecting the lives of women as well as men, black as well as white, limiting our freedom and narrowing our vision.

There is no reason why we should accept these values, which have been consistently questioned by great numbers of people throughout our history as they challenged the established order, relying on a rival analysis and a rival tradition, and campaigned for their replacement by a set of values based on social justice, solidarity and democracy.

Establishment historians ignore our real history. They fear that if it was made intelligible to the mass of the people we would quickly connect past with present, and draw great strength from that understanding. And so indeed we would, as we come to realize that we are engaged on a campaign for justice and freedom that has gone on, in varying forms, for nearly two thousand years. It is not, as the Establishment would have people believe, only a few trouble-makers, perhaps owing their allegiance to some foreign revolutionaries, who are pressing for change.

There is not a single democratic gain made by our people that is not now under some sort of threat, not a single major political issue that has been discussed over the centuries that has not now been placed once more upon the agenda. The role of the Crown, of the Lords, and of the Church are being discussed again. So is the question of Ireland, imperialism, our relations with America and Europe, and the rights of all working men and women.

It is not clear yet how far the Establishment want to go but we would be well advised to be ready for anything, since if they go too far it may be much harder, if not actually too late, to stop them. There is no law of God or Nature that exempts this nation from the fate that befell Germany and Italy, Spain and Portugal in the 1930s, and overtook Greece and Turkey more recently. The only guarantee of our freedom lies with us, here and now, and we had better wake up to that simple truth before it is too late. An ex-imperial power, as we are, with a decaying capitalist system of the kind we have, can be very dangerous to other countries and to its own people too. But even if we are spared the horrors of a domestic struggle to retain or regain our freedom, other countries will not be so fortunate.

Those who live now under corrupt military dictatorships, financed and supported by Washington, or London, to protect Western investments from the danger of a popular uprising, will almost certainly be forced to take to arms to liberate themselves. Herein lies one of the major risks of a global confrontation with nuclear weapons. For it is not the risk of a major invasion by one superpower across a European frontier that we have to fear so much as the danger of war by proxy or by accident, in the absence of any effective democratic control of the fearsome military machines that we have allowed to grow within our own societies. If humanity does survive the appalling dangers that now confront us, it will be, in part, because we have listened to these voices from the past, and have taken seriously those who are warning us now.

Indeed hope must stem from the possibility that we might also allow these voices to reach the people in other countries, where the same calls for justice and peace are to be heard. Although the religious traditions and the historical experiences of these peoples are different from ours, these writings on the wall are to be seen all over the globe, and have appeared in every generation to enrich the understanding of those to whom they were addressed. The only power strong enough to contain and control the unimaginable destructive force released by the splitting of the atom is the greater power that could be generated by the unification of all these voices into one great clamour for justice. Therein lies our greatest hope, and, however it is defined, it must mean radical, if not revolutionary, changes in all societies to make that possible. It must also mean that the United Nations must be reconstituted on a basis of popular consent, as the British Parliament once was, to give it the public acceptance it needs to unite the nations.

Great as the task may seem to be to us, can it really be any greater or more difficult than the ones which faced our forebears when they made their demands? Those demands must have seemed as far-fetched to many of their contemporaries as they were unacceptable to those who stood to lose their privileges. But, as history teaches us, time and time again, it is not enough to speak or write, or compose poems or songs, about freedom if there are not people who are ready to devote their lives to make it all come true. It is only a matter of merest chance who is remembered and who lies forgotten in some graveyard known only to those friends and comrades who lived in the same town or village.

Staying True to the Workers

The next few years in British politics are likely to be marked by severe economic problems and an intensification of opposition to Government policies, and it is these events which will determine the future of the Labour Party, and its commitment to socialism. As the world dips into recession again, as Britain's oil revenues begin to decline, privatisation profits come to an end and we have to fall back on a much weakened manufacturing base, the rosy prospects painted during the election will be seen to have been false.

Then, as the Cabinet begin their task of dismantling public provision for housing, health, and education and introducing the hated poll tax, and resume their frontal attack upon trade unionism and local democracy, they will face the most vigorous – and possibly violent – resistance from those who will suffer as a result. For these policies are dictated by a determination to make working people pay for the crisis so as to secure more wealth, and power, for the rich.

In this way those who own capital are to be assisted at the expense of those who live by selling their labour, which is another way of saying that class politics are central to the strategy being adopted by ministers, and that is also why there is such a determined attempt to deny the existence of class and to ridicule those who refer to class as a factor in the argument. We are told, every day, that the working class has disappeared as a cohesive political force, and that anyone who speaks of class is old-fashioned and destructive. Of course it is obvious that the working class is changing its composition as technical and office workers become an even larger element in the work force, and as more women and blacks enter it.

But what is not mentioned is that many of these groups, like printworkers, teachers and nurses, or Government scientists at GCHQ, have shown the greatest militancy in opposing the measures taken against them. Most of these people, like the dockers, car workers, rail workers and miners in the past, depend for their survival upon collective action through their unions, and many rely for the services they need upon public provision undertaken by local authorities which they elect.

There are very, very few people in Britain who are rich enough to pay, out of their own personal resources, for the housing, schooling, health care and pensions which they need, and are hence strong enough to be able to do without the collective strength that union membership and the ballot box provide. It is for this reason that the need for a Labour Party closely linked to the trade unions and sharing a broad socialist perspective is bound to continue and is likely to seem more and more relevant as the years go by to those who are under attack.

This objective reality necessarily means that all those who have tried to destroy trade unionism and obliterate socialism are bound to fail.

The long list of Labour defectors who have left the party, and those Conservatives who have claimed that they could destroy the unions and bury socialism, can always count on massive Establishment support, but the experience of recent years has converted more and more people to socialism.

That is why the Establishment is now engaged in an attempt to encourage anyone inside the party who might be prepared to attempt the same process by advocating tactical voting, proportional representation, the expulsion of socialists, the weakening of the re-selection process and any moves that might lead the Labour Party towards a harmless and presidential type of American Democratic party. But all this has been tried before, and a Labour Party linked to the unions and espousing a socialist analysis is going to remain strong on the political scene because it is needed. The General Election results proved, in so many constituencies, that Labour candidates did best where a strong socialist challenge had been mounted, as in Liverpool.

Obviously, the Labour Party will need to take account of the changes in the composition of the working class, give more emphasis to issues like peace, internationalism and Green issues, encourage genuine devolution, and accept the need for more autonomous groups to become affiliated. But whatever radical speeches may be made, the key question will be: whose side are we on when the struggles begin outside Parliament, and how much effort do we put into the task of strengthening the Labour movement?

Labour must strengthen and build upon that base and then

we can turn ourselves outwards and address the nation on the central questions that concern our people, confident that they will respond.

Aims and Objectives of the Labour Party

At the 1987 Conference it must be our aim to lay the foundation for a Labour victory at the next General Election, and to begin the development of objectives for the party that will form the basis of our appeal to the electorate, to be followed by detailed policies for presentation to later Conferences, upon which our next Manifesto will be based.

But the problem that confronts us is a deeper one than can be solved by specific commitments, however good in themselves. We are up against a coherent set of ideas and values, which run counter to everything in which we believe, but which have been so consistently advocated by the present Government, that they have become accepted very widely and now constitute something of a consensus. Unless we challenge these ideas and values, and the institutions which now reflect them and administer them, we could remain on the margins of politics for a long, time to come.

Any future Manifesto must take account of the many changes which have occurred in our society over the years including radical changes in technology, the emergence of a new and different pattern of work, and of need, and international developments which may offer better prospects for peace. All these factors will need to be studied most carefully, but none of them really alter the underlying faith which brought the Labour movement into existence, and many of them actually underline the relevance of what we have always deeply believed. There is a real risk that if we are seen to be abandoning our faith in the search for media approval we could come to be seen as a purely opportunistic party that is prepared to say anything to get into office and is ready to sacrifice good policies when the opinion polls swing against us. This could destroy our basic credibility and also fatally damage our electoral chances.

If we are to avoid these dangers the Labour Party should try to make clear – now – the essential aims and objectives which unite it, and publish these at once for discussion in the movement and generally, well ahead of our new policy statements or our next Manifesto.

Here follows a draft of possible *Aims and Objectives of the Labour Party*. I recommend that it be discussed – if necessary amended – and published by the NEC at this year's Conference for the consideration of the party and then adopted, in its final form, in 1988.

The Labour Party is a democratic, socialist and internationalist party, with a membership made up of men and women, young and old, who are widely representative of all aspects of life; closely linked to the trade unions, and other affiliated organizations, in pursuit of the historic role of Labour as a non-doctrinaire party of class struggle.

We work for the election of Labour candidates, in all local and national elections, on the basis of the political programmes put before the electors.

We believe that the party has a duty to defend working people and their families, and to campaign actively for policies that will help them.

This statement of our aims and objectives has been prepared to provide a focus for political discussion and education within the party; to allow those who join the party to understand the policies for which we stand; and to be the basis of our long-term political work.

We Believe:

THAT THERE SHOULD BE CERTAIN RIGHTS WHICH MUST BE WON AND MAINTAINED
  – The right to life, free from fear, oppression, ignorance, preventable ill-health or poverty.
  – The right to useful and satisfying work, balanced with leisure, to meet the needs of society.
  – The right of everyone to receive an income sufficient to maintain a decent standard of living.
  – The right to a good home for all in which to live, bring up children and care for all dependents.
  – The right to receive the best possible medical care, free, and at the moment of need.
  – The right of access, throughout life, to the full range of

human knowledge, through education at school, in college and afterwards.

– The right to mass media which provide accurate news, free from bias or distortion, and a diversity of views.

– The right to enjoy dignity, and a full life, in retirement in suitable accommodation, free from financial anxieties, with proper medical and other facilities, including personal care, necessary to make that possible.

– The right to expect that any government in power will work for peace and justice, and will not provoke international conflict or hostility or divert resources from essential purposes to build up the weapons of mass destruction.

– The right to equality of treatment under just laws, free from all discrimination based upon class, sex, race, life-style or beliefs.

– The right of free speech and assembly, the entrenchment of civil liberties and human rights and the right to organise voluntary associations and free trade unions for the purpose of protecting and improving the prospects for those who belong to them, and in particular, the right to withdraw labour as a means of securing justice.

– The right of elected local and national authorities to provide those jobs and services needed by the community.

IN DEMOCRACY
– We are deeply committed to the democratic process in the political, economic, social and administrative spheres, and believe that no person should have power over others unless they are accountable to, and removable by, those over whom they exercise that power or by elected representatives of the people.

IN SOCIALISM
– We are socialists because we believe that these rights cannot be fully realised in any society under capitalism, which, as in Britain now, has entrenched by law the power of Capital over Labour, and subordinated human values to the demand for profit, at the expense of social justice and peace.

IN INTERNATIONALISM
– We are an internationalist party believing that all people, everywhere, are entitled to demand the same rights.

IN THE RIGHTS OF SELF-DETERMINATION
– We believe that the people of every nation have the right

to govern themselves and to be free from any form of colonial or imperial domination.

IN SOLIDARITY
– We believe that we have a moral responsibility to defend all those who are attacked for protecting their own democratically gained rights, and with this in mind we are establishing work-place branches so that each can help others more effectively.

THAT CONSCIENCE MUST BE ABOVE THE LAW
– We assert the right of all people to follow their own conscientious beliefs even if it involves them in breaking the law; and that while there may be a legal obligation to obey the law there is no moral obligation to obey unjust laws; but we also know that those who break the law on moral grounds, may face punishment for their beliefs, and the final verdict on their actions will rest with the public and with history.

IN THE RIGHTS OF ALL TO THEIR BELIEFS
– We believe that socialist ideas which have been evolved in this country and abroad, over the centuries have given us a rich inheritance; but we do not believe that truth can be captured in any one creed to which all must subscribe under threat of expulsion or exclusion; and we respect the rights of all members of the party to hold their own views, and to organise, within the party to promote them, being convinced that diversity of opinion adds strength to our cause.

IN PROGRESS THROUGH COLLECTIVE ACTION
– We believe, in the light of our own experience, that the only secure basis for social progress must lie in collective action; and that those who have the privilege of representing us, at all levels, must remain accountable for what they say and do, and that no one can demand blind obedience, from us, in the name of loyalty or unity.

THAT WE ARE SERVANTS OF THE COMMUNITY
– We see the Labour Party, and all its representatives, as servants of all those who live and work in Britain.

The Policies We Want:

FOR BRITAIN
– The return to full employment and the adoption of the means necessary for that purpose by, amongst other things, the

common ownership, under democratic control and management, of the commanding heights of the economy, including the banks and finance houses, the land and all the companies which dominate our industrial system, and the development of new forms of social ownership.

– A shorter working week and earlier retirement.

– The establishment, as of right, of a comprehensive welfare system which will safeguard the living standards of our people.

– The elimination of all discrimination and injustice.

– The introduction of a system of taxation which will radically reduce the present gross inequalities of wealth and income.

– The provision of good housing, health and education for all, by absorbing those private facilities that might be necessary to achieve a fully comprehensive system giving real choice to all.

– The introduction of a major programme for the democratic reform of the apparatus of the State including the abolition of the House of Lords; the ending of all patronage in making major public appointments; the democratisation of the magistracy, and lay supervision of the judiciary by the introduction of assessors from all walks of life into the High Court; and the democratic control of the police by elected local authorities.

– The ending of all nuclear weapons and bases in Britain; and the phasing-out of civil nuclear power in favour of coal, conservation and alternative benign sources of energy.

– The provision of cheap and safe public transport for the use of the public, to protect us from the chaos that would follow from leaving key decisions to unrestricted competition.

– The protection of the environment so that this and future generations may enjoy it, free from pollution and exploitation for profit.

– The proper provision for a leisure and multicultural society.

– The protection of the animal kingdom so that this and future generations may enjoy the natural wild life of Britain.

– The upholding and enforcement of existing legislation relating to animal abuse, and efforts to secure the introduction of further legislation making all bloodsports illegal.

IN INTERNATIONAL AFFAIRS

– The adoption by Britain of a non-aligned foreign policy, committed to the United Nations but free of all military alliances, so that this country, with others, could help ease international tensions, reduce arms expenditure and assist the development of the Third World.

– The development of closer economic, industrial, social and political links between working people here and in other countries, free from the control of the Treaty of Rome or NATO.

SOURCES

THE RADICAL TRADITION: PAST, PRESENT AND FUTURE
First published in *Writings on the Wall: A Radical and Socialist Anthology, 1215–1984*, Faber and Faber, 1984.
STAYING TRUE TO THE WORKERS
First published in the *Independent*, 14 July 1987
AIMS AND OBJECTIVES OF THE LABOUR PARTY
Document presented to the NEC, 1987

Index